THE
BRAMBLE
BUSH

The **Legal Legends Series** from Quid Pro Books offers high-quality editions of classic legal scholarship, without formatting errors and misquotes common in such reproductions. Each book is painstakingly checked against original sources. All books in the Series embed the original page numbers for ready citation and consistency with our new eBook editions. Extensive new introductions by recognized legal scholars place the works in historical context and explain the current relevance and application of the original work.

THE BRAMBLE BUSH

ON OUR LAW AND ITS STUDY

by

KARL N. LLEWELLYN

Introduction by Stewart Macaulay

Legal Legends Series

Quid Pro Books

New Orleans, Louisiana

The Bramble Bush

Published in the 2012 *Legal Legends* edition by Quid Pro Books.

ISBN 978-1-61027-804-1 (pbk., trade)
ISBN 978-1-61027-134-9 (pbk., mass mkt.)
ISBN 978-1-61027-137-0 (cloth)

Quid Pro Books

5860 Citrus Blvd., Suite D-101
New Orleans, Louisiana 70123
www.quidprobooks.com

qp

Publisher's Cataloging-in-Publication

Llewellyn, Karl N. (Karl Nickerson), 1893-1962.

The Bramble Bush: on our law and its study / by Karl N. Llewellyn; with a new introduction and notes by Stewart Macaulay.

p. cm. — (Legal legends)

Includes introduction, annotations, and notes of the series editor.

ISBN 978-1-61027-804-1 (trade paperback edition, new 2016 printing)

1. Law—Study and teaching—United States. 2. Law—United States. 3. Law—Education—United States. 4. Law—Philosophy. 5. Jurisprudence. 6. Judges—Judicial Process. I. Macaulay, Stewart. II. Title. III. Series.

KF 273.L55.M6 2012
339.713'52—dc22

2012048748
CIP

There was a man in our town
and he was wondrous wise:
he jumped into a BRAMBLE BUSH
and scratched out both his eyes—
and when he saw that he was blind,
with all his might and main
he jumped into another one
and scratched them in again.

TABLE OF CONTENTS

{Page numbers in brackets reference the author's previous, original editions. That pagination is embedded into the text of this edition, in order to facilitate continuity of citations, referencing, classroom assignment, and new eBook formats; see *Notes of the Series Editor*. The page numbers of this print edition are shown below to the far right of this table and at the bottom of each page. This modern pagination generally follows that of the original editions.}

INTRODUCTION

DODGING THE WORST OF THE
THORNS ON THE BRAMBLE BUSH

The *Bramble Bush* is a book that anyone interested in law schools or law should read. Karl Nickerson Llewellyn was a brilliant man. He loved the British and American legal tradition. A number of great judges were his heroes, and he admired lawyers who solved problems and were skilled crafts people. He offers a Mother Goose nursery rhyme as catching the essence of legal education. In the rhyme, a man falls into a bramble bush and scratches out his eyes. But then he turns to the thorns again and scratches eyes back into his head. Similarly, in law school, law students first lose their old eyes and stumble around for a bit, but then they gain new vision. Llewellyn assumes that, in most cases, the new eyes will be better than the old.

Even if this is true, insofar as the bramble bush story captures something of legal education, it warns those thinking about going to law school that it may be a painful process. I went to law school in the early 1950s, and I can testify that in the first year I faced some measure of education by intimidation and humiliation. Students who displeased one of our professors were insulted and yelled at. Other professors did not yell but were content to question us in ways that showed us and our classmates that we did not understand what we had been asked to read. One professor asked me a question, and I had no idea how to respond. He repeated the question. I remembered a phrase from an old case we had considered in another course and asked timidly, "Could the plaintiff ask for *quantum meruit*?"

The professor dismissed my statement: "Mr. Macaulay! Is it really necessary to discuss this case in Polish?"[1] Needless to say, I heard about

---

[1] The professor was J. Keith Mann. Later in my law school career, I served as his research assistant. He then recommended me for a clerkship with Chief Judge William Denman of the United States Court of Appeals for the Ninth Circuit and later for a position as a Bigelow Teaching Fellow and Instructor at the University of Chicago Law School. In this later role, I got to watch Karl Llewellyn teach and interact with his colleagues at faculty meetings. I have vivid memories of Karl in full flight. Many years afterward, I learned that after my Chicago experience, Professor Mann had recommended me for a job as an assistant professor at the University of Wisconsin Law School. Mann had taught at Madison before he moved to Stanford where we met. Apparently, he left on good terms; I got the job.

that one from my classmates for some time—one remembered it at our fiftieth class reunion. Moreover, several faculty members pointed out to us that usually about a third of the first year class at my law school did not make it to the second year. The bramble bush shows its thorns before you find the raspberries or blackberries—if you ever discover them.

When I was asked to write this introduction, I pulled down my copy of the 1950 re-publication of the book that I bought before I started law school. The price was marked on the inside cover: $3.50.[2] Llewellyn warns that beginners listening to or reading his 1929 and 1930 lectures will understand only a small percentage of what is there. This clearly was true in my case. Yet somehow I kept going that first year and got high grades.[3] Llewellyn's book served to warn me that the game did not involve memorizing collections of clear and certain rules all fit together in a seamless logical structure.

Llewellyn in *The Bramble Bush* looks at legal education, the common law system of precedent, and the American legal system in general. He raises some problems. Nonetheless, Lawrence Friedman, the great legal historian, observes:

> Part of Llewellyn's problem—if we can call it a problem—was that he was quite starry-eyed about the common-law, and the way it moved and worked; basically, he loved the common-law, and this intense love colors all of his work. Everything Llewellyn wrote, he wrote passionately; his style is curious, cryptic, stylized, and at times annoying; but it is full of zest, of boundless enthusiasm. He truly adored the law; and those that made it.[4]

Once we have considered legal education, we will turn to at least a few questions about the adversary system in practice in this country.

I. *The Bramble Bush* and Legal Education

A. Is Anything, or Any One, Over Eighty Years Old Still Worth Listening To?

A skeptic would ask why read a book written over eighty years ago?

---

[2] The Inflation Calculator tells us that this would be $28.43 in 2010 money.

[3] Of course, we must remember the difference between correlation and causation. Perhaps I did well despite reading *The Bramble Bush*. I think otherwise, however.

[4] Lawrence M. Friedman, *Karl Llewellyn and the Riddle of Judicial Decision-Making*, in RECHTSREALISMUS, MULTIKULTURELLE GESELLSCHAFT UND HANDELSRECT: KARL N. LLEWELLYN UND SEINE BEDEUTUNG HEUTE 139 (Ulrich Drobnig & Manfred Rehbinder, eds., 1994).

Why should we think that much in *The Bramble Bush* still applies to today's legal education? Fortunately, we can offer good reasons to read Llewellyn's book. At least some of "classic" legal education may have survived up to almost forty years ago. We can point to the 1973 film *The Paper Chase*, where John Houseman gave us a picture of law professors as nasty people who drove students to think their way. Instead of reading a book, a prospective law student could just watch this film.[5] We can hope that by today Houseman's education by humiliation is not typical.

We know that a great deal of what Llewellyn wrote about is still with us. In *The Bramble Bush*, Llewellyn tells us about first year legal education in 1930. He says:

> The first year . . . aims, in the old phrase, to get you "thinking like a lawyer". The hardest job of the first year is to lop off your common sense, to knock your ethics into temporary anesthesia. Your view of social policy, your sense of justice—to knock these out of you along with woozy thinking, along with ideas all fuzzed along their edges. You are to acquire ability to think precisely, to analyze coldly, to work within a body of materials that is given, to see, and see only, and manipulate, the machinery of law. It is not easy thus to turn human beings into lawyers.[6]

We have a wonderful empirical study of modern legal education by Professor Elizabeth Mertz. Her work, and my experience as a first year law school teacher since 1957, suggest that law schools still are trying to transform beginning students so that they will "think like lawyers."

The Bramble Bush remains a remarkable achievement, well worth reading in the 21st century. Nonetheless, an important part of thinking like a lawyer is a critical perspective. As lawyers, we must presume that no article, book, judicial opinion or institution is perfect. There is always an argument the other way. Llewellyn looks at the common law legal system and American legal education, and he recognizes many flaws. In passages that could have been written today, he points out how much legal scholars do not know about the practice of law and the functioning of the legal system. Nonetheless, in the end, he champions law schools, lawyers, great appellate judges and the common law legal system. In what follows, I will highlight some of major issues raised by *The Bramble Bush* concerning legal education, the practice of law and the functioning legal system. For

---

[5] A student who wanted to read a more recent account could try Scott Turow, ONE L: THE TURBULENT TRUE STORY OF A FIRST YEAR AT HARVARD LAW SCHOOL (1977, rept. 2010).

[6] THE BRAMBLE BUSH, at 101. All page references are to the original pagination, which is embedded into this edition by the use of brackets.

example, if law students lose their idealistic and unrealistic ways of looking at the world, why assume that whatever comes next is an improvement? Instead of a fuzzy concept of justice, do we just get rationalizations for high pay in the service of the well-off? Or is the stuff of classic law school so removed from what lawyers do that it serves only as a hazing ritual while we age students an additional three years so that they are not quite so young when they present themselves to the world as lawyers? Does our legal system approach some measure of justice or are its ideals seldom more than a comforting fantasy? We promise, for example, everyone due process, but typically the best that those who turn to law get is a deal—a compromise rather than a vindication of rights. We price many out of the market for dispute resolution. Does this matter? Can we answer such questions or do we lack reliable knowledge to even begin crafting tentative answers? At the very least, *The Bramble Bush* makes a remarkable contribution to our thought about these issues today.

B. What Does Legal Education Look Like Today?

Clearly, one important thing remains much the same today as was the case in 1930. Law schools almost always begin with classes in contracts, torts and property—common law subjects reflecting a rich tradition.[7] Elizabeth Mertz studied first year contracts classes at eight law schools of varying prestige during the last decade of the 20th century.[8] She found that today's beginning legal education is still very much focused on "thinking like a lawyer." Professors seldom yell at students, but they use "negative uptake"—you are ignored and interrupted until you get on the professor's train of thought. After closely analyzing tape recordings of all these modern classes, she reports: "[L]egal education pushes students to direct their attention toward textual and legal authority, casting aside issues of 'right' and 'wrong,' of emotion and empathy—the very feelings most likely to draw the hearts of lay readers as they encounter tales of human conflict."[9] She tells us that students are required to defend points of view

---

[7] Llewellyn first wrote after the great stock market crash but before the election of Franklin Roosevelt and the implementation of his "New Deal" policies. Those brought us the development of the regulatory state, and statutes and administrative regulations came to play a role in the practice of law that would have been hard to anticipate in 1930. Nonetheless, first year law students today seldom see many statutes and administrative regulations. Criminal law and civil procedure are common first year courses that involve statutes, but they differ from the Internal Revenue Code, the Bankruptcy Act, or the various attempts to regulate aspects of the economy.

[8] Elizabeth Mertz, THE LANGUAGE OF LAW SCHOOL: LEARNING TO "THINK LIKE A LAWYER" (2007).

[9] Elizabeth Mertz, *Teaching Lawyers the Language of Law: Legal and Anthropo-*

whether or not they actually believe in them. Lawyers learn not to have much humility about language or their ability to deal with the fields of others. Thinking like a lawyer means that one can take almost any social situation and convert it into legal categories. The lesson is that language is fundamentally manipulative and truth is highly contingent. Compare Llewellyn, writing about seventy years earlier, in the part of *The Bramble Bush* that is directed to third year law students:

> Already you are almost lawyers. Three years you have been study-ing the law. Are you still unaware that every doubtful point is regularly answered both ways by authority? Are you still blind to the fact that rules do not *control* decision when the case is troublesome? In every field, on every point, when there is doubt, the law will offer you technique and rules, respectable, respect-ed, to work to *either* goal.[10]

I think it clear that we can put aside any concern that *The Bramble Bush* is dated and no longer worth reading if we are concerned with mod-ern legal education. Of course, in some important ways the social context when Llewellyn wrote his book was very different from today. Women and minorities, for example, have stormed the barricades that guarded legal education and law practice for white males in the 1930s.[11] Still, women and minorities go through the classic process of learning to think like lawyers. Today's students may be taking notes on a computer, but the notes they are taking will resemble those taken with pen and ink at the time of the Hoover Administration.

C. Changing Perspective for the Better?

Both Llewellyn and Mertz raise the major problem with the bramble bush approach to first year law school education—it is one thing to scratch

---

logical Translations, 34 JOHN MARSHALL L. REV. 91, 99 (2000).

[10] THE BRAMBLE BUSH, at 149 (emphasis in original). Compare Mertz, THE LANGUAGE OF LAW SCHOOL, at 216: "The legal epistemology taught in the prototypical first-year U.S. law classroom, embodied in the practice of learning to read cases, employs a set of linguistic procedures to generate knowledge that is at once flexible enough to encompass almost any conceivable context, while still generating certainty . . . and rules with knowable parameters . . . that nevertheless change as they are applied."

[11] As was the customary practice at the time, Llewellyn refers to lawyers and judges as "he" and "him." Although there were some brave women who were pioneers attending law school at earlier times, it was not until the 1970s that there were more than a very few women students at any American law school. See Nancy J. Reichman & Joyce Sterling, *Sticky Floors, Broken Steps and Concrete Ceilings in Legal Careers*, 14 TEX. J. WOMEN & LAW 101 (2005); Cynthia Epstein, WOMEN IN LAW ch. 3-4 (1993, rept. 2012).

out the eyes that students bring to law school, but why do we assume that they will scratch in new eyes that are better? Llewellyn said: ". . . this tendency of our teaching has caused me worry, in its aspect as developing the technician at the cost of the whole man."[12] In his typical style, he commented:

> There is a brand of lawyer for whom law is the making of a live-lihood, a competence, a fortune. Law offers means to live, to get ahead. . . . He whose desires have shrunk to meat and drink and income tax evasion, to bowing butlers and the bejewelling of his wife—he has his happiness if he can gain the coin. I would not say that "more law" had brought him vision. But neither do I see that he desires vision, or could use it.[13]

Mertz may sing to a modern beat instead of Llewellyn's Harlem jazz or Broadway shows, but her song is much the same. She notes: "As the semester wears on, poignant, glaring, pitiful stories of human drama and misery begin to sail easily past you, as you take them expertly in hand and dissect them for the 'relevant' facts."[14] She worries that those who entered law school to help those in need will abandon such goals as their idealism is replaced by cynicism. We hide behind an apparent neutrality, but with all of the advantages of the 'haves' who come out ahead. In the first year of law school, most students confront contracts, torts and property—all governed by the common law that reflects capitalist ideas rather than statutes that suggest that the market isn't the perfect solution to all human problems.[15]

While it may or may not be unfair to former Prime Minister Tony Blair, an article in *The Financial Times* reflects a common criticism of lawyers:

> [B]e sure to get the right kind [of lawyer]. You probably don't want one on the model of Tony Blair, the UK's most recent lawyer-prime minister. A classic English barrister, Mr. Blair was eloquent, quick-witted and persuasive. He constructed arguments that slid almost imperceptibly back and forth between the general and the particular, using convenient facts if any were to

---

[12] THE BRAMBLE BUSH, at 124.

[13] *Id.* at 119.

[14] Mertz, THE LANGUAGE OF LAW SCHOOL, at 8.

[15] Compare Note, *'Round and 'Round the Bramble Bush: From Legal Realism to Critical Legal Scholarship*, 95 HARVARD L. REV. 1669 (1981).

hand and elegant sophistry[16] if they were not.

> Ultimately, his skill in weaving a compelling narrative out of scraps of circumstantial evidence ended with the British army crawling over Iraq looking for non-existent weapons of mass destruction. His conviction, as it were, turned out to be unsafe.[17]

This passage makes Blair sound like the product of some American first year law school instructors. Mertz stresses that, as compared to any social science field, law professors seldom worry about the accuracy of their factual assumptions. Indeed, they are quick to use their intuition to fashion plausible hypothetical cases to test the limits of what courts have said.

I am one of a group of law professors who have sought to have their cake and eat it too. We do teach how to think like a lawyer and stress the relevant legal questions that come before the courts. Neither Llewellyn nor I am against teaching the classical topic of first year law school classes. The point is, rather, that it is not enough—and if we do no more, we may produce negative results. We also make great efforts to put the appellate opinions in context, to tell students about the dispute and the consequences of what happened before the courts.

The work of Professor Judith Maute offers a rich example. Many contracts courses teach *Peevyhouse v. Garland Coal & Mining Co.*[18] The Peevyhouses entered into a contract whereby Garland Coal could strip mine land that the Peevyhouses used to raise cattle. The location of their land gave them bargaining power because Garland Coal needed it in order to strip mine some of their neighbors' property. The Peevyhouses insisted on a contract clause calling for Garland Coal to restore the land after the strip mining. Garland Coal abandoned the project, and it breached the contract when it failed to restore the Peevyhouses' land. The evidence indicated that it would have cost almost $30,000 to fill in the holes so cattle could move from one side of the property to the other. However, over objection, Garland Coal offered evidence that the diminution in the value of the farm resulting from Garland Coal's failure to do the work was only about $300. The Peevyhouses' lawyer offered no evidence on this point. The jury awarded the Peevyhouses $5,000, at best a rough compromise. The Supreme Court of Oklahoma, by a five-to-four vote, reversed and ordered the judgment modified to only $300. In legal theory, this protected their expectation interest: they were put where they would have

---

[16] That is, clever but fallacious arguments.

[17] Alan Beattie, *Take a Deep Breath, Economists, It's Time for the Lawyers*, FINANCIAL TIMES, June 18, 2011, at 7.

[18] 382 P.2d 109 (Okla. 1960).

been had the contract been performed.

Professor Maute produced a 123 page study of the background of the case that was published in the *Northwestern University Law Review*.[19] She advocates this kind of "legal archaeology" because it will often take our students and us away from abstraction and force us to confront basic questions of justice.[20] In her study of the *Peevyhouse* case, she makes one thing very clear: the Peevyhouses were not put where they would have been had the contract been performed. The majority of the Oklahoma Supreme Court did just what *The Financial Times* charged former Prime Minister Tony Blair of doing. Her article is illustrated with photographs of the Peevyhouses' land; it is an ugly mess. Even if we assume that the award accurately measured the amount by which the resale value of their land had been diminished, the land had not been restored to its original state as Garland Coal had promised. Maute does consider the arguments for the Oklahoma court's majority opinion, but you never are in doubt that she thinks that the Peevyhouses were treated very badly by the American legal system. Much of the responsibility for the unsightly mess with which they were left with falls on their lawyer. He took the matter on a contingent fee arrangement, and this likely influenced how he tried the case. We learn why Garland Coal abandoned the project, and why it failed to carry out its explicit promise. We even get to consider the effect of a bribery scandal involving justices of the Supreme Court of Oklahoma who decided the case.

Professor Maute's study is but one of many attempts to put contracts and tort appellate opinions in context.[21] Some law professors are very critical of such efforts because this material is "irrelevant."[22] They argue

---

[19] Judith L. Maute, *Peevyhouse v. Garland Coal & Mining Co. Revisited: The Ballad of Willie and Lucille*, 89 NORTHWESTERN U. L. REV. 1341 (1995).

[20] Judith L. Maute, *Response: The Values of Legal Archaeology*, 2000 UTAH L. REV. 223, 223-24.

[21] I review a number of these contracts stories in Stewart Macaulay, *Contracts, New Legal Realism, and Improving the Navigation of* The Yellow Submarine, 80 TULANE L. REV. 1161, 1176-79 (2006). We focus on putting problems in their real world context in Stewart Macaulay, Jean Braucher, John Kidwell & William Whitford, CONTRACTS: LAW IN ACTION (3d ed. 2010).

[22] Richard Danzig, THE CAPABILITY PROBLEM IN CONTRACT LAW (1978), offered a collection of stories about the background and context of a number of appellate opinions often found in first year contracts casebooks. Professor Tierney objected: "[T]he trouble with Professor Danzig's book is that it is an oblique attack on the legal concept of relevance without any offer of a substitute. In general, first year law students need to be taught a sense of relevance, and weaned off the habit of crass generalization, with which many of them have grown up." Kevin Tierney, *Book Review*, 32 HASTINGS L.J. 1071, 1091 (1981). William Whitford and I wrote an article dealing with the background of *Hoffman v. Red Owl Stores*, 26 Wis.2d 683,

that all we need is the rule and the facts reported by the court. Those who see themselves as teaching lawyers some of their craft, see these stories as very relevant. Often they teach that we cannot understand the legal system in action if all we study are the rules. We can wonder also how much exposure to these stories offsets the bramble bush effect. I think that it helps at least some law students learn the new language that they are being taught without losing their ability to see many of its consequences and judge them normatively. I see no reason why one cannot learn a new language without forgetting everything about her native tongue.

D. Will There Be Jobs When Law School Has Scratched My Eyes Back In? The More Things Change, the More They Remain the Same?

In other ways, as well, there is at least some similarity between then and now. Llewellyn's students faced the uncertainty about their careers as a result of the stock market crash and bank failures. Llewellyn, in *The Bramble Bush,* notes:

> For you come to us disillusioned as few other generations have been disillusioned. I meet and talk with you. . . . Our economic system you find neither the best of all possible worlds, with captains of industry to gape at in admiration, nor yet a crying injustice to be fought. Nay—at the captains you lift your eyebrows with a sneer compound of envy and contempt: servants of the commonwealth? . . . Great men? Twaddle! Yet not in revolt: you know the revolters for the beaten at the game.[23]

How far would this describe present day law students? Today's students

---

133 N.W.2d 267 (1965), a contracts decision that appears in many casebooks. See William Whitford & Stewart Macaulay, *Hoffman v. Red Owl Stores: The Rest of the Story,* 61 HASTINGS L.J. 801 (2010). The late Professor Larry E. Ribstein objected: "As legal analysts, the case matters to us because it's law. What makes it law is the court's holding, which turns on the facts the court articulates rather than on the additional facts Whitford & Macaulay discover. We might now rest easier that justice was done in the actual facts of the case. But Hoffman . . . warrants discussion only because of its role as law, and the new story is completely irrelevant to that." <http://busmovie.typepad.com/ideoblog/2009/08/tales-of-hoffmann.html.> Bill Whitford and I think Ribstein's comment fits the conventional model of legal education that Mertz found common today. We think that it is an odd way to train lawyers who have to cope with the law in action, and we do rest easier that justice was done in the actual facts of the case. For another book that puts classic contracts cases in context, see Douglas G. Baird, ed., CONTRACTS STORIES vii (2006) ("Context always matters, and much is lost when controversies are reduced to simple hypotheticals and black-letter maxims.").

23 THE BRAMBLE BUSH, at 123.

also are worried about the opportunities that will await them when they graduate. As a result of an economic crisis, the practice of law now is changing in ways that do not favor recent graduates.[24]

Llewellyn's students were going to face the political realities of big cities, corruption and favoritism. These problems have not been solved during the past eighty years. Indeed, we now face the issue of elected state supreme court judges who are or appear beholden to interest groups that fashion television campaigns that got them elected.[25] Presidents seek to staff the federal judiciary with judges who reflect the views of their political parties. Senate confirmation hearings are highly politicized. Scholars have discovered that you can predict the results in certain types of cases before federal appellate courts by knowing the political party of the presidents who nominated the three judges on the panel hearing the case.[26]

Students come to law school with some awareness that there is a gap between the laws on the books and the law in action. Despite what they may answer to an interviewer, Americans do not obey all of the laws all of the time. Yet classic law school's focus on pure theory helps professors avoid such uncomfortable dirty secrets. When Llewellyn wrote, organized crime supplied an illegal drug—alcohol—not far from the Columbia Law School. Few in his audience would have been unaware of this at the end of the "roaring twenties." I suspect that a member of the Columbia community would not have to go far from that institution today to obtain other

---

[24] Elite law firms have moved to outsourcing much work formerly done by young associates. Indeed, a firm in India has moved to Texas where it hires American lawyers as temporary workers at much less than the salaries typically paid associates in large law firms in the United States. Heather Timmons, *Where Lawyers Find Work*, N.Y. TIMES, June 3, 2011, at 1. See also John Markoff, *Armies of Expensive Lawyers, Replaced by Cheaper Software*, N.Y. TIMES, Mar. 5, 2011, at 1 ("Now, thanks to advances in artificial intelligence, 'e-discovery' software can analyze documents in a fraction of the time for a fraction of the cost [of 'a platoon of lawyers and paralegals.']").

[25] See *Caperton v. A.T. Massey Coal Co., Inc.*, 556 U.S. 868 (2009); Editorial, *Can Justice Be Bought? Soaring Spending on Judicial Elections Requires Tighter Rules for Disqualifying Judges*, N.Y. TIMES, June 16, 2011, at 34; Erwin Chemerinsky & James J. Sample, *You Get the Judges You Pay For*, N.Y. TIMES, April 18, 2011, at 23; Adam Liptak, *Justices Issue a Rule of Recusal in Cases of Judges' Big Donors*, N.Y. TIMES, June 9, 2009, at 1; Ian Urbina, *West Virginia's Top Judge Loses His Re-election Bid*, N.Y. TIMES, May 15, 2008, at 25; Dorothy Samuels, *The Selling of the Judiciary: Campaign Cash "In the Courtroom,"* N.Y. TIMES, April 15, 2008, at 22; Adam Liptak & Janet Roberts, *Campaign Cash Mirrors a High Court's Rulings*, N.Y. TIMES, Oct. 1, 2006, at 1; Adam Liptak, *Judicial Races in Several States Become Partisan Battlegrounds*, N.Y. TIMES, Oct. 24, 2004, at 1.

[26] Cass R. Sunstein, David Schkade & Lisa Michelle Ellman, *Ideological Voting on Federal Courts of Appeals: A Preliminary Investigation*, 90 VIRGINIA L. REV. 301 (2004).

kinds of illegal drugs. Legal scholarship in 1930 or in 2012 seldom had or has much to say about the gap between the law on the books and the law in action. Whatever people wanted to say about Americans in 1930, they would not have called them totally law abiding.[27] Indeed, fiction tells us that breaking the prohibition laws was exciting and fun in the "jazz age." Is the business of supplying and the practice of buying illegal drugs much different today? Are Americans any more law abiding? Should this matter to those who fashion theories about the functions of law in this country?

II. Including and Going Beyond Legal Education: *The Bramble Bush* and the Legal System

Legal education and scholarship would improve if we broadened our subject. When *The Bramble Bush* was written, law schools largely ignored much of what lawyers did. While we do more today, we largely still focus on appellate opinions and the rules. Llewellyn recognized that lawyers drafted documents and created legal devices needed to support ever-changing forms of business. He certainly knew that they negotiated transactions, and he understood the complex role of the lobbyist for organized interest groups. We have long shared anecdotes and war stories about law practice. If we are to understand the legal profession, and appraise both what lawyers do and the functions served by the legal system, we need better information.

Llewellyn anticipated some of the problems facing today's legal education and scholarship. His focus in the book is on the techniques for reading the opinions of appellate courts. Yet Llewellyn defined law as what officials—"whether they be judges or sheriffs or clerks or jailers or lawyers"[28]—do about disputes. In *The Bramble Bush,* he tells us:

> More; for a thousand cases on trial in the higher courts of trial—the County Court, or Circuit, or Supreme—there are again ten or twenty thousand settled *finally* in some lesser court of trial: a small claims court, a municipal court, the court of a magistrate or justice of the peace. Here in this moving mountain of the cases *un*appealed, is the impact of the officials on society—even within the realm of litigation. Beyond, there is the massive impact of the administrative machine. By my own showing, on my

---

[27] Sonny Greer, Duke Ellington's drummer, said "The Club Kentucky was something, and the money was flying. . . . We had all the gangsters, all the big gangsters you read about, Legs Diamond, Lucky Luciano and all the Brooklyn gang. They'd rendezvous." Stuart Nicholson, Reminiscing in Tempo: A Portrait of Duke Ellington 51 (1999).

[28] The Bramble Bush, at 12.

own premises, these are what count. I pass them by. Out of my own mouth, damned.[29]

He defends the top-down practice of legal education in terms of what was available. Appellate opinions arrived at the professor's mailbox, nicely printed and bound.[30] There still is no easy way to study the work of trial courts. At least, the scholar would have to step outside the law school's doors, something many of them seem to fear.

In the past sixty years, scholars specializing in sociology and psychology of law have studied juries, the kinds of cases brought to trial courts, lawyers settling cases with insurance adjusters, contingent fee practice and the whole wide variety of other-than-legal ways to deal with disputes in ways that pass under the label "alternative dispute resolution."[31] Moreover, some have studied the decision whether to see a lawyer and seek legal redress. Others have contrasted a legal approach with relying on other not-always-consistent normative systems that are supported by various sanctions. This is the new legal realism that has accepted Llewellyn's challenge to look beyond high courts and legal rules.[32] However, my experience suggests that relatively little of what these scholars have found has made it into the first year legal education. It is still focused largely on how to think like a lawyer. We can hope that the decisions of the highest courts have some influence on trial judges and magistrates, and what the highest court might do if a case were appealed is at least one influence on lawyers trying to settle a case. Yet we know that a lot more is involved.

Llewellyn saw a need eighty years ago that is still largely unmet. What beyond precedent and doctrine should be studied and taught by legal scholars and law students? As he put it in *The Bramble Bush:*

> What, then, do you need that we do not offer you? . . . It is hard to answer that question. It is hard . . . because we still know so

---

[29] THE BRAMBLE BUSH, at 90.

[30] Today appellate opinions arrive at our computers via LexisNexis and Westlaw.

[31] See, e.g., Marc Galanter, *Reading the Landscape of Disputes: What We Know and Don't Know (and Think We Know) About Our Allegedly Contentious and Litigious Society*, 31 UCLA L. REV. 4 (1983); David M. Trubek et al., *The Costs of Ordinary Litigation*, 31 UCLA L. REV. 72 (1983).

[32] See, e.g., Elizabeth Mertz & Mark Suchman, *A New Legal Empiricism: Assessing ELS and NLR*, 6 ANN. REV. LAW & SOC. SCI. 555 (2010); Victoria Nourse & Gregory Shaffer, *Varieties of New Legal Realism: Can a New World Order Prompt a New Scholarly Agenda?*, 95 CORNELL L. REV. 61 (2009). See also Theodore Eisenberg, *The Origins, Nature, and Promise of Empirical Legal Studies and a Response to Concerns*, 2011 U. ILL. L. REV. 1713. Compare John Henry Schlegel, AMERICAN LEGAL REALISM AND EMPIRICAL SOCIAL SCIENCE (1995).

little of what constitutes the practice of law today. How much of the old-time practice has been taken over by trust and title companies, and how many lawyers do they use? How much of their "law" is in the cases, on the statute books, how much is based upon their own practices and understandings? How much of law practice lies in trial of cases, and with what differences between New York and Wichita and Cedar Forks? How does trial practice in the city court differ from trial practice before the federal courts or the supreme? Where does appeal work fit into the picture? How much of practice lies in interviews with the dock commissioner or the tax commissioner, or the claim agent for the New York Central? Is there a special workman's compensation bar? How much of law practice lies in drafting contracts, how much in closing titles, how much lies in dispossessing tenants? How much in business strategy? How much in journeying to Albany or Washington to lobby; how much of the lobbying occurs when the committee has adjourned? How much of practice lies in getting business, and whose business, and how is it got? How much of practice lies in marrying the senior partner's niece, and which of them—and again, how? To these and some hundred other questions we can answer: for some men, more or wholly; for some, less or not at all; for how many, or how much of any, we can only guess.[33]

While I think that our guesses are much better than they could have been when Llewellyn wrote, we still are a long way from being able to answer his questions with more than anecdotes and war stories. Although, these may be the best methods to deal with Llewellyn's question about succeeding in practice by picking the right niece of the right partner.

III. Getting Outside The Law Schools' Doors and Looking at Lawyers

In the past few decades, some scholars have begun studying the practice of law. Many have tried to cope with the seemingly innocent question: what is it that lawyers do? Of course, some law professors know at least a few of the answers as a result of their own experience and their contacts with the practicing bar. Yet many law professors have little firsthand experience of practice—they have done no more before they turned to teaching than hold a clerkship with a prestigious judge and work in a large law firm for a very few years. Many make little effort to stay in touch with the bar. More and more law schools run elaborate clinical programs that

---

33 THE BRAMBLE BUSH, at 134.

take students into law offices, courts, jails, prisons and other places where lawyers work. However, professors who teach the basic courses and clinicians in law schools often have a distant and strained relationship. This may be changing as law schools are now under pressure to produce young lawyers more nearly ready to practice. Law firms want to push the costs of apprenticeship back on the law schools. Some clinicians have joined forces with social scientists to write articles dealing with the law in action that they must cope with daily.[34] This looks like a promising trend.

Professor Mertz has a recent paper in which she notes the many current calls for drastic reform of legal education.[35] Most of these proposals push for more contact with what Llewellyn calls the craft skills of law, such as negotiation, planning and drafting. Mertz argues that law professors must stay in contact with the state of law practice. However, she warns:

> But assessing the state of practice requires more than collecting anecdotes. Here is a place where social science has a contribution to make, providing more accurate pictures of law practice than might be available from a sprinkling of conversations with individual practitioners. On the other hand, social science studies by themselves will not bridge the gap between theory and practice. As any good enthnographer knows, we need to hear from the people who are actually practicing law—and who are being represented by lawyers—to create a truly integrated approach to training lawyers.[36]

Mertz warns, however, that social science isn't a cookbook that can be applied to law without an understanding of both its research methods and their limitations, as well as an appreciation of what legal scholarship is about. "Understanding the limits of our expertise is an important component of good interdisciplinary work."[37] She worries that:

> [A]n "add social science methods and stir" approach to training law students—in which, for example, incipient lawyers might be required to take a statistics course—may simply produce future lawyers with only partially digested and rudimentary statistical

---

[34] See, e.g., Michele LaVigne & Gregory J. Van Rybroek, *Breakdown in the Language Zone: The Prevalence of Language Impairments Among Juvenile and Adult Offenders and Why It Matters*, 15 U.C. DAVIS J. JUV. L. & POL'Y 37 (2011).

[35] Elizabeth Mertz, *Social Science and the Intellectual Apprenticeship: Moving the Scholarly Mission of Law Schools Forward*, 17 J. LEGAL WRITING INSTITUTE 427 (2011).

[36] *Id.* at 439.

[37] *Id.* at 435 n.22.

skills. Recognizing the limits of expertise in both law and social science may well be the first necessary step to reaching a new kind of synthesis—one that truly integrates two disciplines rather than merely layering somewhat incompatible forms of experience on top of one another without thought. . . .[38]

[W]hat is needed is a reformulation of the intellectual mission of legal education to integrate the knowledge generated by social science with the existing expertise of legal professionals skilled in moving from law-on-the-books to law-in-action.[39]

Mertz is clearly right. However, the "add social science and stir" approach seems to appeal to a group whose members are not noted for their humility—law professors.

IV. How Should We Evaluate Legal Education and the Legal System?

Finally, *The Bramble Bush* is an evaluation of our legal system by a noted legal realist scholar. While Llewellyn recognizes many problems, he defends law and lawyers against their critics—most notably the poet Carl Sandburg.[40] For example, Llewellyn says:

The closer I can come to seeing law whole, the more nearly do I, of the skeptic's clan, find myself bordering on mysticism. There is such balance and such beauty and such consummate skill in this whole—seen whole; balance and beauty and skill beyond the little powers of the individual judges.[41]

He looks at three of his heroes, Lord Mansfield, Judge Cardozo and Justice Holmes, and tells us that in their work: "there is poetry, in these things there is life, in these things there is beauty. If this be not culture, I do not know where to find it."[42]

When *The Bramble Bush* first appeared, Jerome Frank reviewed it in

---

[38] *Id.* at 434-35.

[39] *Id.* at 435-36.

[40] Llewellyn quotes all of Sandburg's poem "The Lawyers Know Too Much." THE BRAMBLE BUSH, at 142. It ends: "The lawyers—tell me why a hearse horse snickers hauling a lawyer's bones." Llewellyn mounts a major counterattack against Sandburg. "The unpopularity of our profession, the accusations against it, must not and cannot be permitted to hide its finer service from our eyes." THE BRAMBLE BUSH, at 150.

[41] THE BRAMBLE BUSH, at 125.

[42] *Id.* at 128.

the *Yale Law Journal*.[43] Frank and Llewellyn were two of the most noted legal realists. Frank had much favorable to say: "Written primarily for students—but appealing to all intelligent lawyers—this book discusses admirably in the homeliest terms some of the most difficult and important legal problems."[44] But Frank then offers a great deal of criticism of Llewellyn's "too emphatically favorable appraisal of the old ways."[45]

Frank notes that you can find in *The Bramble Bush* effective criticism of the "evil consequences of the conventional theory"[46] about the legal system. Llewellyn argues that rules do not control behavior; at best rules influence it in some circumstances. Judges have techniques for reading a precedent very broadly or very narrowly. Usually, judges prefer to follow a middle-of-the-road reading of the law. This helps them when they are pressed for time, and it reinforces the pressures to conform to the received wisdom about the boundaries of the judicial role. Moreover, judges must persuade other judges—some sit on panels composed of several judges, while others face the possibility of an appellate court reviewing their work. They will be seen as more persuasive if they seem to play by the rules of the game. Llewellyn argues that the constraints placed on weak judges and the freedom given to strong ones produce good results. Frank objects: We do not know how much effect the rule system and the norms that influences judges to follow rules in most situations really has. Moreover, these legal techniques can help an intelligent but bad judge rationalize wicked decisions. Frank sees Llewellyn as exposing many of the problems with our precedent system but, at the same time, insisting that we only repair rather than destroy the traditional tools of legal thought. Frank advocates much more change.

If we really wanted to evaluate the common law system of dealing with disputes, we would have to add to Llewellyn's argument some clear information about the common law system in action. As I have said, Llewellyn pointed out that little was known about what goes on in trial courts. Judging from what we have learned over the past eighty years, there are still real questions that need answering. Llewellyn is realistic about the way lawyers and judges "create" the facts,[47] and he recognizes that the jury is counted on to accept some blend of the extreme claims of

---

[43] Jerome Frank, *Book Review*, 40 YALE L.J. 1120 (1931).

[44] *Id.* at 1120.

[45] *Id.* at 1125.

[46] *Id.* at 1124.

[47] Llewellyn says: "One thing is clear: the raw events as they happened are not before judge or jury; there has been a straining process. The plaintiff's lawyer has, with an eye to *legal* relevance, and with an eye to winning, done some selection." THE BRAMBLE BUSH, at 31 (emphasis in original).

the parties. Similarly, Jerome Frank believed: "Legal rules do not control the trial courts since they cannot, no matter how intelligent the judge, control the subjectivity of the fact-finding process."[48]

If somehow we could learn all we wanted to know about trials, we would still need more information to assess the American system of dispute resolution and the role of courts and law in it. Today, we know some of what we need to know to evaluate the living law and the law in action.[49] Here I can only sketch a little of what we know relevant to such an appraisal. Samuel Gross and Kent Syverud claim that the primary function of trials in our legal system is not dispute resolution in the particular case. Rather, the real function is to deter other trials, and this function is carried out very successfully.[50] Trial judges work hard to push the parties to settle.[51]

The late Judge Robert R. Merhige, Jr., was a master at this.[52] In one cluster of cases, he dealt with the claims of major utilities against Westinghouse which concerned nuclear power plants, a guaranteed price for the fuel, and the problem of disposing of nuclear waste. Merhige demanded that executives of Westinghouse and each of the utilities meet at his home, sometimes without their lawyers present. In the courtroom, he pushed the lawyers by demanding that they work on weekends as well as late hours most days. He appointed a special master to aid in the negotiations as well as a committee of expert engineers not connected with the parties. He drove the parties to settle.[53] Similarly, several studies suggest

---

[48] Steven Richman, *Edgar Lee Masters and the Poetics of Legal Realism*, 31 CAL. W.L. REV. 103, 108 (1994).

[49] See Eugen Ehrlich, FUNDAMENTAL PRINCIPLES OF THE SOCIOLOGY OF LAW (Walter L. Moll, trans., 1936); David Nelkin, *Law in Action or Living Law? Back to the Beginning Sociology of Law*, 4 LEGAL STUDIES 157, 166-68 (1984). Such sources tell us that law in action focuses on the gap between the law on the books and the actual practices of legal officials and the public in cases of disputes. Ehrlich's idea of the living law refers to the "norms recognised as obligatory by citizens in their capacity as members of associations." Much of the work that we think of as legal, actually is carried out by various kinds of "private governments." See Stewart Macaulay, *Private Government*, in Leon Lipson & Stanton Wheeler, eds., LAW AND SOCIAL SCIENCE 445 (1986).

[50] Samuel R. Gross & Kent D. Syverud, *Don't Try, Civil Jury Verdicts in a System Geared to Settlement*, 44 UCLA L. REV. 63, 63 (1996).

[51] See, e.g., Marc Galanter, "*. . . A Settlement Judge, Not a Trial Judge": Judicial Mediation in the United States*, 12 J. LAW & SOC'Y 1 (1985); Marc Galanter & Mia Cahill, "*Most Cases Settle": Judicial Promotion and Regulation of Settlements*, 46 STANFORD L. REV. 1339 (1994).

[52] R. J. Bacigal, MAY IT PLEASE THE COURT: A BIOGRAPHY OF JUDGE ROBERT R. MERHIGE, JR. (1992).

[53] See Stewart Macaulay, Jean Braucher, John Kidwell & William Whitford, 2 CON-

that today we face "the vanishing trial," as few cases actually get past all of the filters that ward off litigation.[54]

How should we evaluate a system that pushes parties to settle? Or judge one where access to the courts is rationed by cost barriers to litigation? Marc Galanter and Mia Cahill stress that "[s]ettlement is not intrinsically good or bad, anymore than adjudication is good or bad. Settlements do not share any generic traits that commend us to avoid them *per se* or to promote them."[55] On the other hand, *The Bramble Bush* recognizes that there is a tendency for the best lawyers to work for clients who can pay the most, and this dynamic is at work whether cases settle or proceed to trial. Llewellyn tells us:

> [I]t is clear that the activity of most skillful lawyers will be upon the side of the Haves and not upon the side of the Have-nots; conscience-sturdy activity, too, impassioned skill; one cannot live with Haves for twenty years without contagion. The best talent of the bar will always muster to keep Ins in and to man the barricade against the Outs. And while in theory legal contests may be equal, ... the man with the longer purse who can hire the better, the more skillful man, has his advantage and will have it in the time to come. Where long-run legal strategy is called for, the marshalling of counsel and of cases through a generation, this advantage will be piled up twentyfold.[56]

TRACTS: LAW IN ACTION 666-71, 675-99 (3d ed. 2010), for an account of Judge Merhige's "coercive mediation" of Westinghouse's contract problems with nuclear energy.

[54] See, e.g., Marc Galanter, *The Vanishing Trial: An Examination of Trials and Related Matters in Federal and State Courts*, 1 J. EMPIRICAL LEGAL STUDIES 459 (2004). Compare John Lande, *Shifting the Focus from the Myth of "The Vanishing Trial" to Complex Conflict Management Systems, or I Learned Almost Everything I Need to Know about Conflict Resolution from Marc Galanter*, 6 CARDOZO J. OF CONFLICT RESOLUTION 191, 211 (2005) ("Before becoming horrified at the possible demise of the trial in general, we should have a clearer picture of the actual changes and their consequences. In the meantime, the insights of legal pluralism can help provide a balanced analysis by recognizing that much adjudication occurs before trial and outside the courts.")

[55] Marc Galanter & Mia Cahill, *"Most Cases Settle": Judicial Promotion and Regulation of Settlements*, 46 STANFORD L. REV. 1339, 1388 (1994). Ezra Friedman & Abraham L. Wickelgren, *Chilling, Settlement, and the Accuracy of the Legal Process*, 26 J. LAW, ECON. & ORG. 144 (2010), offer a model suggesting that "even if damages are set optimally, allowing settlement can reduce social welfare." This is because settlement "reduces the accuracy of legal outcomes."

[56] THE BRAMBLE BUSH, at 144-45.

In his classic article, Galanter shows us why "the haves come out ahead."[57] He points to the advantage that "repeat players" hold over "one-shot" parties. Those who anticipate having to go to court to deal with multiple cases involving similar issues can invest in legal work and plan strategy. They also can afford to invest in lobbying to try to change the rules to their benefit.

Furthermore, much takes place before anyone files a complaint and formally starts a legal action. Professor Nora Engstrom, for example, reports that high volume personal injury law firms are running what she calls "settlement mills."[58] They press the claims of their clients against insurance companies through negotiation and gain relatively quick settlements. Most of the settlements can be defended, but Engstrom argues that these law firms do not even attempt to litigate when a settlement offer is very low in light of a client's injuries. Insurance companies have worked to rationalize settlement practice. Twelve of the twenty leading automobile insurers use Colossus, a computer program that recommends settlement amounts by comparing the details of an accident claim with a database of what the insurance company had done in similar cases.[59] Plaintiffs' lawyers have not been happy with the way these databases were constructed.

Obviously, there are cost barriers to litigation. Somehow, one wishing to make a claim must find a way to pay lawyers, expert witnesses and court costs. For many, the contingent fee solved the problem. The lawyer was paid a percentage of what, if anything, she won for her client. Jurors often awarded subjective damages that did not have a clear market value as compensation for emotional distress. Business interests organized the American Tort Reform Association, and it has been very successful in lobbying legislatures to limit plaintiffs' lawyers actions. Its website says:

> ATRA supports an aggressive civil justice reform agenda that includes:
>
> Health care liability reform
>
> Class action reform
>
> Promotion of jury service
>
> Abolition of the rule of joint and several liability

---

[57] Marc Galanter, *Why the 'Haves' Come Out Ahead: Speculations on the Limits of Legal Change*, 9 LAW & SOC'Y REV. 95 (1974).

[58] Nora Freeman Engstrom, *Sunlight and Settlement Mills*, 86 N.Y.U. L. REV. 805 (2011).

[59] Dawn R. Bonnett, *The Use of Colossus to Measure the General Damages of a Personal Injury Claim Demonstrates Good Faith Claims Handling*, 53 CLEVELAND ST. L. REV. 107 (2005).

Abolition of the collateral source rule

Limits on punitive damages

Limits on noneconomic damages

Production liability reform

Appeal bond reform

Sound science in the courtroom

Stopping regulation through litigation[60]

As we might predict, ATRA is met in combat before the legislatures by the American Association for Justice.[61] This association, primarily made up of trial lawyers, fights tort reform before the legislatures and before the courts. Moreover, corporate lawyers have drafted standard form contracts that often contain arbitration clauses which send consumer and employment cases to a private dispute resolution system. Some have argued that many of these systems are captives of the large corporations that hire them. Thus, there are many levels at which those with more money and power can influence the delivery of legal services and the ability to vindicate rights.

Finally, we can add that Americans have very mixed feelings about bringing a law suit.[62] There are many barriers to asserting a claim. One can sue one's employer and even win, but then where is the next job? Being a plaintiff in significant litigation can take over one's life. Family and friends are not sure to support bringing the claim. At the minimum, anyone appraising the American system of handling disputes must look far beyond the legal rules.

Thus, one cannot get a clear picture of the American system for resolving disputes just by reading appellate cases—judicial opinions do not reflect a random sample of what is going on both inside and outside our courts. Llewellyn recognizes:

> You will find one great group of litigated cases which were predestined to be litigated. . . . They are in court because they are so exceptional that the normal ways of society have afforded no solid basis for deciding them, or even because the ordinary ma-

---

[60] <www.atra.org/about>

[61]

[62] See William L. Felstiner, Richard L. Abel & Austin Sarat, *The Emergence and Transformation of Disputes: Naming, Blaming, Claiming . . .,* 15 LAW & SOC'Y REV. 631 (1980-81); Catherine R. Albiston, *Bargaining in the Shadow of Social Institutions: Competing Discourses and Social Change in Workplace Mobilization of Civil Rights,* 39 LAW & SOC'Y REV. 11 (2005).

chinery of adjusting cases in society has no teeth which fasten on them.[63]

If one were to attempt to evaluate the American legal system, she would have to consider all these facts involved in the law in action—and probably more as well. Increasingly, we are beginning to be able to do this. The picture is complex and messy; simple theories are just wrong. Llewellyn's eighty year old book touches on only part of the picture. But it is the part that is stressed in the first year of law school, and it is a part of the skill set required of most lawyers.

Jerome Frank listed many problems with *The Bramble Bush,* and I've raised a few more. Nonetheless, as Frank told us: "Here is a book to read many times, be you law school student or that somewhat humbler type of student, a sensible practicing lawyer. You will find it hard-headed yet (or, rather, and) vigorously idealistic."[64] Whether it is a testament to this classic text or a comment on the state of legal education in the 21st century, that assessment remains true today.

STEWART MACAULAY
Malcolm Pitman Sharp Professor and
Theodore W. Brazeau Professor Emeritus,
University of Wisconsin Law School

Madison, Wisconsin
April, 2012

---

[63] THE BRAMBLE BUSH, at 58.

[64] Frank, *Book Review,* 40 YALE L.J. at 1121.

NOTES OF THE SERIES EDITOR

As the series editor for *Legal Legends* at Quid Pro Books, I can say that we have tried as much as possible to recreate *The Bramble Bush* exactly as Karl Llewellyn published it and intended it in 1951 and 1960: as an accessible and helpful collection he edited from his lectures given to students at Columbia University Law School. The other contemporary reproductions of this classic book (even by established presses), which I compared to the original source, all failed to produce it accurately. I infer that they were created by scanning without an awareness of the limitations of that technology, and then run through a spellchecker that did not discriminate between words and usages as the author intended (e.g., he refers to canons of case precedent, not "cannons"). They sometimes deleted whole lines of text, altered key phrases, and in any event used nonstandard page numbering (which in turn skewed the cross-references). This approach made it harder to navigate through or understand this great work—and made Llewellyn's careful and lyrical (and occasionally difficult) prose harder than it had to be ... with simply an accurate rendition of his actual text. A reprinting's presentation should not distract the reader from the work, misstate the author's intent, or make it difficult to assign and reference.

Thus, the principal goal of this new edition was simply to let Llewellyn be Llewellyn, yet speak to a new generation of students with modern formatting that is accessible to them. We emphasized accuracy of text and usefulness to readers. To that end, this version includes all the original page numbers, from the standard 1951 and 1960 editions of *The Bramble Bush* produced by Oceana Publications and reprinted over two decades (up to the 1981 printing, when it was inexplicably reworked and altered). Fortunately, the pagination for these editions remained standard over that time (when in doubt the 1960 edition is used). The page numbers are reintroduced into text by the use of {brackets} so that the work may be accurately assigned, cited, and referenced. This also allows consistency with the new eBook edition of the book, which likewise embeds this standard pagination.

Anything else in brackets is material we have added. For example, in occasional places we've added and bracketed a word or two to complete a shorthand from that era that would not be understood by today's students. In a few passages where Llewellyn refers to a specific legal procedure, we provide the modern name for that concept or rule, just so that readers can relate his point to terminology they would face in a current first-year class. We have annotated in brackets some historical references, to make his point clear to present readers. We also added the first name, in brackets, where he referred to a legal figure known at the time but perhaps unknown to new readers.

These additions are relatively few and, we hope, not a serious imposition on his actual wording, which remains unaltered. In any event, except for a few set rules below, the text follows his original editions and is true, most pointedly, to the accepted 1960 edition which as noted is the author's best and final version of this work. The overriding intent was to respect Llewellyn. Notably, his timeless advice permits that without much in the way of deviation.

Even so, producing this classic work for a modern format (to include eBooks) required a few alterations that were necessary today, even under the goal of carefully recreating his work. Some notes to keep in mind:

- We have made minor, consistent spacing changes throughout for legibility without changing the words or quotability in any way (for example, adding more space around his few blockquotes, to set them off clearly).

- All of Llewellyn's prose is reproduced as he had it, without editing. Keep in mind that it was delivered as a *lecture* series, and the pace and comma structure make more sense when it is read that way, as if spoken. The book is also quite evocative with that image in mind. But in a few passages where there was an obvious misprint (two periods in a row, the wrong word printed, that sort of thing), we took the liberty of correcting the printer error.

- In a few passages, where an older spelling he used could be confusing to a modern student, we updated the spelling to be clear as to his intent. Yet this license was used rarely, and you will see many older phrasings and words throughout left untouched because they will not unduly confuse the current reader.

- A lengthy Acknowledgments section that he included in his first edition is omitted here, just as he omitted it in both of the later editions used for this version. It was quite a summary and footnote-laden review of the literature that influenced this work and, though not particularly necessary as part of the purpose and target of this book, could be a useful bibliography to researchers in legal history and jurisprudence; it is recommended to them. It is not the usual Acknowledgments, in the sense of thanking his typists and friends; it is his *intellectual* acknowledgment. Its length and depth is hinted at in the present Acknowledgments, where he admits he thanked everyone in history but his cats. At any rate, his later Foreword certainly is included, and it explains a lot of what was the first reaction (and perhaps overreaction) to the most famous quote from his first edition. The earlier Preface is not reproduced, both because he omitted it in later printings and because its text is largely subsumed into the present Foreword. The book's helpful Afterword, which he added to the end of later editions, is reproduced at the back.

- Special thanks are extended to Professor Stewart Macaulay, an inspirational teacher and leader in the law and society movement, for contributing his new Introduction and notes. Painstaking copy-editing was volunteered by Lee D. Scheingold, along with detailed design consultation by Michele Veade and research expertise by Bonnie Shucha. We thank them profusely as well.

As noted, this edition was designed to include a digital platform, where the gap in availability is stark. Nonetheless, even in print it corrects the scanning errors and undisclosed editing found in current republications as well. Other classic works, in eBook and print formats, are available at multiple retail sites and at *www.quidprobooks.com*.

STEVEN ALAN CHILDRESS
Conrad Meyer III Professor of Law,
Tulane University Law School

New Orleans, Louisiana
May, 2012

THE
BRAMBLE
BUSH

FOREWORD

{page 7}

These lectures grew out of an attempt in 1929 and 1930 to introduce the students at Columbia Law School to the study of law. They were privately printed in 1930, and met with reasonable favor. But I found out early that their bite for a beginning law student lies rather in November than in September; and a man's own ideas—especially on perspective and whole-view—change as he gains experience. Hence for ten years I planned and worked over a rewrite.

Then it slowly became clear that I have no business to rewrite. The young fellow who wrote these lectures just isn't here any more, and the job he did has its own virtue, and I have no right to mess it up with Monday morning quarter-backing which has used two decades in getting from Saturday to Monday morning. Hence I republish with no more change than is normal as a man corrects page-proof: a comma deleted here, a clarification wrought there—but within the limits of one line or two.

How to accomplish any introduction is a problem as perennial as it is perplexing. Of one thing I remain persuaded: across the problem of material, and indeed of method, cuts that of manner. The primer type of textbook introduction has been well done and yet found wanting. The materials-to-work-with type is, thank Heaven, today a flourishing line of thought, work and publication, and already beginning to bear.

But a right text is a different thing. It should be a *standing* introduction. It should be simple. It should seem to lie open to a student who has never met the law, and give him a footing. He need not fully understand it all, or any of it; but out of each page, each sentence, he should get enough to help him in his work.

But the work of a right text-"introduction" has then only begun. It ought to invite, excite, to a second reading and to a third and to a fourth. Each reading, in the measure that the reader has moved on into the law and gained a further wherewithal to read, should introduce him further. This is the only right goal. With all its surface simplicity, an introduction must cut as deep as its author has wit and strength to see the way. It must cut for that deepest simplicity which is true meaning.

I still think this ideal obvious. An introduction, like a teacher, must gain and not lose in retrospect, or be a half-thing. Hence no man's solution is likely either in matter or in manner to seem sufficient to himself, much less to others. But as we begin slowly to discover how to approach these {8} vital matters simply, it becomes vital in a new way to remember that the sound quest cannot be for the simple-via-the-shallow; it must drive on despite all defeat toward the simple-via-the-deep.

Meantime, in regard to presentation, let me repeat a full sentence from the earlier preface. It states doctrine I still stand to: "And I care little for propriety, and less for manner, if—as I believe—occasional lapses from the accepted taste and dignity of print give more hope of making vivid to the students who are a teacher's life some of the more passionately held convictions which motivate his living."

Acknowledgments

The only persons who seem to have been left out of the list of acknowledgments in the prior private printing {in 1930} are Adam, Euripides, Genghis Khan, Alpha Centauri and my cats.

These errors of omission are obvious, but are they significant? The discussion here proceeds on a horse-sense basis to lay out for seeing various things which I take to be obviously so to any moderately experienced eye which will take time to look and think. Is a lyric poet to waste time giving acknowledgments to the first guy who happened to put on paper that a lily of the valley is a loveliness?

The young man who prepared these lectures had sense enough to know that he was offering no original ideas, that he was merely drawing on and attempting to shape into a thing *seen* some stuff from a great and noble common reservoir of observation. What the young man had not yet discovered was that Cititis was a disease abroad in the land. Victims of this mental disorder hold the delusion that nothing *is*, except in print; and that even what is in print is taboo to use unless some print is cited. I have been fighting Cititis, especially in law reviews, now for many years. (The cure is to ask: Where did Aristotle get his stuff from?) I shall not here contribute to its spread.

Correcting an error: "What these officials do about disputes..."

On the old page 3 and on the present page 12 appear the words: "What these officials do about disputes is, to my mind, the law itself."

{9} These words express a deep and often sad truth for any counselor: he can get for his client what he can actually get, and no more. They express a deeper and often even sadder truth for any litigant: "rights" which cannot be realized are worse than useless; they are traps of delay, expense and heartache. The words pose the problem of the reform of institutions and press upon us the eternal problem of the need for personnel careful, upright, wise. They signal the possibility of differential favoritism and prejudice on the one hand; the possibility, on the other, of much good being brought out of an ill-designed and limping machinery of measures. In so far the words are useful words, and true ones, and I have let them stand.

They are, however, unhappy words when not more fully developed, and they are plainly at best a very partial statement of the whole truth. For it is clear that one office of law is to control officials in some part, and to guide them even in places where no thoroughgoing control is possible, or is desired. And it is clear that guidance and control *for* action and by others than the actor cannot be had out of the very action sought to be controlled or guided. Moreover, no man sees law whole who ever forgets that one inherent drive which is a living part of even the most wrongheaded and arbitrary legal system is a drive—patent or latent, throbbing or faint-pulsed, impatient or sluggish, but always present—to make the system, its detail and its officials more closely realize an ideal of justice. That drive works in ways so complex and varied as to be but dimly suggested in "what these officials do," in regard to any given occasion. Thus the words fail to take proper account either of the office of the institution of law as an instrument for conscious shaping or of the office and work of that institution as a machinery of sometimes almost unconscious questing for the ideal; and the words therefore need some such expansion and correction as the foregoing.

But there is more to the matter than this. The history of these thirteen short words sheds troubling light on the methods, manner and ethics of a style of controversy in jurisprudence which is now happily waning but against which it still pays to warn. Let me note that at the time of the tentative printing {the 1930 edition} I had already served four years as a Commissioner on Uniform State Laws and had completed the drafting for the Commissioners of a rather ambitious statute, and that a few months before *The Bramble Bush* I had brought out a book on Sales with what is I think still the most detailed discussion in print of the use of cases and statutes in advocacy and in counseling, and with a sustained critique of the rules in that field, looking not only to a more effective analytical statement but also to that reform of them which now forms the core of the Uniform Commercial Code. Against that background came the teapot tempest in which "realism" (which was and still is an effort at more effective legal {10} technology) was mistaken for a philosophy and made the scape-goat for all the sins (real and supposed) of administrators and autocrats and the ungodly in general. No piece of ammunition in the whole teapot compares in the frequency of its use, nor yet in the irresponsibility thereof, with our little thirteen-word passage. With its help, I was shown to disbelieve in rules, to deny them and their existence and desirability, to approve and exalt brute force and arbitrary power and unfettered tyranny, to disbelieve in ideals and particularly in justice. This was painful to me. But it was even more painful to observe that none of the attackers, exactly none, gave any evidence, as they slung around the little sentence, of having looked even at the rest of *Bramble Bush* itself. A single sentence, if it made a good brick-bat for a current fight, was enough to characterize a whole man and his whole position. And that ought to be painful to anybody. I have in mind at the moment passages from twelve different writers in which the poor sentence was marshalled to convict me of one or more intellectual crimes; and the passages are by no means all signed by inexperienced youth: Dickinson, Goodhart, Kantorwicz, Kocourek, Patterson, Pound, e.g., are names of power. And I take a perverse pride in one passage in which "BRAMBLE BUSH, page 3," alone, leads off a list of eighteen citations whose every other member is a full article or a full book.

In retrospect it is amusing, and the story reads like rather grotesque farce. I think that is because our methods, manners and ethic of controversy in jurisprudence have tremendously improved. All over the country, as all over the Western World, jurisprudes have begun to try to read a man as they should: for his wheat, sorting out his chaff. It is interesting that Cardozo was at work on that line on the "realists" by 1932, while the hurricane was already in full sweep across the tea leaves.

And so to work

As indicated already, and as is developed in the *Afterword*, this is not the book that I should write today. I feel a lack especially in the failure to get before the reader at the outset the idea of the crafts of law, of their value to the prospective craftsman, of his obligation to those crafts. But there is at least this to be said in mitigation: the first craft of law a man must learn is the craft of the law-student; and to that one the lectures as written attempt to give both body and meaning.

K. N. LLEWELLYN

Columbia University Law School
December, 1950

THE BRAMBLE BUSH

I · WHAT LAW IS ABOUT

{*page* 11}

You have come to this school to embark upon the study of the law. Most of you have in the back of your heads an idea that as a result of that study you will become lawyers. Some of you have some notion of what it is that a lawyer does. You think of a man who tries cases before courts. Or do you think particularly of a man to whom to turn in case, for any reason, you happen to get arrested? But what a court does, what a lawyer does in court, and what he does outside, what relationship either court or lawyer has to the law, what relation the law school has to any of these things—around these things, I take it, there floats a pleasant haze. If it were not pleasant, you would not be here. Perhaps you would not, if there were no haze.

What I propose to do is to take up successively a series of questions. First, and today, what is this law about, which you propose to study? Second, and tomorrow, what is the machinery for going about this study; what are you going to have to do in this school and how can you best go about doing it? Third, what are the opportunities that the school offers and what are some of the problems that you will have to solve here, and what are some of the ways of their solution? And lastly, how does the study of the law here bear upon the work that you will do and the life that you will live when you leave this school and go into the practice?

We have no great illusions, my brethren and I, as to how much good it will do you to be told these things in advance. We have learned by bitter experience that you will not take the things we tell you very seriously. You conceive this, I take it, to be somewhat in the nature of the pep meeting to which you were exposed when you first entered college. You expect me to tell you that you should be earnest about your work, and get your back into it for dear old Siwash, and that he who lets work slide will stumble by the way. You sit back with a cynical detachment, prepared in advance to let this anticipatory jawing slide comfortably off your neck and rump. Let him have his say. That is what he gets his pay for. But we, the sophisticated youth of this new century, we know that he means little of what he says, and what he does mean, as far as *he* is concerned, means nothing to us. The ungovernable hand of fate has put him in the chair; no help for that.

The workings of society require us to let his mouthings fan our ears. Another of the conditions to admission to the bar.

We have, I say, no great illusions as to how much good this talking at you is to do. Still we must perform our duty as we see it. Not only that, {12} but after some sweat of spirit we have arrived at the conclusion that some things need saying, even to the wilful deaf. They shall be said!

There is yet another thing upon which experience long and sad has caused us disillusion. We have discovered in our teaching of the law that general propositions are empty. We have discovered that students who come eager to learn the rules and who do learn them, *and who learn nothing more*, will take away the shell and not the substance. We have discovered that rules *alone*, mere forms of words, are worthless. We have learned that the concrete instance, the heaping up of concrete instances, the present, vital memory of a multitude of concrete instances, is necessary in order to make any general proposition, be it rule of law or any other, *mean* anything at all. Without the concrete instances the general proposition is baggage, impedimenta, stuff about the feet. It not only does not help. It hinders. And since what I am to say to you is said while there is vacuum in your heads, the likelihood of its taking hold, or its taking on meaning, of its having utility for you at the present time, is very slight. It would be slight enough if you had any will to hear.

Yet it needs saying. It needs saying because there is great joy in heaven when even one lost sheep is gathered to the fold. It needs saying because there is always an odd chance, an odd chance worth eight hours of your time and mine, that something of what is said may stick long enough to be on hand *when the concrete problems do develop* before you, on hand to help your thinking when they come.

What, then, is this law business about? It is about the fact that our society is honeycombed with disputes. Disputes actual and potential; disputes to be settled and disputes to be prevented; both appealing to law, both making up the business of the law. But obviously those which most violently call for attention are the actual disputes, and to these our first attention must be directed. Actual disputes call for somebody to do something about them. First, so that there may be peace, for the disputants; for other persons whose ears and toes disputants are disturbing. And secondly, so that the dispute may really be put at rest, which means, so that a solution may be achieved which, at least in the main, is bearable to the parties and not disgusting to the lookers-on. This doing of something about disputes, this doing of it reasonably, is the business of law. And the people who have the doing in charge, whether they be judges or sheriffs or clerks or jailers or lawyers, are officials of the law. *What these officials do about disputes is, to my mind, the law itself.**

There are not so many, I think, who would agree with me in thus re-garding law. It is much more common to approach the law as being *a set of rules of conduct*, and most thinkers would say rules of *external* conduct to distinguish them from the rules of morality: be good, sweet {13} maid, and let who will be clever. And most of the thinkers would probably say rules *enforced by external constraint*, to distinguish them not only from rules of morality, but also from some phases of custom, such as wearing ties and Paris garters. And many thinkers would add, rules *laid down by the state*, in order to distinguish them from the commands of a father, or the regula-tions of a university, or the compulsion to be a Democrat in Georgia. Most thinkers, too, would take these rules as *addressed to the man on the street* and as telling him what to do and what not to do. To most thinkers, I say, *rules* are the heart of law, and the arrangement of rules in orderly coherent system is the business of the legal scholar, and argument in terms of rules, the drawing of a neat solution from a rule to fit the case in hand—that is the business of the judge and of the advocate.

All of which seems to me rather sadly misleading. There is indeed much, in some part of law, to be said for this view that "rules laid down *for* conduct" are the focus, quite *apart from disputes*. Rules that everyone's income tax return must be made out on the same type of form do not look to disputes so much as to convenience of administration. Rules as to fencing elevator shafts look primarily to avoiding not disputes, but inju-ries. And indeed it may properly be said that as civilization grows more complex there is a widening slice of law in which disputes as such sink out of sight, and the focus of law becomes the arrangement or rearrangement of business or conduct to get things done more quickly, more easily, more safely. It may properly be said that in many such cases there is not even (as there is in requiring travel on the left side of the road or on the right; or in fixing *the* one effective form for validating will or deed) a purpose of dispute-avoidance running *beside* the purpose of convenience. It may properly be said, finally, that even where the purpose clearly is dispute-avoidance, that purpose in turn often sinks into the background, and men talk about contracts, and trusts, and corporations, as if these things exist-ed in themselves, instead of being the shadows cast across the front stage by the movements of the courts unheeded in the rear. All of this, however, goes not so much to the importance of "rules" as to the *non-exclusive* importance of *disputes*. Whether about disputes, or about when wills are valid, or about the form for income tax reports, we come back always to

---

* *For necessary expansion and correction, see e.g. pp. 22, 42, "(3)"; 58-9; 71-74; 75 ff. — and especially 8-10.*

one common feature: The main thing is what officials are going to *do*. And so to my mind the main thing is seeing what officials do, do about disputes, or about anything else; and seeing that there is a certain regularity in their doing—a regularity which makes possible prediction of what they and other officials are about to do tomorrow. In many cases that prediction cannot be wholly certain. Then you have room for something else, another main thing for the lawyer the study of how to make the official do what you would like to have him. At that point {14} "rules" loom into importance. Great importance. For judges think that they must follow rules, and people highly approve of that thinking. So that the getting of the judge to do a thing is in considerable measure the art of finding what rules are available to urge upon him, and of how to urge them to accomplish your result. In considerable measure. Rules, too, then, and their arrangement, and their logical manipulation, make up an unmistakable portion of the business of the law and of the lawyer.

In any event, and whether I am right or whether I am wrong in this analysis, it is certain that you will spend much of your time attempting to discover and to study and to remember and to see the meaning of these so-called *rules of law* which judges say they are bound by, which judges say they have to apply. If I am wrong you can perhaps rest content when you have found out what the judges say. If I am wrong, you can believe what they say and be happy. But if I am right, finding out what the judges *say* is but the beginning of your task. You will have to take what they say and compare it with what they *do*. You will have to see whether what they say matches with what they do. You will have to be distrustful of whether they themselves know (any better than other men) the ways of their own doing, and of whether they describe it accurately, even if they know it. Nor is this all. If I am right you will also have to look into the question of what difference what the judges do is going to make to you, or to your client, or to any other person who may be affected by the judges' rulings on disputes. And even that will not be all. For when you find out what difference the judges' acts will make, you will then be confronted with the task of figuring what you, or your client, are to do about it. If the judges say a contract with your buyer that he will not resell below a certain price will be illegal, and not enforceable, if they are likely to fine you or send you to jail for making such a contract, but you still want your goods resold throughout the country at a single price—what can *you* do? That is a problem for invention, for ingenuity; the problem of inventing a method of action which will keep you free of difficulty and will produce the results you want in spite, if you please, of what the judges in a case of dispute may be expected to do. If I am right, in a word, the action of the judges past and prospective becomes a piece of your environment, a condition of your living—like the use of money—with which you must reckon if you want to get where you would go to. And you cannot then rest content upon their *words*. It will be their *action* and the available means of influencing their action or of arranging your affairs with reference to their action which make up the "law" you have to study. And *rules*, in all of this, are important to you so far as they help you see or predict what judges will do or so far as they help you get judges to do something. That is their importance. That is all their importance, except as pretty playthings. But you will discover that you can no more afford {15} to overlook them than you can afford to stop with having learned their words.[*]

You will have noted, I hope, that I have been talking chiefly about disputes, whereas the ordinary man's thinking about law is in terms of "axmurderer breaks up love nest" or of "bobbed-haired bandit loots three banks"—or at the very least, of Mr. Volstead. But, as a matter of logic, crime and those who commit crime and the conviction or acquittal of those who say that they have not committed crime, although the district attorney alleges savagely they have, all belong under the head of disputes. As a matter of logic they are but one such class of disputes: those which are deemed to affect less two particular private parties who may be incidentally concerned than they affect the whole body of the public, as represented by the state officials. Not merely as a matter of logic, but as a matter of practical importance, *disputes* is a larger and more important category than the category *crimes*. The criminal business of the courts bulks large, yes; but in terms of quantity it does not bulk so large as the civil business. We can afford, therefore, to think of law as relating primarily to disputes, and to think of crimes as only one piece of the business of the law. On the other hand, crimes are a peculiarly important piece of that business. They are the piece which it seems so essential to deal with that we do not always wait for the aggrieved party to act before the state official steps in; that indeed we do not trust the aggrieved party to handle the affair, even when he has made a complaint. So that if you have looked over the list of courses offered in the school, it may already have struck you as somewhat strange that you find but one course in the undergraduate curriculum allotted to this whole field of crime, while all the rest is taken up with the civil side of law. I suppose that the reason for this somewhat astounding fact is that we expect very few of you to practice on the criminal side. Some of you, to be sure, and especially those who have some ambitions in a political way, may for a time go into the public prosecutor's office. A few of you may go further and undertake to emulate the noted defenders of those accused of crime. But in the main it will be an accident if five percent of you touch criminal practice more than incidentally in the course of your professional

---

[*] For needed correction of this passage, see page 12, n.

careers. That is more than regrettable, as it is also regrettable that the criminal bar in the large enjoys anything but an enviable reputation. But regrettability does not change conditions, and I surmise that the curriculum has been constructed with reference to conditions and not with reference to regrettabilities.

But I should say here, as I shall say again, that whatever the nature of your prospective practice, it would be a misfortune for you, and for us, and for the public whom you, supposedly, will later service, if you were {16} to confine your training in this school to what I may describe as bread-and-butter courses, to those which seem to you of most immediate practical importance, to those which you conceive adapted to butter your bread, or to give you bread to butter.

At this stage of the game I wish to do no more than to indicate one of the huge discrepancies between the set-up of the law curriculum and the importance of law in life. *In the world outside the criminal law cuts to the essence of things legal.* In the law school curriculum it appears almost as an excrescence upon the body of the private law. There are reasons for this which are defensible. But one thing I would drive home before you begin your study: that it will not do to take your picture of the importance of the law to society or of the relative importance of various fields of the law from any law curriculum alone.

Within the field of civil law, however, it may well be that the divisions of the law curriculum afford a more trustworthy guide to actual importance. And no division is more vital, or more necessary for your immediate understanding, than that between so-called substantive law and so-called adjective {i.e., procedural} law. The idea behind that division is something like this: That certain bodies of law, which we call substantive— the substance of the law—deal with what ought to be, with whether contracts ought to be enforced at law, and when; with what formalities are necessary to make a last will stick; with how to form a corporation and how to issue its stock, and how to keep investors from having any say in it; with what words are necessary to make an effective lease or deed of land; and so on. The idea, so far as I get it, is that these are matters which can be thrashed out without immediate reference to the courts; that these are matters which can be determined and are determined in terms of what ought to happen, and that rules can be laid down by legislatures or by courts, and are, making clear what ought to happen in such cases.

Adjective law, on the other hand, is supposed to be the mere regulation of the work of the courts. The business procedure, if you please, by which they go about doing what they ought to do and go about solving disputes to ends already indicated by the substance of the law. That some procedure is necessary should be fairly obvious. There may once have been a society so simple that all one had to do when there was a dispute was to go up to Uncle Obediah, pull him away from his plow for ten minutes, talk the matter over, and listen to what he had to say. But when there are enough disputes to take up all the time of ten or a thousand Uncle Obediahs, an *order* of business becomes necessary. We cannot all run in on the same judge at once, or none of us will get our business done. We cannot even all run in upon the particular judge who has been assigned to our case, or most of us will sit around for three weeks waiting for the others to have their cases heard. Moreover, there are defendants who will not {17} be willing to come to court with us when we have a dispute against them, and there must be some regular procedure for getting them there and some regular means for letting them know what the row is about. Indeed, there is some importance in getting the disputes fairly well stated in advance so that the judge, too, will know what the row is about. And so it goes. To economize the time of judges and parties, to make the issues clear in advance, to give due notice and due chance for a hearing to defendants, and again due notice and chance for a hearing to plaintiffs in regard to what defendants claim by way of a defense, to make the trial itself orderly; again, to economize time and make regular and fair the presentation of the case to an upper court when one side claims that the lower court has not acted according to the proper rule; finally, to have a record of just what dispute was litigated, so as to prevent its being brought up a second time—these things make up procedure. And from one angle it is perfectly clear that this procedure has nothing whatever to do with the subject matter, the substance, of the dispute, nor with the desirable way of deciding it. From one angle, I say, it is clear that procedure has nothing whatever to do with substantive law. For these reasons it is worthwhile to take a distinction between the two. It is worthwhile to mark off a course in procedure, a course in trial practice, a course in evidence, and set them apart as technical studies which run free of any particular substantive subject matter. From this angle these procedure courses appear as the technical tools of the trade and nothing more; as books of etiquette through which one learns to use the legal oyster fork for legal oysters and to avoid the knife when picking bones from legal fish.

But from another angle this distinction tends to disappear. For if you whistle your soup you may be looked at queerly, you may be laughed at; you may even fail to be invited out again, another time. But if you slip in your legal etiquette it is not a question of queer looks or laughter or of what may happen later; it is likely to cost you your case right here and now; your case, and your client's case. The lawyer's slip in etiquette is the client's ruin. From this angle I say procedural regulations are the door, and the only door, to make real what is laid down by substantive law. Procedural regulations enter into and condition all substantive law's becoming actual when there is a dispute. Again this is no reason for not marking off procedure and evidence and trial practice as fields for special and peculiar study apart from substantive law. They should be marked off. They should be marked off for the most intensive study. But they should be so marked off not because they are really separate, but because they are of such transcendent importance as to need special emphasis. They should be marked off not to be kept apart and distinct, but solely in order that they may be more firmly learned, more firmly ingrained into the student *as conditioning the existence of any substantive law at all.* Everything {18} that you know of procedure you must carry into *every* substantive course. You must read each substantive course, so to speak, through the spectacles of the procedure. For what substantive law says should be means nothing except in terms of what procedure says that you can make real.

You will have observed that I do not take too much stock in this demarcation of substantive law from adjective, as *meaning* much. I see the distinction as offering simply a certain convenience in one's thinking. Substantive law presents the problem of where officials *would like* to get with a problem, and of where they say that they *are going* to get—either because they want to, or because tradition forces them. But discussions of substantive law become so easily misleading; one falls so easily into thinking that because he would like to get somewhere, he has arrived. *If wishes were horses, then beggars would ride.* If rules were results, there would be little need of lawyers.

Nonetheless the demarkation is convenient, and convenient especially to help classify the *types* of problem law must reckon with. So, too, within substantive law, one can make various rough groupings for convenience. I suppose the most vital one is that between what we call public and what we call private law. Public law is that part of law which deals with the framework of the state, the operations of the state and the more direct relations between the state and the individual or the various groups of individuals, like corporations. The Constitution states the framework for all our law. Legislation is one great tool of legal change and readaptation. The administrative officer, from the Secretary of the Treasury issuing regulations on income taxes down to the traffic policeman with his stop-and-go, affects the lives of each of us and is, to that extent, the state itself. The study of their work is public law. And into the field of public law of course go crime and all dealing with crime. In this first year you meet public law only in the second semester when you take up the process and interpretation of legislation, and the criminal law. You begin essentially on the other side, the private side, the side of the legal relations between individuals. And perhaps this is well, precisely because that is the side of law with which you have thus far been least concerned.

The field of private law can be split perhaps into four grand divisions of major importance. The first is that of contracts, of agreements between people and the legal effects of such agreements. This is the branch of law which plays primarily into what economists know as the market, the balance wheel of a money economy, the social machine which makes possible our regime of specialization. The second grand division is the law of property, and more particularly the law of real property, of land. Here one goes into the fact behind the economist's theory of value, the fact of scarcity; and into its legal side, to wit, the monopoly of the things which are scarce. It is hardly necessary to point out that so far as the state safeguards {19} such a monopoly and at the same time makes possible the free transfer of the things monopolized, it sets the framework within which the market, the agreement, the contract moves. And that exchange is possible only within the limitations thus set and with the advantages thus created for some men over others, and along the lines and by way of the devices which law officers lay down. The third great field of private law I suspect to be that of associations and the ways in which men can come together in groups to accomplish their purposes, and of the limitations as well as the powers which legal officers place upon the activities of such groups. At this point the law plays especially into the phase of economic life we know as industrialism, of capital aggregation, and the concomitants thereof, the labor organizations. The fourth major field I take to be the left overs, and more particularly, the attempted general regulation of matters in the field of free play which fall outside of the field of agreement. There are contacts which cause trouble but which were not intended or agreed upon—the motor accident. There are aggressions which raise problems not only of the criminal law, but of compensation for the damage caused. There are uses of land, as for a soap factory in a residence district, which are obnoxious to the neighborhood. There are instances of competition carried too far, which call for regulation or for compensation. A good part of this we lump together under the head of torts—of private wrongs.

I do not mean in this classification to make mutually exclusive groups. The heads are convenient for description, not the framework of a logical system. Things overlap. Associations, e.g., are formed by contract, and hold land. Property is transferred by contract, and there are torts peculiarly connected with property. Some torts arise either out of contract or out of interference with contract. Some of the most puzzling questions of tort law deal with associations. The suggestion is therefore not of mutual exclusiveness, but rather of striking divergence of focus. Neither do I mean to suggest that all private law can conveniently be brought under one or another of these main heads. I know of some topics which I should find a good deal of difficulty in assigning to one rather than another of the heads, or in assigning to any one of them at all. But that, too, is of small import, if the heads are sufficient to give you some rough picture of how the bulk of private law divides, the bulk of private law, I mean to say, in its importance to the community. There is, for example, a huge number of legal rules relating to the family, which you will observe that I have not mentioned at all, and did not think I needed to. For I suspect that the thing which marks those rules off rather strikingly from those I have been attempting to classify is the fact that in the main the rules of family law are of relatively *little* importance to family life, whereas the rules on economic life play a very considerable part in business living.

{20} Thus far I have told you that what law was about was the dealing with disputes. That it was made up largely of what officials do about disputes. That the rules of law were important in so far as they give us a guide to what the officials will do or to how we can get them to do something. And then I have told you a little of the main divisions of the subject matter of law: into substantive law and procedure on the one hand and into public law and private law on the other. And I trust that it has become clear that the law curriculum, while it gives considerable attention both to procedure and to public law, still puts its major emphasis upon private law on the one hand, and substantive law on the other.

All this only presents the setting for the final thing I wanted to talk about today, to wit, what does this law business really come to? What does it mean to people in society? In a word, what difference does it make whether or not there are any courts, or lawyers, or law schools, or law students? The first difference, I suppose, that it makes, is that the removal of all these would somewhat add to the current crowd of unemployed. Perhaps it is harsh to a high profession to urge that that by itself is no particular reason for the existence of courts and lawyers. Nevertheless I shall take the position that a job needs some further justification than the fact that if it is present someone can make a living holding the job down. Which brings us back to the problem: What difference do courts and lawyers make?

For you will observe that it is not enough to say merely that they deal with disputes, because there are so many disputes they do not deal with. That little difference of opinion with your father as to whether you should go to Chicago or Harvard or as to how much your monthly check should be was not, I take it, settled by a court or by a lawyer. The higgling of the market presents a constant series of disputes that reach their adjustment by negotiation and by bargaining. Rancorous rivalries between competing firms are worked out mostly by skill and by endurance, with no appeal to law. Strikes are called and fought through and settled. Often some phases of them reach the courts. Often none do. Almost never does the main question in a strike occupy a court. But perhaps the case of the strike is as good as any to bring out the part that law does play. Law (in the person of judges, police and sheriffs) does lay down rules within which strike and lockout and struggle of employer and employee are to be worked out. "Rules" of the game: no beating, no shooting, no intimidation, no blacklisting. Does it follow that these rules of the game are always observed? It does not. The games are few in number in which the rules are *always* observed. But what is vital is to see that the law official functions somewhat like an umpire in *attempting to see* that they are. Somewhat like an umpire, but not wholly. Like an umpire in that he does not always see the breach of the rules. Like an umpire in that at times he is {21} severely partial to one side, or stubborn, or ignorant, or ill tempered. Like an umpire, at least on the criminal side, in that he reaches in to decide and control on his own motion. But on the civil side, on the side of private law, less like an umpire in this: that he does not reach in on his own motion, but waits to be called upon. Always, however, and on both civil and criminal sides, like an umpire, I repeat, in that when acting he tries in the main, and in the main with some success, to insist that the rules of the game shall be abided by; in that he takes the rules of the game in the main not from his own inner consciousness, but from existing practice, and again in the main from authoritative sources (which in the case of the law are largely statutes and the decisions of the courts). Like an umpire finally in that his decision is made only after the event, and that play is held up while he is making it, and that he is cursed roundly by the losing party and gets little enough thanks from the winner.

But whereas a ball game is tightly organized and must move swiftly, society at large is loosely organized, so loosely that *individual* disputes do not in the main hold up the workings of the whole. It is not therefore necessary for the law official, save at a crowded traffic corner, to be on hand announcing the rules, applying them to particular situations, all the time. For the bulk of the disputes of life he can simply wait and be sure that sooner or later the parties will iron their own difficulties out with no need to call upon him. Law and the law official are not therefore in one real sense what *makes* order in society. For them society is given and order is given because society is given. Apart from order there is no meaning in that word. Furthermore, most minor maladjustments and readjustments of order work out in one way or another without calling on the law official. They are not worked out without suffering: over-production means unemployment. But worked out, in the main, they are.

The law then, the interference of officials in disputes, appears as the means of dealing with disputes which do not otherwise get settled. Less as *making* order than as *maintaining* order when it has gotten out of order. This is its first aspect, its most ancient aspect, its fundamental aspect. But you cannot have officials to be appealed to, you cannot have them acting in fairly regular and predictable ways, without a great many people finding it desirable and useful to orient their action in advance to what the officials will do if they do happen ever to be called upon. I spoke before of the law as a part of your environment, like the weather, or the party system. As long as the officials are present and capable of being called upon, you must reckon with them. What they will do shapes what you can do. What they do shapes how you can effectively go about getting what you want. You must chart your course to keep free of trouble with them, if a dispute should arise. You can perhaps chart your course so that, if they are called {22} upon, they will be for you and not against you; you can so shape your bargain as to thrust the legal risks upon the other party.

And is it not clear that to the extent that lawyers and their clients and even men who might be clients, but who have no lawyers, shape their conduct with an eye to what the courts would do if they were called upon, to that extent the court decision reaches out beyond the individual case and enters into molding and channeling the action of the community? It ceases to be merely a regulation of actual disputes and becomes a regulation, and if all goes well, an anticipation and prevention, of potential disputes vastly greater in number than the actual. It ceases to function merely as a last-resort machinery to take care of disputes that by no other means work out to settlement, and becomes indirectly but potentially a factor in regulating what people *do*, *before* disputes, how people actually go about their ordinary business and, at times, even, where there are legal prohibitions, what businesses people go about.

And it is this fact that people in some important measure orient their action to the possible action of officials which makes *legislation* such a valuable tool of social readjustment. For legislation is an authoritative command to the official, whether judicial or executive, henceforward to act in new described ways, whenever a certain type of case may come before him. Or, in the case of legislation on crimes, even a command to some officials to hunt up some new types of case which they had theretofore been told to let alone. These commands are public. They can be learned of by the interested parties. And to a large degree the interested parties foresee what the officials will now do, and reshape their own affairs in consequence.

You may have missed in this discussion the common idea that the law is right, that rules of law are to be obeyed because they are right, that men have duties to uphold the law. Such ideas are not missing because they have been overlooked. They are left out because you may fairly be expected to be well aware of them already. They are left out, too, because they contain truth so partial, so faulty, as to cry out for revision in the light of some such analysis as I have been presenting. They are left out because *at this stage* of your approach to law your common sense is rather in the way than otherwise. Let me here say only this about rightness of the law. That if most people did not stand behind the officials, however passively, there would be little law to talk about. That if most people did not most of the time when they looked at a rule look to its *purpose* as well as to its exact and narrow form, and fit their conduct roughly to that purpose, then the officials would have a burden on their hands they could not bear. And, finally, that if most people shaped their conduct really with reference to the law and to their legal rights, for any serious fraction of their time, rather than with reference to the patterns of action, the patterns of thought, the standards of judgment which they inhale as the social atmosphere they {23} breathe, then life in our society would become unlivable. Lawyers are lawyers because they alone among men devote themselves with some constancy to studying out what courts are going to do; and if there are people more unpleasant to deal with professionally, who are they?

Courts affect people quite directly, then, by their action taken in individual disputes. Courts affect people indirectly because *to some extent* people concern themselves ahead of time with what courts may do to them, or for them. But whereas *people* are only incidentally concerned about the courts, the *lawyer* is professionally concerned. He is the point of contact between the people and the law official.

And as an *advocate*, the lawyer is interested in the work of the courts in individual cases. This is his oldest job. This is still a most important job. This is the job which in England is the sole business of the most respected portion of the profession, the barrister. But as *business counsel* the lawyer is interested rather in this indirect effect of the work of legal officials which I have just described, in anticipating what the courts might do and in shaping his client's conduct to his client's desires in view of that anticipation. And this is a phase of law practice which is becoming of steadily increasing importance in this country and of transcendent importance in this city.

I stop at this place only to call your attention to one fact. It should be clear, it should be clear even to the blind, that the work of business counsel is impossible unless the lawyer who attempts it knows not only the rules of the law, knows not only what these rules mean in terms of predicting what the courts will do, but knows, in addition, the life of the community, the needs and practices of his client—knows, in a word, the *working situation* which he is called upon to shape *as well as* the law with reference to which he is called upon to shape it. It has seemed to some students in the past that they had come to law school to "learn the law", and that the law was made up of legal rules and nothing more, and that all other matter was irrelevant, was an arbitrary interference with their proper training for their profession. I have been told by some that social science was for social scientists, in the graduate school; that what law students wanted was the law. I have met with resentment, sometimes bitter, at the so-called cluttering up of our law curriculum with so-called non-legal material. If I have made my point just now it should be clear to you that this is the language of men who do not see far enough beyond their noses to measure even their own job in life. If I have made my point it should be clear that for most lawyers the job of advocate is half, nay, less than half the job they have to do. Even as advocates, I am prepared to argue, they need, desperately, full knowledge of the facts of the life of the community, against which law must play. But when it comes to their task as business counsel there is no need for argument. The case is clear. {24} The stones speak. What the courts will do means nothing save in relation with how people are to act in the light of the court's doing. For the meaning of the law in life and in the practice of lawyers is its meaning not to courts, but to laymen.

Your faculty offers, then, no apology for "cluttering" up the curriculum with such useful data as it can discover as to what law means to those whom it affects. Your faculty knows no other way of making law mean anything. Your faculty welcomes you into a study of law which deals not with words, but with practice, not with paper theory, but with living fact. And if that be treason, make the most of it.

II • THIS CASE SYSTEM: WHAT LIES BEHIND THE CASE

{25}

A law school, setting up a course of study, must face two different jobs. In part, they overlap; but they cannot be assumed in advance to coincide at all. The one job is to discover what you need in order to practice your profession, to pick out such parts of that equipment as are either most fundamental or best teachable in school, and to devise means of getting these things across to you. The second job begins where the first leaves off, and begins irrespective of how well the first is done, and is a problem peculiarly of the first year. Granted that the curriculum is, wisely or unwisely, to take a given line, what do you need to know in order to handle, not the practice of law, but the practice of law school? In part, I say, these two problems overlap, and it is well they do. But I am concerned today but little with their overlapping, or with the first, the long-run job, save as a passing reference to it may shed some light upon the other. The question today is immediate and intensely practical. It has been decreed that you are to study law largely by "the" case system. What do you need to know to make that study go? I warn you again that you will find my words empty, find them even likely to mislead, to the extent that you have incurred the danger of a "little knowledge". But the concrete basis is already being provided day by day in your assignments and your use of the case-books. It will pay promptly, therefore, if you follow. Certain it is that students who are simply pushed off the dock into case-method-study flounder rather longer than if they have some inkling of the underlying theory. For however different the methods of your various instructions are (and they diverge amazingly), there are some theories common to the teaching of them all.

I shall discuss first what the so-called cases are, and in that connection, I shall sketch our judicial system far enough for you to place the so-called case a little in its setting. That done, it will be time to turn, tomorrow, to how the case is used, in class and out.

A case, it is obvious, is made up for lawyers not of a dozen bottles, but of a dispute, and the term "case hardened" is to be read in this connection. But for purposes of the case system not every dispute will be a case. We deal with law, and it must be a case at law—that is, a case in court. Even when fancy ranges, and we put this case or that for your discussion, the fiction of the "case-class" is always that the case supposed has come before a court.

But again, there are two kinds of courts, *trial courts*—or as they are also called, lower courts, or courts of first instance; and *courts of review*: i.e. appellate or upper courts. Now a case never reaches a court of review until it has first been through a tribunal of trial—else there would {26} be nothing to review. But the cases, so-called, in your case-books are almost exclusively chosen from courts of review. To understand them, therefore, you must get at least some quick picture of what has gone on before they got there. Before attempting that sketch there is one thing to hammer home, to orient the sketching: a court of review has as its business of review to listen to complaints that a lower court has done some job improperly, i.e., as the phrase goes, *has been in error*, has made some ruling *not* in accord with the rules of law, correctly understood. That, and that alone, in legal theory, will come up for decision: did the trial court, in the points complained of, act according to the rules? Has there been "error" in those points? It is essential to grasp this theory, and to grasp it firmly, and to work with it till it has become familiar, before it pays to try to criticize it much.

Hence we turn to the trial court to look over what it does. Our eye is out for the type of thing the losing party may later accuse it of having done against the rules.

In the first place, the trial court may not be the proper court to try this kind of case at all. There are rules about that—rules dividing the power to try cases among the various trial courts of the state and of the country. Those we call rules of jurisdiction of courts. Some courts for instance—such as the municipal court in New York City—can as a rule take on a case only if it involves $1000 or less. Other courts, such as the federal courts when the only ground for bringing the case before them is that the parties are citizens of different states, can handle only cases which involve $10,000 or more {or, as of 2007, a $75,000 "amount in controversy" for such "diversity jurisdiction," which is one type of "subject matter jurisdiction"}. And so it goes. Some of the rules seem arbitrary; some seem very sensible. Like all rules of procedure, they aim to get business done more quickly and effectively; convenience, efficiency and fairness are their aim. Like all rules of procedure, they tend to degenerate into red tape. In any event, the court must be the right court, or, at least, one of the right courts for the kind of case. A court of review can inquire into that.

And second, the trial court must have power over the defendant {or "personal jurisdiction"}. We rarely need to worry about power over the plaintiff. He wants action, he comes in, he submits himself. The defendant, however, may want delay, or he may (as some people sometimes do) distrust the particular court, or it may be inconvenient for him to stand suit just there. And as to this the theory of our law seems in the first instance to be based on the idea of physical power to coerce: if the defendant has goods or land within the territory inside of which the court can act, or if an officer of the court can find the defendant in that territory and summon him in (which shows that he might at need have taken him in by the neck), or if the defendant submits, then the court has jurisdiction enough over him to go ahead. Into this, too, the court of review can inquire.

{27} These matters have been mentioned only to get them out of the way. We now assume that our trial court has jurisdiction both of the case and of the parties. We turn to inquire what it does, with both.

In the first place it informs itself of what the row is about. This is accomplished in one way or another by the *pleadings*. To bring his case, the plaintiff's lawyer must prepare a statement of what he claims to be the facts, and of what he wants from the defendant: this is the complaint, the declaration, the petition, or the bill. First, the facts, the statement of his cause of action; and second, what the plaintiff wants, his prayer for relief. Please note these things. They go to the root of any understanding of a case. They must become a matter which you look for as automatically as you blink your eyes when a June-bug buzzes at them. But experience shows that the plaintiff's statement is not at all there is to say. Some of the plaintiff's so-called facts the defendant wishes to deny. Some other matters, which change the color of the picture, and on which the plaintiff kept his thumb, the defendant wishes to assert. As a price for letting him do these things when he needs to—which we do by letting him put in a so-called *answer* to the plaintiff's *complaint*—we have to take the risk that he will seize upon the answer merely to make trouble: to deny what is so, to assert what is false. Just as we must risk false claims by plaintiffs, if just claims are to be allowed. In any event, sooner or later we come to an *issue* on the facts, or to a set of issues—we know what facts are in dispute. Of course this process is not the simple thing that I have made it. Like all procedure, it is a technical affair. And either lawyer may slip, and the court may make rulings (right or wrong) upon these technicalities, and these rulings may be presented for review.

And one other thing must be noted, here and throughout. We have not thus far, you will have noticed, found out anything definite about the facts of the original event, about what really happened. We have the plaintiff's statement, we have the defendant's. But both may be mistaken, both may even be lying. The things that happened are not yet before us, and they may never be. Again and again we shall find courts of review testing the legal significance not of what happened outside to the parties, *but of something that may be assumed to have happened outside*. Testing the legal significance of say what the plaintiff claims in his complaint, or of the most favorable inferences for him that can possibly be derived from the evidence he brings in. This—and this, too, is basic to our understanding of the cases—is because our system of law lets the parties fight their own battles, in the main. What they do not claim, they cannot have. What they do not or cannot prove, is irrelevant to the court. It is, to the court, as if it never had occurred. Let them make their own cases. If they are fools, then leave them to their folly. This, I say, is basic to an understanding of the cases. It is no less basic to an understanding of {28} your responsibility as an advocate: you must become a good technician: when you slip, it is your client who falls.

So in our trial court we may find the defendant not raising an issue on the facts, but saying to the court (by demurrer, or by motion to dismiss): even if what this fellow says is true, it makes no difference; those are facts of which the court takes no account.—There are such facts. A green and pink checked jacket may offend your eyes, but you cannot do anything at law against the wearer. And there are words which he may call you which will burn your collar, without the judge's catching fire at the sparks.—Or, in a more technical day whose marks are with us still, the defendant may have said to the court even if this fellow's facts are so, they entitle him not to what he asks for, but to something else; he has chosen the wrong *form* to bring his action. You have this in a mild form in the family: "Peter, I *will* not listen to you when you whine!" "John, this is neither the time nor the place. See mother after dinner." These rulings do not, in one sense, go to the merits. They are not rulings on what will be done if all the proper etiquette is once observed. But they affect the outcome.—And we shall, later in the trial, find rulings of a similar character: when the evidence on one side or on both sides is all in, it may be claimed that, even indulging all inferences in favor of an opponent, his facts will not touch the court or induce the action he desires: so the motion for a directed verdict, or for a non-suit {or, in modern phrasing, for "judgment as a matter of law" or, especially before trial, for a "summary judgment"}. And, finally, the same type of fact assumption appears when objection is made to evidence as immaterial: even if true, it makes no difference; therefore it is to be excluded as cluttering up the place.—And any of these rulings, when appealed from, when reexamined by a court of review, give us light on what courts will do, and on what a lawyer must do. They help show—whether the "facts" assumed really occurred or not—what the court would or would not do, if they had occurred; what facts have importance to courts, and what not—and for what purposes.

But I must come back to my trial court and my issue on the facts. Here are our plaintiff and defendant, with their divergent stories, and the judge has settled that the outcome will be different according to whose tale is believed. How to determine? Who is to be believed? And even before that, *who* is to determine? Solomon, you remember, did it himself: a king, and so a judge. In somewhat similar fashion once in England. Shortly, however (a king has other business), the job got delegated to king's representatives, the judges; and after some centuries (for use breeds right, use breeds exclusive privilege) the king found that he could no longer intervene. The relics of this situation, of this turning of decision over to the judge, we, too, still have: in admiralty—cases involving ships—where there has never been a jury; nor is there in equity cases—cases which trace their roots back to the Court of Chancery, which came into existence {29} partly to cure some troubles that the common law courts were caught in, due to jury trial. Finally, when for one reason or another the parties do not want a jury, and are content to take the court's decision on the facts, or in the petty courts in which men think it does not pay to have a jury. In all these cases the judge hears the two stories and the judge makes his own decision as to what the true facts may have been.

But it is still the common practice, in some states—and at least a common practice in all—for that job to go over to a jury. And what is important for us, whether the jury is called upon in a particular case or not: the one-time regular presence of that body has left its marks all over the way the trial court works.

It is not my present task to weigh the jury as against other possible machinery for deciding on contested facts. Nor to take up the origin of the jury in a group of men from the neighborhood whom gossip and keen knowledge of their neighbors had made aware of most that had gone on: a body who did not try facts, but were summoned to supply from their own heads the needed information on what the facts were. It is not my task to trace how that body of knowledgeable persons turned into the impartial blankly ignorant jury of the present day, who begin knowing nothing, and only reach their decision upon the conflicting tales of the contestants. I do not know the detailed process of the transformation, nor am I sure that it is known to anyone. My task is much simpler. It is to hammer on the fact that the jury are and have been with us; that they are a lay body, and never lawyers; that they begin the trial in ignorance, but make the decision about disputed facts. And then to hammer on certain consequences which have come to cluster around these three things.

In the first place, this introduction of a lay body into the court, in this form, *splits* the court. We are left with a judge to preside, and to speak the law, but with a jury of laymen to decide on facts. A jury of laymen, whom judges often did not trust too far, and whose action they have through at least two centuries sought somewhat to restrict by an intricate sieve of rules. Because the jury are laymen, not trained in weighing evidence, not case-hardened by legal experience, they must not, save in peculiar cases, be permitted to hear mere statements of opinion nor to hear repetitions of reports about events, mere *hearsay*, lest they be led unduly into inference. Because the jury are laymen, untrained in sifting issues, not experienced in legal nicety, the common law trial must be confined to a two-party trial, one against one, a supposedly *simple* type; and must be reduced if possible to a single, precise issue. Because the jury are laymen, but must pass on the facts, it is necessary before they render verdict to *charge* the jury, to *instruct* them on the law, and the judge's instructions to them must conform to the rules of law; and much of our study will be taken up with reexamining such instructions, when {30} complained of by the losing party. And because the jury, after hearing the instructions, brings in in most cases only a single, shotgun, general verdict ("We find for the plaintiff in the sum of $1400", or "We find for the defendant") it is almost impossible to know whether they paid any attention at all to the instructions, whether they even understood them—so that much of our study will be spent upon the learning of an *etiquette* of instruction, which must be executed well nigh letter-perfect by the winning lawyer if the verdict he has won is to be proof against appeal, but whose value to the community is strangely dubious. Finally, because the jury is a body of laymen, to be informed, but lacking organization or experience for extracting information, a mighty forward thrust is given to our system I have already mentioned, of *party*-presentation, of leaving the heavy burden of the conduct of the trial, the main control of trial discretion, the choice and handling of the evidence, in the hands of the two lawyers—our system {often called the "adversary system"}, in short, of making the trial in good part a battle of strategy and wits, a judicial duel between counsel—and may Heaven help the client.

Now let me break in upon myself quickly, to avoid misunderstanding. I have spoken of consequences which clustered about our jury system: I have not said that these were consequences inevitable upon the introduction of a jury, or inevitable upon the type of jury that we know. You have no understanding of a causal sequence in society if you know merely that *b* has followed upon *a*. You need to know also why *a* did not persist; you need to know also why it was *b*, not *c* or *d*, which followed *a*. It is not enough, either, to know that *a* has shown at other times a tendency to result in *b*, nor even that *a* alone is enough to produce *b*. You must know also why other twisting, or balancing, or negating factors were not present which would have substituted *x* for *b*. So with this jury. Each of the consequences I have mentioned the jury favored; some, it may be, would hardly have been possible without the jury; none of them is, however, an inevitable consequence. We find on the Continent, for instance, juries but few rules of evidence, and the control of the trial much more than with us in the hands of the judge. Nor will it do to waive that off because the jury there is relatively recent and the procedure took its major shape before the jury came. For we can compare the present English jury with our own, two shoots off the same stock: the general system of party-presentation there has not resulted in eliminating the judge as an important factor in the conduct of the trial, nor has it in the mine run of our federal courts; indeed the instructions to a jury can be of moment, of great moment, often decisive, when a strong judge moves in a state court to the limit that procedure will allow, in his arrangement, in his emphasis, and in his language, to clear up concretely the bearing of rules of law upon the contested fact-situation in the case. Finally, it is surely not {31} the institution of the jury, but primarily the inertia of the human mind, which is responsible for carrying over into trial at common law even where there is no jury the limitation to the sharp two-party issue, and for carrying over into trials before the judge alone, even in equity, those rules of evidence which were designed to screen the inexperienced laymen from misleading testimony.

But whatever the causal sequences, I repeat, the jury has played midwife in our system to a host of consequences. And to those consequences we must have an eye as, after delays that bear comparison to those at law, our trial in the trial court is finally reached. You will recall that the court is a proper one for our particular case, that the defendant has been duly served with process calling on him to appear, that plaintiff and defendant have duly filed complaint and answer, and that the court is now persuaded that their allegations are of legal consequence. The question is: which one of them can *prove* the things he *claims*. We shall pass over the impanelling of the jury, the testing of the prospective jurors one by one to make sure that they are uninformed, and free of bias. What of the trial?

The plaintiff's lawyer makes his opening statement, explaining to the jury what he intends to prove, and how his side of the case will hang together as a whole. He then proceeds. The handling of the evidence is almost wholly in his hands. He brings in what he wants, what he thinks favorable. He tends quite definitely not to bring in more. There is indeed an interesting rule which works to my mind directly against any theoretical duty he may have to bring fairly and fully before the court what evidence there is: the rule that a man is bound by the testimony his own witness offers; one will go slowly, with that rule at hand, in making witnesses "his own".

The plaintiff's proof will be by documents, if he has any which are relevant; outside of that, it will be mostly by the testimony of witnesses. Whether counsel questions point by point, or lets the witnesses tell their own story and puts further questions to make clear important points or matters they leave out, depends on him. One thing is clear: the raw events as they happened are not before judge or jury; there has been a straining process. The plaintiff's lawyer has, with an eye to *legal* relevance, and with an eye to winning, done some selection. Some facts, he may himself not have discovered. Moreover, he is by no means wholly free in presentation. There are rules within which he must move and which the defendant's lawyer will do his best to keep him, or the court, from overlooking. These rules may keep him, sometimes, from proving vital facts. Each time that such an issue on the rules comes up, the judge decides it. Each time, the loser can "note his exception." Each exception can, if the exceptor ultimately loses, be made the basis for demanding a review.

{32} Each witness, as the plaintiff finishes with him, is turned over to the defendant for cross-examination. There may be further points to be brought out which change the whole tone of that person's story; it may be possible, too, to show that his observation was poor, or his memory bad, or his good faith in doubt; he may, for instance, have made prior contradictory statements. Such matters are the focus of the cross-examination; and the jury presumably looks not merely to what the witness says, but to his appearance. Does he look honest? Is her hat cute?

As with the plaintiff, so with the defendant. Then the plaintiff again, this time exclusively for the purpose of rebutting what the defendant may have produced. The defendant combines his main case with his rebuttal.

Then counsel address the jury—first, commonly, for the defendant, then for the plaintiff. Here the job is to analyze the testimony as a whole, to put it together, to stress the points which speak for you, to slight or explain away those which do not. In a word, to persuade, to persuade that your story is the right one. The judge then gives his charge. In most state courts he may not comment on the evidence and thus risk undoing all the work of counsel. That would offend the rules of the judicial duel.—The jury gives its verdict.

I have spoken of the judicial duel. The figure has not all the accuracy one might wish. In our courts one misses often the courtesy and the grave dignity which seem to have been common in the duel. Nor do both sides start even, in the courts. {Charles E.} Clark speaks neatly of the *handicapping* of the one side or the other by practices and rules, built as are all wise handicaps out of judgment based on past experience. The first great handicap rests on the plaintiff: he carries the *burden of proof*; that is, he carries the burden of bringing in evidence enough *to let a reasonable man conclude* that the facts necessary to his case exist, and then the further burden of *persuading* the tribunal to believe that evidence, despite all contradictions. This is a handicap. A trial is no debate. The defendant has no legal need to make a case, to win, unless the plaintiff makes a case against him first.

Such is the theory of our law: the sleeping dogs will lie, unless the plaintiff finds power in his foot to stir them. There is no inherent virtue in this theory; other systems have dealt otherwise. The popular mind still feels an accusation to have elements of proof. One might in proper circumstances draw from experience quite as well a rule that claims are not made without cause, and so handicap the defendant with the burden of clearing himself. And in a closer-knit community, where false charges would probably be known and even more probably be frowned upon, where charges made would come attested by a "suit" of people evidencing the plaintiff's good faith by their presence, this has been done. Our present theory, however, is as described above—and in a loose-knit community of shifting, distant contacts, this handicapping of the plaintiff seems wise {33} enough. So, likewise, in the main, do the lesser incidental handicaps one meets throughout the trial: presumptions. If the plaintiff proves making and possession of a note, then it is *presumed* that he gave value for it, and came by it honestly, and has not yet been paid. The handicap—although it is a lesser one—runs against the defendant now. He must lift the burden of showing enough against such presumptions to force the plaintiff to his proof. This, you can see, is sense. This trial is made to profit by the experience of the cases of the past.

At various times in all this trial procedure questions come up which we have glanced at, but which it pays to remember here. When the plaintiff's story is concluded, the defendant may test its adequacy in law: even granting that everything he says is so, with all the inferences a reasonable man could draw from it—So what? This is the motion to dismiss. That motion may be made, too, at the end of the testimony. Or either side may ask for a directed verdict {or "judgment as a matter of law"}—which comes to this: on all the evidence, even when read most favorably to my opponent, nò reasonable man could see facts which get in the way of my victory. His case is completely insufficient. Mine is completely sufficient.—You will observe again that all of these questions deal with hypothetical, not actual, states of fact, yet with the legal consequences of such hypothetical facts. One thing more: in about half our states, if *both* sides ask for a directed verdict, the jury disappears from the case, and the court—so to speak by mutual consent—takes over the determination of what the true facts shall be assumed thenceforth to be.

Once the jury has rendered its verdict, or the court has (so to speak, acting as a jury) done the like, the legal situation changes. From then on— providing only first, that the proper etiquette has been observed throughout the trial, and second, that enough evidence is present to support a "finding" by that omnipresent hypothetical "reasonable man" who rules our legal theory—conflicting evidence on all material points has been resolved for keeps against the losing party. We have therefore moved one farther step away from the reality of raw events. From now on, the facts of this case, for purposes of anything that will be done at law, are "settled"; whatever "facts" are needed to support the verdict, and are themselves supported by the evidence, *are* for this case *"the facts"*. And this is the situation presented by a motion for judgment notwithstanding the verdict {or for "judgment as a matter of law" after a verdict is decided}: not "even if the facts were ruled against me", but "even although the facts have been ruled against me", and on all points, those facts still show my right in law, and not my adversary's. But you will see how many weaknesses in a case, and, indeed, how many slips made by counsel in trying a case, a verdict will "cure", if it is once obtained. *Any* "facts" the pleadings and evidence would permit to be {34} "found" are now by main strength treated *as if found*, if that is "necessary to sustain the verdict".

One last point. If what is objected to is an alleged departure from the proper rules of trial, the losing counsel must normally give the trial judge a chance to correct his own error before making an appeal. He moves for a new trial, moves to discard the old trial and start over. If he is right, this will save time and trouble. A ruling which the judge has made in error in the pressure of the trial he may perceive, when more at peace, to have been wrong. But if the loser does not prevail in this, the judge will enter judgment. The losing party, within the fixed time set for the purpose, can now appeal.

If he does not, there is the matter of enforcing judgment. If the defendant won (and if he has not filed a counter-claim, a claim against the plaintiff like the plaintiff's against him), the judgment for him will cover only so-called costs—the fees for filing papers, and for the jury; perhaps a nominal sum supposed to cover his expense for counsel. If the plaintiff wins, typically he has become entitled either to be put in possession of land, or to a sum as damages, or both—as well as costs. The sheriff, when proper application has been made, will order the defendant off the land, and put the plaintiff in. The order ordinarily will be enough; even the order will be hardly needed. Defendants have no wish to go to war against the state. But with the damage judgment things are different. For it can be realized, even when the sheriff has been duly called upon, only by seizing goods or land of the defendant. They must be found, to be seized. They must exist, to be found. Here again procedure conditions substantive law—not only in that you must know what to do, and do it right, but this time also in that there must be something to be done, some assets of the defendant for procedure to work upon. Sumner in one of the neat turns that mark his essays hits home on this: "A man who has no property may break his contract with impunity."

However, these troubles with the sheriff which do afflict the man with property can commonly be staved off by an appeal. And why can he appeal? Observe, pray, that his appeal is brought at a heavy price; but not to him. His power to appeal is simultaneously a right to delay for more long months the realization of a just claim by his adversary. Security, by an appeal bond, the adversary may demand. But security solves the problem only half. The appeal remains as a power to put the adversary to time, and trouble, and expense. Assuredly, this is not the purpose of the power. That purpose looks to an adversary who never should have had temporary success below. But note the expense and delay of dilatory appeals as you meditate upon the values of the proper ones—and raise the question in your minds for pondering: is there no way of having what good this gives, at lower social cost? {35}

What is that good—why do we recognize appeals?

I suspect chiefly, if not entirely, because there is more than one trial judge within the state. More than one trial court means two things. The first is that where several men hold like jobs, no matter how good they are, there is always a chance of getting a smaller group of better men. Or, when (as so long in England) the several men sit separately, and under pressure of business, they may be able to do materially better on difficult problems if they sit together, and at leisure. All of this looks to deciding *this case right*. There is a strong feeling, which seems to lie deep in human nature, that disputes at law should be decided right. At the very worst, that they should be decided right within the presuppositions and the terms of the particular legal system in which they are decided. And indeed some legal systems have at times attempted no more with the appeal than this. Some again have not been so much worried with this problem: it was not till 1907 that appeals in criminal cases were allowed in England.

But there is another result of having several trial courts; distinct, however closely related to the first. Different trial courts, indeed different appellate courts—different coordinate courts, in short—will inevitably from time to time decide like cases in different ways. This is uncomfortable. Partly, people like to think of the law as definite—even while it is not. Partly, many people have an idea there can be but one right solution of a legal problem. Partly, it is much harder to arrange affairs with an eye to what courts will do, when different courts before which a matter may be brought will with some certainty act differently about it. One of the grand functions of the appeal, and of a single supreme court to which to appeal, lies certainly in the reducing of this difficulty. Reducing—not eliminating. It is still present. Except that we are hardened to it, we might say present in alarming measure. It is present, as among the several states, under our system of 50 distinct civil, criminal, and commercial jurisdictions; it is present as between state and federal courts in some instances; it is, despite state supreme courts, present to a large degree within the states. Judges do not cease to be human because they wield a gavel. Divergencies in training, ability, prejudice, and knowledge still occur, and lead to differences in the results upon like facts. Yet the supreme court and the appeal to it go far to limit the trouble. One excellent evidence we have in the history of Georgia, which for half a century struggled on with trial courts alone. Divergent decisions drove the judges there into informal conferences to iron out their differences. They would not iron out; some men are stubborn. A supreme court was finally introduced; once introduced, it had come to stay. The need, I may say in passing, was clear some thirty years before the plaster was applied. This gives suggestion of the speed of basic law reforms.

{36} I have said that these two reasons for having courts of review were not the same. Certainly not in their tendencies. For if the main job be to get this individual case decided right, it should go up on law and facts and both together. Ideally, there should be a new trial entire before the upper court. Short of that—to save time and duplication—the whole written record should go before the reviewing body, and they should have power where things seemed doubtful or obscure or overlooked to call new witnesses. And some such procedure was in vogue in Germany. Some such procedure was the practice of the English chancery. Some such procedure, although without the procurement of any further light that may seem needed, is the procedure before the Appellate Division in New York.

But if the main job be to fix a single practice for all the trial courts of the territory, then a review of the facts, of the doubtful testimony, even a review of all the details of admitted facts, in reference to the legal consequences, seem to lose their importance. What looms large is the *rule* to be laid down—a general proposition. The facts seem relevant only in highly abstracted form, and only to build the general setting of the rule. The facts of the case in hand, be they admitted or contested, seem interesting chiefly as illustrating one of a thousand possible "applications" of "the rule". So we have the highest court of France presented with the most painstakingly abstract of problems; and those of Germany and of New York explicitly limited in theory (in distinction to their own intermediate courts of review) to questions "of law", and barred from consideration of questions "of fact". The rule alone is for them to be relevant. They are to specialize in setting rules for all.

So far the theory. Yet the facts are hardy weeds. They will not down. Whatever the theory, courts of review of "pure law" feel the pressure of the individual case, and strain to decide it right. "Judgment for the plaintiff", runs the old anecdote of Marshall; "Mr. Justice Story will furnish the authorities". And we have similar testimony, in individual cases, from many judges in many lands and times.

From all this two things follow: first, in approaching any case upon review, we need to know what the kind of review is, what the court is undertaking to do, or we shall fail to understand its action. And secondly, even when it in theory is confined to rulings on the law, we shall be somewhat canny as we watch its work, and look for evidence as to how far the proposition which seems so abstract has roots in what seems to be the due thing on the facts before the court.

And from the second viewpoint, that making clear doubtful rules is the main job, we shall understand the growing tendency of our law to cut down on appeals, to deal with them not as matters of right, as things to which a man has claim merely because there is a lawsuit, but as matters {37} primarily of public interest, which need occupy the highest court only when it arrives at the conclusion that a question of general interest is at stake. And we shall understand from this viewpoint also and peculiarly why it is so necessary, in studying the case on appeal, to look for *the particular lapse complained of*. For it is only the claim that the lower court in some point has gone counter to the law which gives the upper court a law-point to review.

When we turn now to what goes on in the appeal, we find again that most of it lies in the background, where we do not get to see it. The losing counsel gets together, from the proceedings below, a statement of the case; more accurately, a statement of *so much of what came before the trial court* as is necessary to make clear what he complains of. If the winning party will agree that he has stated the question fairly, that is that. If not, he must make a statement which the trial court will approve. To this he adds, as a brief, what he complains of, his argument that, as the phrase goes, there "was error", and that the error, if such there was, was prejudicial to him. For our courts do not sit to decide questions if they do not matter. To be sure that the question matters, the rule is clear, and it is rigorous. What is complained about, on the complainant's showing, must have hurt him, must have hurt him or had clear tendency to hurt him, in his legal rights. Finally, the appellant weaves into his argument the authorities on which his argument is based. The other party replies in similar fashion; the papers are printed, exchanged, submitted to the court—a court, this time, which regularly consists of more than one judge, to get the benefit of consultation; a court, this time in which there is no jury, in which lay members (wisely or unwisely) do not sit. It may or may not occur, according to the practice of the court and the agreement of the lawyers, that over and above the briefs an oral argument is made. But whether it is or not, *you* do not get to see it.

What do you see? You see the so-called "case", as reported from the court of review. Its name or "style", the court that decided it, the date of decision, the briefest of statements as to how it got before this court, a summary of the facts, the names of the counsel on both sides, perhaps a listing of the points they made, even a summary of how they made them. The ruling of the court of review. And the opinion. Especially the opinion. Almost you can say, the opinion for purposes of case-books *is* "the case".

What then, is the opinion? It is the justification, prepared by one judge whose name it bears, and concurred in by the court, for the court's deciding the case as they have done. How it comes into being differs from court to court. Sometimes there is a consultation and if possible a decision of the case before any opinion is prepared. Sometimes one judge is assigned before consultation to report upon the case, and brings in as a report what if all goes well will then be the opinion. Sometimes {38} the opinion is viewed by the whole court as its own responsibility: "the opinion of the court, delivered by Judge X". Sometimes the court purports only to render judgment, without too heavy obligation to the reasons as put forward by the judge who writes. Always, however, the opinion is an explanation, a justification of the decision, and one at least acceptable to the court which decided. Almost always the opinion is all that you see. Behind it lies the whole course of transaction, trial and appeal which has been sketched.

And one vital point is here again to be hammered home. Obviously the case cannot be decided, or rather the bearing of the decision cannot be made plain, nor the decision justified, without some statement of the facts. That is, of the facts the court *assumes*, adopts as the basis for its decision. Sometimes the judge prepares the statement himself, whether he writes it into the opinion, or prints it before. Sometimes it is prepared by the reporter—be he an official of the court or a private observer—who gets the decision ready for publication. But whoever prepares it, it is prepared with reference to the opinion, and peculiarly if the judge prepares it, it is prepared to make the opinion look sound, look right, persuade. What is the relation of this statement of "the facts" to the brute raw events which happened long before? What is left in men's minds as to those raw events has been canvassed, more or less thoroughly, more or less skillfully, by two lawyers. But canvassed through the screen of what they considered *legally* relevant, and of what each considered legally relevant to win his case. It has then been screened again in the trial court through the rules about what evidence can be admitted. The jury has then reached its conclusion, which—for purposes of the dispute—determines contested matters for one side. The two lawyers have again sifted—this time solely from the record of the trial—what seemed to bear on points upon appeal. Finally, with a decision already made, the judge has sifted through these "facts" again, and picked a few which he puts forward as essential—and whose legal bearing he then proceeds to expound. It should be obvious that we may now be miles away from life. Again, we may not. By some miracle it may be there is no distortion. Or by some other each successive distortion may have neatly cancelled out the last. But it is current doctrine that the age of miracles is past.

Yet even if all I say and hint is true, that in no slightest part destroys the value or the power of the court's opinion. For the decision plus the opinion go far to show what this court that speaks will do again *upon like facts to those assumed.* They are the court's pronouncement as to what we may expect. From the side of orienting ourselves to what the court will do they are essential. Moreover, the court in its opinion has laid down a rule, or five. These, too, have been pronounced, as things we are to reckon with.

We shall do well to heed them.

{39} On the other hand, two things this long-continued sieving of the facts through different screens has hidden from us. In the very last of the sievings, that undertaken by the judge who wrote the opinion, we have had removed from our sight a very considerable number of hard facts, which may, for all we know, have much affected the actual outcome of the case. I pointed out before that even an appellate court officially concerned with rules alone has been known repeatedly to strain itself and to strain the rules that it laid down in order to produce what seemed a just result in the case in hand. Put differently, although the outcome in the case may be (and commonly is) a function of the rule laid down, the rule laid down may be (and commonly is) a function of the outcome of the case—partly sought for, shaped and phrased for the purpose of justifying the result desired. Now so far as facts or factors not shown in the report were at work in the court, and so far as they really bore upon the outcome, the opinion gives us a misleading picture of what happened, and therefore, a misleading basis for prophecy of what will happen in the future. Fortunately for us, however-er, the *basis for prophecy* is somewhat firmer than is the *record of what happened* in the case. Fortunately for us we know that judges will, in future cases, take account of what the opinion records pretty largely *as if* the opinion itself contained a true record of the events. To that extent, they in their canvassing of what has been done in the past in order to predict or to influence their decision in the new case, and we in our canvassing of what has been done in the past in order to predict or to influence their decision in the new case, will be working with a common equipment on a common basis. Yet in another aspect of prediction, the facts which the judge has hidden from us consciously, or, as in most cases, unconsciously, are badly needed. For we may expect that in future cases, as in the case in hand, *one* of the possibilities will be that rules will be twisted out of their apparent shape in order to produce what seems a just result. In order to reckon with that possibility it is vital to us to see something of the twisting that has gone on in the past, to get at its extent, at its nature, at the facts which have induced it. I shall have more to say on this when I come to a discussion of dissenting opinions. At this time I wish merely to remind you that here is an aspect in which the judge's justification for the decision often may and often will prove to be inadequate if taken as a *description* of how the decision really came about and of what the vital factors were which caused it.

But even more has the long continued sifting of the facts hidden from us another aspect of what we would gladly be equipped to gather from the case. I have said before that we could measure the meaning, either of rules of law, or of the actual decisions of the courts—could measure their meaning in life only as we observed what difference these rules and these decisions made to people. And every law case is obviously {40} an instance where the court's behavior has had an influence on people. But the influence on people cannot be gathered with any sureness from the hypothetical states of fact with which, too often, the issue in the case presents us. The influence on people and our understanding of it depend upon what I have described as the brute events outside. If we are to understand what the rule means, then we must typically go far outside the opinion. We cannot typically trust the facts given in the opinion all the way, even as a record of a single concrete instance of what the rule has meant. This is not always true. Or better, there are cases in which this typical situation happens by good fortune to be absent. There are cases in which the facts recorded in the opinion carry what historians would call internal evidence to guaranty that they are really close to life. Such cases deserve your careful study of the facts as such, over and above their relation to the action taken by the court. But in other cases your hunger must be directed partly to something not found in law books, but lying beyond and still to be explored.

In this discussion of what lies behind a case as it appears in the opinion I hope it has become clear to you that through all the technicality of mere procedure there run threads of purpose, sane purpose, useful purpose. Indeed, I find it very difficult to imagine your ever coming to grasp these technicalities and to master them unless you keep in mind these threads of purpose as the strings to thread your single beads upon. Save for a recognition of the jobs procedure has to do, the rank growth of technical detail becomes impassable.

Yet, I hope, on the other hand, that it has grown clear that purpose alone is no guide through procedure. It is no guide through any human institution. The nature of institutions is that they grow around our needs and partly serve them. The nature of institutions is also that they almost never serve those needs to satisfaction. Hence all the detailed technique of our law procedure is not only better seen, but better judged, by following the purposes concerned. In their light and in their light only you see whether the technique is a good one or a bad, a wasteful one or an efficient, a fossil or a living organ. Yet to know it as a fossil, as an instrument of impediment, delay, confusion, is not to remove it from the scene. It is there. You see it more clearly and know better how to reckon with it when you know how and how far it is out of its due place and in the road. But regard it you must. It stands between you and a successful conclusion of your case. Challenge it you may. If you have any sense of what your profession owes to our society, challenge it you will with such skill as you know. But overlook it you may not. It is there, a part of your environment, to be reckoned with, to be worked with,—or to be challenged. And to be reckoned with, worked with, even while you challenge it.

III • THIS CASE SYSTEM: WHAT TO *DO* WITH THE CASES

I have now sketched for you in charcoal outline—an unkind critic might remark, in bastard caricature—the part that law and law's minions play in our society, and the general history of a case at law. All this, for your ordained affairs, is background; you will be getting restive. Indeed, in delivering these lectures orally, I have felt the need, before the second hour, of setting to work to dynamite the foreground stumps: cases in casebooks have been assigned to you; what, then, are you to do with them?

Now the first thing you are to do with an opinion is to read it. Does this sound commonplace? Does this amuse you? There is no reason why it should amuse you. You have already read past seventeen expressions of whose meaning you have no conception. So hopeless is your ignorance of their meaning that you have no hard-edged memory of having seen un-meaning symbols on the page. You have applied to the court's opinion the reading technique that you use upon the Satevepost {*Saturday Evening Post* magazine}. Is a word unfamiliar? Read on that much more quickly! Onward and upward—we must not hold up the story.

That will not do. It is a pity, but you must learn to *read*. To read each word. To understand *each* word. You are outlanders in this country of the law. You do not know the speech. It must be learned. Like any other foreign tongue, it must be learned: by seeing words, by using them until they are familiar; meantime, by constant reference to the dictionary. What, dictionary? Tort, trespass, trover, plea, assumpsit, nisi prius, venire de novo, demurrer, joinder, traverse, abatement, general issue, tender, mandamus, certiorari, adverse possession, dependent relative revocation, and the rest. Law Latin, law French, aye, or law English—what do these strange terms mean to you? Can you rely upon the crumbs of language that remain from school? Does *cattle levant and couchant* mean *cows getting up and lying down*? Does *nisi prius* mean *unless before*? Or *traverse* mean an upper gallery in a church? I fear a dictionary is your only hope—a law dictionary—the one-volume kind you can keep ready on your desk. Can you trust the dictionary, is it accurate, does it give you what you want? Of course not. No dictionary does. The life of words is in the using of them, in the wide network of their long associations, in the intangible something we denominate their feel. But the bare bones to work with, the dictionary offers; and without those bare bones you may be sure the feel will never come.

The first thing to do with an opinion, then, is read it. The next thing is to get clear the actual decision, the judgment rendered. Who won, the plaintiff or defendant? And watch your step here. You are {42} after in first instance the plaintiff and defendant *below*, in the trial court. In order to follow through what happened you must therefore first know the outcome *below*; else you do not see what was appealed from, nor by whom. You now follow through in order to see exactly what *further* judgment has been rendered on appeal. The stage is then cleared of form—although of course you do not yet know all that these forms mean, that they imply. You can turn now to what you want peculiarly to know. Given the actual judgments below and above as your indispensable framework—what has the case decided, and what can you derive from it as to what will be decided later?

You will be looking, in the opinion, or in the preliminary matter plus the opinion, for the following: a statement of the facts the court assumes; a statement of the precise way the question has come before the court—which includes what the plaintiff wanted below, and what the defendant did about it, the judgment below, and what the trial court did that is complained of; then the outcome on appeal, the judgment; and finally the reasons this court gives for doing what it did. This does not look so bad. But it is much worse than it looks.

For all our cases are decided, all our opinions are written, all our predictions, all our arguments are made, on four certain assumptions. They are the first presuppositions of our study. They must be rutted into you till you can juggle with them standing on your head and in your sleep.

1) *The court must decide the dispute that is before it.* It cannot refuse because the job is hard, or dubious, or dangerous.

2) *The court can decide* only *the particular dispute which is before it.* When it speaks to that question it speaks ex cathedra, with authority, with finality, with an almost magic power. When it speaks to the question before it, it announces *law*, and if what it announces is new, it legislates, it *makes* the law. But when it speaks to any other question at all, it says mere words, which no man needs to follow. Are such words worthless? They are not. We know them as judicial *dicta*; when they are wholly off the point at issue we call them *obiter dicta*—words dropped along the road, wayside remarks. Yet even wayside remarks shed light on the remarker. They may be very useful in the future to him, or to us. But he will not feel bound to them, as to his ex cathedra utterance. They came not hollowed by a Delphic frenzy. He may be slow to change them; but not so slow as in the other case.

3) *The court can decide the particular dispute only according to a* general *rule which covers a whole class of like disputes.* Our legal theory does not admit of single decisions standing on their own. If judges are free, are indeed forced, to decide new cases for which there is no rule, {43} they must at least make a rule as they decide. So far, good. But how wide, or how narrow, is the general rule in this particular case? That is a troublesome matter. The practice of our case-law, however, is I think fairly stated thus: it pays to be suspicious of general rules which look too wide; it pays to go slow in feeling *certain* that a wide rule has been laid down at all, or that, if seemingly laid down, it will be followed. For there is a fourth accepted canon:

4) *Everything, everything, everything, big or small, a judge may say in an opinion, is to be read with primary reference to the particular dispute, the particular question before him.* You are not to think that the words mean what they might if they stood alone. You are to have your eye on the case in hand, and to learn how to interpret all that has been said *merely* as a reason for deciding *that* case *that* way. At need.

Now why these canons? The first, I take it, goes back to the primary purpose of law. If the job is in first instance to settle disputes which do not otherwise get settled, then the only way to do it is to do it. And it will not matter so much *how* it is done, in a baffling instance, so long as it is done at all.

The third, that cases must be decided according to a general rule, goes back in origin less to purpose than to superstition. As long as law was felt as something ordained of God, or even as something inherently right in the order of nature, the judge was to be regarded as a mouthpiece, not as a creator; and a mouthpiece of the general, who but made clear an application to the particular. Else he broke faith, else he was arbitrary, and either biased or corrupt. Moreover, justice demands, wherever that concept is found, that like men be treated alike in like conditions. Why, I do not know; the fact is given. That calls for general rules, and for their even application. So, too, the "separation of powers" comes in powerfully to urge that general rules are made by the Legislature or the system, not the judges, and that the judge has but to act *according* to the general rules there are. Finally, a philosophy even of expediency will urge the same. Whatever may be the need of shaping decision to individual cases in the juvenile court, or in the court of domestic relations, or in a business man's tribunal for commercial cases—still, when the supreme court of a state speaks, it speaks first to clear up a point of general interest. And the responsibility for formulating general policy forces a wider survey, a more thorough study of the policies involved. So, too, we gain an added guarantee against either sentimentalism or influence in individual cases. And, what is not to be disregarded, we fit with the common notion of what justice calls for.—All of which last, I may say in passing, seemed to me once too pat to be convincing. In point of fact, the clearing up by courts of points of general interest does not require any constant {44} strain to make a *rule*; and the felt need to make a rule that would be safe has often led our courts to over-caution. Responsibility for formulating general policy is not, as European practice shows, essential to fine, firm and conscientious work of judges, nor does it guarantee with us the absence of disturbing factors. And, finally, the man in the street can understand so little of the distinctions lawyers take that his reliance for justice is now just what it would be under a different system: the traditional respect for and training of the bench, the character of the personnel, the substantial soundness of its output.—I take time to say this because I deem it important that early, very early in this game you meet some counterweight against what I may call the unconscious snobbery of social institutions: against the bland assumption that because things social are, therefore they must be; against the touching faith that the current rationalizations of an institution, first, fit the facts, second, exhaust the subject, third, negate other, negate better possibilities. Nowhere more than in law do you need armor against that type of ethnocentric and chronocentric snobbery—the smugness of your own tribe and your own time: *We* are the Greeks; *all* others are barbarians. For the partial cure which is provided in the arts, in business organization, and most magnificently in science, by the international character of the data, of their application, their communication— these in law are no more. Law, as against the other disciplines, is like a tree. In its own soil it roots, and shades one spot alone. Atoms and x-rays seem to behave indifferent to whether the laboratory be in Paris or Chicago. A German appendix acts much like an American; the knife can speak a tongue more international than Volapluk. But the day when the Roman sources as modernized by Bartolus "and the other old mastiffs of the law" were serviceable equally in Italy and Germany and France—that day is past. The day is over when a dispute in Bristol could be referred to two Italian merchants, because the Italian cities were the root and flower of commercial customs of the world. If you would keep perspective, then—if you would really *see* the common law, you must beware of letting it submerge you. Perhaps when you see it, when you weigh it against other possibilities, you will look upon its work again and find it good. That, as a common lawyer, I may hope, and do. But I should think it a cheap valuation of our wayward, wilful, charming Mistress to feel that she must be kept from comparison, or even scrutiny, lest her charm should fail.

Back, if I may now, to the why of the two canons I have left: that the court *can* decide only the particular dispute before it; that all that is said is to be read with eyes on that dispute. Why these? I do believe, gentlemen, that here we have as fine a deposit of slow-growing wisdom as ever has been laid down through the centuries by the unthinking social sea. Here, hardened into institutions, carved out and given line by rationale. What is this wisdom? Look to your own discussion, look to any argument. You {45} know where you would go. You reach, at random if hurried, more carefully if not, for a foundation, for a major premise. But never for itself. Its interest lies in leading to the conclusion you are headed for. You shape its words, its content, to an end decreed. More, with your mind upon your object you use words, you bring in illustrations, you deploy and advance and concentrate again. When you have done, you have said much you did not mean. You did not mean, that is, *except* in reference to your point. You have brought generalization after generalization up, and discharged it at your goal; all, in the heat of argument, were over-stated. None would you stand to, if your opponent should urge them to *another* issue.

So with the judge. Nay, more so with the judge. He is not merely human, as are you. He is, as well, a lawyer; which you, yet, are not. A lawyer, and as such skilled in manipulating the resources of persuasion at his hand. A lawyer, and as such prone without thought to twist analogies, and rules, and instances, to his conclusion. A lawyer, and as such peculiarly prone to disregard the implications which do not bear directly on his case.

More, as a practiced campaigner in the art of exposition, he has learned that one must prepare the way for argument. You set the mood, the tone, you lay the intellectual foundation—all with the case in mind, with the conclusion—all, because those who hear you also have the case in mind, without the niggling criticism which may later follow. You wind up, as a pitcher will wind up—and as in the pitcher's case, the wind-up often is superfluous. As in the pitcher's case, it has been known to be intentionally misleading.

With this it should be clear, then, why our canons thunder. Why we create a class of dicta, of unnecessary words, which later readers, their minds now on quite other cases, can mark off as not quite essential to the argument. Why we create a class of *obiter dicta*, the wilder flailings of the pitcher's arms, the wilder motions of his gum-ruminant jaws. Why we set about, as our job, to crack the kernel from the nut, to find the true rule the case in fact decides: *the rule of the case.*

Now for a while I am going to risk confusion for the sake of talking simply. I am going to treat as the rule of the case the *ratio decidendi*, the rule *the court tells you* is the rule of the case, the ground, as the phrase goes, upon which the court itself has rested its decision. For there is where you must begin, and such refinements as are needed may come after.

The court, I will assume, has talked for five pages, only one of which portrayed the facts assumed. The rest has been discussion. And judgment has been given for the party who won below: judgment affirmed. We seek the rule.

The first thing to note is this: *no rule can be the ratio decidendi from which the actual judgment* (here: affirmance) *does not follow*. Unless {46} affirmance follows from a rule, it *cannot* be the rule which produced an actual holding of affirmance. But the holding is the decision, and the court speaks ex cathedra only as to the dispute decided, and only as to the decision it has made. At this point, too, I think you begin to see the bearing of the *procedural* issue. There *can* be a decision (and so an ex cathedra ratio) *only* as to a point which is before the court. But points come before a court of review by way of specific complaint about specific action of the court below, and in no other way. Hence nothing can be *held* which is not thus brought up.

You will have noted that these two statements are not quite the same. For the losing party may have complained of five, or fourteen, different rulings by the court below, but the final judgment below is affirmed or reversed but once. If you see what is ahead you will see that—on my argument to date—I am about to be driven either into inconsistency or into an affront to common sense. For obviously the court will in many or most instances take up the objections made before it, one by one. Now in that event we shall meet either of two phenomena, and very likely both at once. I shall assume this time, to set my picture more neatly, that the court *reverses* the judgment below. Then *either* it will say that the court below was wrong *on all five points,* or it will say that although right on less than all, it was nonetheless wrong on *at least one.* Suppose, first, it says: wrong on all. It is clear that *any one* would be sufficient for reversal. It is more than likely that the court will not rest peculiarly on any of the five. Any one of the five rulings would then be enough to justify a reversal, and four of them are by consequence wholly unnecessary. Which, now, are which? Further, under the canon I so proudly wheeled before you, the court can decide only the particular dispute before it. Which was that particular dispute?

Again, take a case where the court rules on four points in favor of a man who won below, but reverses, for all that, on the fifth point. Of the four rulings, not a single one *can* be a premise for the actual holding. They are, then, dicta merely?

Here, I say, common sense and my canons seem to be at odds. The fact is, that they are both right, and yet both wrong. To that, as a phase of the doctrine of precedent, I shall return. Here merely the solution. One of the reasons, of the sound ones, often given for weighing dicta lightly, is that the background and consequences of the statement have not been illumined by the argument of counsel, have not received, as being matters to be weighed with brows a-wrinkle, the full consideration of the court. In the case put the first reason does not fit; the second, if it is to be put on at all, hangs loose and flaps. No one point being the only crucial point, and the points decided which do not lead to judgment {47} not being absolutely necessary to decide, it may be the court has not sweated over them as it would had each stood alone. But sweated some, it has; and with due antecedent argument. Hence we have, in what we may call *the multi-point decision*, an intermediate type of authority. If a decision stands on two, or three, or five legs, any one of them is much more subject to challenge than it would be if the decision stood on it alone. Yet prima facie there remains "a decision" on each one of the points concerned. It is, as {Edmund M.} Morgan well says, within the province of a court to instruct the trial court how to act on points disputed and argued in the case in hand. The same reasoning in form, yet with distinctly lesser cogency in fact, applies to the multi-points ruled in favor of the party which ultimately loses the appeal. Authorities of a third water, these; and getting watery.

But our troubles with the ratio decidendi are not over. We meet forthwith a further formal one. Our judge states his facts, he argues his position, he announces his rule. And lo, he seems but to have begun. Once clean across the plate. But he begins again, winds up and again he delivers his ratio—this time, to our puzzlement, the words are not the same. At this point it is broader than it was before, there it is narrower. And like as not he will warn you another time, and do the same job over—differently again. I have never made out quite why this happens. A little, it may be due to a lawyer's tendency to clinch an argument by summarizing its course, when he is through. A little, it may be due to mere sloppiness of composition, to the lack, typical of our law and all its work, of a developed sense for form, juristic or esthetic, for what the Romans knew as *elegantia*. Sometimes I get a wry suspicion that the judge repeats because he is uneasy on his ground, that he lifts up his voice, prays his conclusion over loud and louder, to gain and make conviction, much like an advertiser bare of arguments except his slogan. At other times I feel as I read opinions the thrill of adventure in an undiscovered country; the first and second statements of the ratio, with all that has led up to them, are like first and second reconnoiterings of strange hills; like first and second chartings of what has been found and what surmised—knowledge and insight growing as the opinion builds to its conclusion. But whatever the reason, recurrent almost-repetition faces us; also the worry that the repetition seldom is exact. Which phrasing are we then to tie to?

Perhaps in this, as in judging how far to trust a broadly stated rule, we may find guidance in the facts the court assumes. Surely this much is certain: the actual dispute before the court is limited as straitly by the facts as by the form which the procedural issue has assumed. What is not in the facts cannot be present for decision. Rules which proceed an inch beyond the facts must be suspect.

{48} But how far does that help us out? What are *the* facts? The plaintiff's name is Atkinson and the defendant's Walpole. The defendant, despite his name, is an Italian by extraction, but the plaintiff's ancestors came over with the Pilgrims. The defendant has a schnautzer-dog named Walter, red hair, and $30,000 worth of life insurance. All these are facts. The case, however, does not deal with life insurance. It is about an auto accident. The defendant's auto was a Buick painted pale magenta. He is married. His wife was in the back seat, an irritable, somewhat faded blonde. She was attempting back-seat driving when the accident occurred. He had turned around to make objection. In the process the car swerved and hit the plaintiff. The sun was shining; there was a rather lovely dappled sky low to the West. The time was late October on a Tuesday. The road was smooth, concrete. It had been put in by the McCarthy Road Work Company. How many of these facts are important to the decision? How many of these facts are, as we say, legally relevant? Is it relevant that the road was in the country or the city; that it was concrete or tarmac or of dirt; that it was a private or a public way? Is it relevant that the defendant was driving a Buick, or a motor car, or a vehicle? Is it important that he looked around as the car swerved? Is it crucial? Would it have been the same if he had been drunk, or had swerved for fun, to see how close he could run by the plaintiff, but had missed his guess?

Is it not obvious that as soon as you pick up this statement of the facts to find its legal bearings you must discard some as of no interest whatsoever, discard others as dramatic but as legal nothings? And is it not clear, further, that when you pick up the facts which are left and which do seem relevant, you suddenly cease to deal with them in the concrete and deal with them instead in *categories* which you, for one reason or another, deem significant? It is not the road between Pottsville and Arlington; it is "a highway". It is not a particular pale magenta Buick eight, by number 735207, but "a motor car", and perhaps even "a vehicle". It is not a turning around to look at Adorée Walpole, but a lapse from the supposedly proper procedure of careful drivers, with which you are concerned. Each concrete fact of the case arranges itself, I say, as the *representative* of a much wider abstract *category* of facts, and it is not in itself but as a member of the category that you attribute significance to it. But what is to tell you whether to make your category "Buicks" or "motor cars" or "vehicles"? What is to tell you to make your category "road" or "public highway"? The court may tell you. But the precise point that you have up for study is how far is it safe to trust what the court says. The precise issue which you are attempting to solve is whether the court's language can be taken as it stands, or must be amplified, or must be whittled down.

This brings us at last to the case system. For the truth of the matter is a truth so obvious and trite that it is somewhat regularly overlooked by

{49} students. *That no case can have a meaning by itself!* Standing alone it gives you no guidance. It can give you no guidance as to how far it carries, as to how much of its language will hold water later. What counts, what gives you leads, what gives you sureness, *that is the background of the other cases* in relation to which you must read the one. They color the language, the technical terms, used in the opinion. But above all they give you the wherewithal to find which of the facts are significant, and in what aspect they are significant, and how far the rules laid down are to be trusted.

Here, I say, is the foundation of the case system. For what, in a case class, do we do? We have set before you, at either the editor's selection or our own, a *series* of opinions which in some manner are related. They may or may not be exactly alike in their outcome. They are always supposedly somewhat similar on their legally relevant facts. Indeed, it is *the aspects in which their facts are similar* which give you your first guidance as to what *classes* of fact will be found legally relevant, that is, will be found *to operate alike*, or to operate *at all*, upon the court. On the other hand, the states of fact are rarely, if ever, quite alike. And one of the most striking problems before you is: when you find two cases side by side which show a difference in result, then to determine *what* difference in their facts, or *what* difference in the procedural set-up, has produced that difference in result. Those are the two problems which must be in your mind as you examine the language of the opinions. I repeat them. First, what *are* the significant categories of facts, and what is their significance to the court? Second, what *differences* in facts or in procedural set-up produce differences in the court's action when the situations are otherwise alike?

This, then, is the case system game, the game of matching cases. We proceed by a rough application of the logical method of comparison and difference.

And here there are three things that need saying. The first is that by this matching of facts and issues in the different cases we get, to come back to where we started, some indication of when the court in a given case has over-generalized; of when, on the other hand, it has meant all the ratio decidendi that it said. "The Supreme Court of the United States," remarks the sage Professor T. R. Powell, "are by no means such fools as they talk, or as the people are who think them so." We go into the matter expecting a certain amount of inconsistency in the broader language of the cases. We go into the matter set in advance to find distinctions by means of which we can reconcile and harmonize the outcomes of the cases, even though the rules that the courts seem to lay down in their deciding may be inconsistent. We are prepared to whittle down the categories of the facts, to limit the rule of one case to its new whittled narrow category, to limit the rule of the other to its new other narrow category—and thus to make two cases stand together. The first case involves a man who makes an offer {50} and gets in his revocation before his offer is accepted. The court decides that he cannot be sued upon his promise, and says that no contract can be made unless the minds of both parties are at one at once. The second case involves a man who has made a similar offer and has mailed a revocation, but to whom a letter of acceptance has been sent before his revocation was received. The court holds that he can be sued upon his promise, and says that his offer was being repeated every moment before the time that it arrived until the letter of acceptance was duly mailed. Here are two rules which are a little difficult to put together, and to square with sense, and which are, too, a little hard to square with the two holdings in the cases. We set to work to seek a way out which will do justice to the holdings. We arrive perhaps at this, that it is not necessary for the two minds to be at one at once, if the person who has received an offer thinks, and thinks reasonably, as he takes the last step of acceptance, that the offeror is standing by the offer. And to test the rule laid down in either case, as also to test our tentative formulation which we have built to cover both, we do two things. First and easiest is to play variations on the facts, making the case gradually more and more extreme until we find the place beyond which it does not seem sense to go. Suppose, for example, our man does think the offeror still stands to his offer, and thinks it reasonably, on all his information; but yet a revocation has arrived, which his own clerk has failed to bring to his attention? We may find the stopping-place much sooner than we had expected, and thus be forced to recast and narrow the generalization we have made, or to recast it even on wholly different lines. The second and more difficult way of testing is to go to the books and find further cases in which variations on the facts occur, and in which the importance of such variations has been put to the proof. The first way is the intuitional correction of hypothesis; the second way is the experimental test of whether a hypothesis is sound. Both are needed. The first, to save time. The second, to make sure. For you will remember that in your casebook you have only a sampling, a foundation for discussion, enough cases to set the problem and start you thinking. Before you can trust your results, either those which you achieve yourselves, or those which you take with you from the class, you must go to the writers who have read more cases and see what they have to say.

In all of this I have been proceeding upon the assumption— and this is the second further point about case method that I had in mind—that all the cases everywhere can stand together. It is unquestionably the assumption you must also make, at first. If they can be brought together you must bring them. At the same time you must not overlook that our law is built up statewise. It is not built up in one piece. With fifty supreme courts plus the federal courts at work, it is inevitable that from time to time conflicting rules emerge. The startling thing is that they have been {51} so few. And where a given state, say Pennsylvania, has laid down one rule, but another state, New York, say, has laid down another, the mere fact that fifteen further states go with New York is unlikely in the extreme to change the Pennsylvania point of view. A *common* law in one sense is therefore non-existent on that point. What we have is fifteen states deciding one way, one state deciding another way *and thirty states whose law is still uncertain.* Yet in these circumstances, we do speak of "common law", and for this reason: True though it is that each state sticks, in the main, to its own authorities, when it has them, yet common to all the states is a large fundamental body of institutions which show at least a brother-and-sister type of likeness, which, to a surprising extent, as I have indicated, can even fairly be called identical. Furthermore, the *manner* of dealing with the legal authorities, the *way* of thinking, the *way* of working, the *way* of reading cases, the reasoning from them—or from statutes—these *common law techniques* are in all our courts in all our states substantially alike. And finally, if in a given state a point has not been settled, the court will turn to the decisions of the country as a whole as to a common reservoir of law. If there is but a single line of decision that court, although it never decided on the point before, is likely to lead off its argument: "It is well settled". If the decisions are divided on the point, the court is more likely than not to go with any substantial majority which may exist. But whether it goes with the majority or with the minority or picks a third variant of its own, it works with the materials from the other states almost as if they were its own, save that there is rarely any one of them which carries the sanction of transcendent authority.

Hence, in your matching of cases, you may, as a last resort when unable to make the cases fit together, fall back upon the answer: here is a conflict; these cases represent two different points of view.

You must, however, before you do that, make sure that they come from different jurisdictions, else one will have to be regarded as flatly overruling the other. Which brings me to the point of dates. Not the least important feature in the cases you are comparing will be their dates. For you must assume that the law, like any other human institution, has undergone, still undergoes development, clarification, change, as time goes on, as experience accumulates, as conditions vary. The earlier cases in a series, therefore, while they *may* stand unchanged today, are yet more likely to be forerunners, to be indications of the first gropings with a problem, rather than to present its final solution even in the state from which they come. That holds particularly for cases prior to 1800. It holds in many fields of law for cases of much more recent date. But in any event you will be concerned to place the case in time as well as in space, if putting it together with the others makes for difficulty.

{52} The third thing that needs saying as you set to matching cases, is that on your materials, often indeed on all the materials that there are, a perfect working out of comparison and difference cannot be had. In the first case you have facts *a* and *b* and *c*, procedural set-up *m* and outcome *x*. In the second case you have, if you are lucky, procedural set-up *m* again, but this time with facts *a* and *b* and *d*, and outcome *y*. How, now, are you to know with any certainty whether the changed result is due in the second instance to the absence of fact *c* or to the presence of the new fact *d*? The court may tell you. But I repeat: your object is to *test* the telling of the court. You turn to your third case. Here once more is the outcome *x*, and the facts are *b* and *c* and *e*; but fact *a* is missing, and the procedural set-up this time is not *m* but *n*. This strengthens somewhat your suspicion that fact *c* is the lad who works the changed result. But an experimentum crucis still is lacking. Cases in life are not made to our hand. A scientific *approach* to prediction we may have, and we may use it as far as our materials will permit. An exact science *in result* we have not now. Carry this in your minds: a scientific approach, no more. Onto the green, with luck, your science takes you. But when it comes to putting you will work by art and hunch.

Where are we now? We have seen the background of the cases. We have seen what they consist of. We have seen that they must be read and analyzed for their facts, for their procedural issue and for their decision. We have seen that they are to be matched together to see which are the facts which have the legal consequences, and in what categories we must class the facts with that in view. And out of this same matching process we can reach a judgment as to how much of the language, even in the ratio decidendi, the court has really meant.

But if you arrive at the conclusion that a given court did not mean all it said in the express ratio decidendi it laid down, that the case must really be confined to facts narrower than the court itself assumed to be its measure, then you are ready for the distinction that I hinted at earlier in this lecture, the distinction between the ratio decidendi, the court's own version of the rule of the case, and the *true* rule of the case, to wit, what *it will be made to stand for by another later court*. For one of the vital elements of our doctrine of precedent is this: that any later court can always reexamine a prior case, and under the principle that the court could decide only what was before it, and that the older case must now be read with that in view, can arrive at the conclusion that the dispute before the earlier court was much narrower than that court thought it was, called therefore for the application of a much narrower rule. Indeed, the argument goes further. It goes on to state that no broader rule *could* have been laid down ex-cathedra, because to do that would have transcended the powers of the earlier court.

You have seen further that out of the matching of a number of related cases it is your job to formulate a rule that covers them all in harmony, {53} if that can be done, and to test your formulation against possible variants on the facts. Finally, to test it, if there is time, against what writers on the subject have to say, and against other cases.

It does not pay to go too early to the writers. To do so is to come under strong temptation to skip through the process of case matching on your own. If your chin is square enough, then you may risk it. If you can take what the writer says not as an answer, but as an hypothesis, if you have patience to test it against the cases in your book, and to read, too, some of those the writer cites to see how far they bear out his own conclusions, then you are better off when you consult the writer early. But otherwise, and if you try to use him as a trot, you court disaster.

Now you come into class. There you find the instructor carrying on the same process I have been describing, save that he is more skillful, that he has more knowledge and more insight. He points distinctions which had not yet occurred to you. He tries cases on you you had never thought about. He speaks from a background rich with knowledge of specific states of fact and of their background. Precisely for that reason it is necessary, it is vital, it is the very basic element of case law study, for you to have done your matching of the cases before you meet with his. For it is not by watching him juggle the balls that you will learn. It is by matching his results against your own, by criticizing the process you have gone through in the light of the process he is going through. Indeed if you have not tried the game yourself, *you will not follow him.* The man who sees line-play in the football game is the man who once tried playing on the line himself. A Harlem audience responds to niceties in tap-dancing you do not even know are hard to do. Let me repeat: you will get little out of your instruction unless daily, repeatedly, consistently, you try the game out to the end the weary night before. At the same time, with growing skill, you will bring criticism to bear on the man behind the desk as well. You will, if he is human, find inconsistencies between his work today and what he did or said five weeks ago. That will be useful for him. It will be infinitely more for you.

What now of preparation for your case class? Your cases are assigned. Before they can be used they have to be digested. Experience shows that it is well to brief them. Briefing is valuable if only for the impending discussion. Briefing is well nigh essential when it comes to the review. Make no mistake in this. Day to day, at ten or fifteen pages every day, it still is possible to keep your material well enough in mind to follow much that will go on in class. But when you come to attempting to review 300, 400 or 500 pages at once, you will find that your mind is blank as to most of the cases, and there is no time to fill that blank with meat. There is one answer and there is only one: your brief, or abstract, or digest.

There is another point at which the brief is valuable. You cannot take adequate notes on class discussion in your casebook, yet you need in one {54} place the substance of a case and the notes on its discussion. The classic plan is briefing on gummed paper, and the pasting of the briefs into the relevant passages in your notes. At this point I would make one remark. The class discussion will show you often that your brief is bad. The thing to do before you paste it in is to make it over. *Before* you paste it, make it over right.

And one thing more. Briefing, I say, is valuable. Briefing, I say, is well nigh essential. Briefing is also the saddest trap that ever awaited a law student, if he does not watch his step. For the practice under pressure of time, as eyes grow tired in the evening, or the movies lure, is to brief cases *one by one*, and therefore blindly. Now if I have made one point in this discussion it should be this: that a case read by itself is meaningless, is nil, is blank, is blah. Briefing should begin *at the earliest* with the second case of an assignment. Only *after* you have read the second case have you any idea what to do with the first. Briefing, I say again, is a problem of putting down what in the one case bears upon the problem stated by the other cases. Each brief should be in terms of *what this case adds to what I already know about* this subject. Hence at least two cases must be read before any can be intelligently briefed. And as you pass to the third case and the fourth case, you have accomplished nothing unless both in your reading and your briefing of them you work at them with reference to the cases that have gone before. What does the case *add, what difference does it make*, to what I already know? This is the keynote of the brief. For this same reason, when you ever do any research in law, you must distrust your briefs, and distrust most the earliest ones you made. The earlier in the research the brief was made, the less you knew when you made it; hence, the more worthless it is. Read through the first-found case again, and see! The chances are the first half of the briefs made in any one job of research belong on the ash-heap. The cases blossom under further study, under new reading. They yield more wisdom as your wisdom grows.

What, now, should a brief contain? (1) First, as a finder: the title and its page in the casebook. (2) Second, to orient it in the law, the state and date. From now on, the order becomes largely immaterial. I give you one possible and useful order. (3) What, precisely, did the plaintiff want? What did he ask for? This is one most vital and one almost regularly overlooked feature of a brief. This is the first start in coming to the *question*. (4) Contrariwise, what did the defendant want and how did the case come to an issue? (5) What did the trial court do; that is, what was the judgment below? (6) Finally, what action of the trial court is complained of? When you have these things in your brief, and only then, are you prepared to look for either relevant facts or relevant rules of law. When you have found these things, and only then, have you your cross-lines laid to spot *the question* in the case. (7) I find it useful to put down next the outcome of appeal. You see why {55} that is useful. It at once makes clear whether the language of the court in a given passage was or was not necessary to the decision. (8) Then come the facts of the case as assumed by the court. I warn you, I warn you strongly, against cutting the facts down too far. If you cherish any hope of insight into *what difference the rules make* to people, you will have to keep an eye out to some of the more striking details of the facts, as the court gives them. I know you will lose patience with them. But observe this, my friends. *You will be impatient with the facts to the precise extent to which you need them.* If you do not need them, if you already have some knowledge of the background of the case, the facts will not be boring; they will interest you. If they pester and upset you, that is a sign that you know so little about what the case means in life that these facts need desperate study.

Which facts, then, are significant? I recur again to my proposition. One case will not tell you. Only the group of cases will give you any start at solving that. The more cases you read, therefore, before you brief any, the better off you are, provided only that you brief them each one in the light of all.

And finally, remember this: it is where the facts (as illumined, as *selected*, as *classified* in the light of other cases) *cross* with the issue given by the procedural set-up, that the narrow-issue question of the case is found. *And only there.*

(9) After the facts, the ratio decidendi, phrased preferably substantially along the lines taken by the court. (10) If you do not like the language of the court, in the light of the other cases, here is the place to note down how you think it should have phrased the rule.

Beyond this, notes are a matter of discretion. (11) I have always found it useful to indicate something of the line of argument the court indulged in, for reasons which I hope to make appear. (12) A beginning law student, moreover, finds in cases many remarks as to the law, which although they have no bearing on the subject he is studying, are highly interesting and informative. It was my practice when a student to note those down, but to note them by themselves, where they helped memory but did not get in the way of review.

So much for the brief. And if you follow this advice you will discover that by the time the last brief is made the class is well prepared. For you cannot brief four cases each with reference to the other without having *already* put them together, without having *already* phrased the results that you have come to on them all. Your last brief will have incorporated, at least by implication, all the rest. And let me say once again, that till they all are put together, and some of the bearings of your phrasing thought over, you will not be prepared, you will not know what *any* of them is about.

IV · THIS CASE SYSTEM: PRECEDENT

There are psychologists who delight in talking of an apperceptive mass. I am not quite sure what such an apperceptive mass may be, nor of whether it is at all. But I am very sure that these psychologists have a strong truth by the tail. The only question, as A. G. Keller used to put it, is whether, for all our firm grip on the tail, we shall have skill and patience to work up over the rump.

The truth that we have seized upon is this: you see in your case almost exactly what you brought to it, and hardly more. If you bring much, you see much. If you bring nothing, that is what you see. A *little*, each case will add to what you knew. The measure of what it adds, again, is what you bring.

This point I dwelt on lovingly in the last lecture, in regard to briefing. I shall dwell on it now again, in reference to review. Case study progresses slowly. It works intensively. It works, because it must work intensively, upon a *tiny* body of material day by day. Hence you can *seem* to do the work, and *seem* to follow, although each day you have in mind the cases for the day, and nothing more. At this point, gentlemen, we meet the rump. You *seem* to do the work. But if you are to *do* it, you require, each day, each week, to build your new material together with your old. You require to enlarge, above all you require to consolidate, your apperceptive mass in law. You require to bring to each new case and each new briefing the *whole* of the body of the knowledge you have that far met. The crux of your briefing: "What does this case *add*?" develops value to you in exact proportion to the size and quality of the existing stock of skill to which the new addition will be made.

Now I know well that you have heard all this before. I know that you have met before our old familiar frog: three feet a day he climbs out of the slickery pit, two feet each night he slides down as he sleeps. The benighted frog does not dig in betweenwhiles. He takes no thought about his apperceptive mass. He does not, in the military jargon, consolidate his position. Having no tail he does not see the problem of surmounting rumps.

Yet you perhaps lay claim to being more than frogs. Presumably, at least in theory, you own intelligence. The Dean's office vouches that you have got by our private lunacy commission. You should thus *understand* me, when I tell you that the only road to making the slow-moving case instruction gain momentum is to *accelerate* the learning process day by day. The quantity of new material studied you will not much increase. The quantity and quality of what you *get out of* your new material can jack up daily. But in one way only: by daily, by weekly, going over, arranging, consolidating what you have. Our class instruction is invaluable to you. But, I insisted {57} yesterday, valuable only as you labor through the problems first yourself, as you prepare yourself to see what goes on in the class. And, I insist today, valuable only as you work through the problems *afterward* yourself (or in a group), build what you have seen into a *working* part of your equipment for tomorrow. Our class instruction, as a catalyzer, is all that you have hoped. But *by itself* it is a poorer show than Keith's {Theatres}, at higher prices.

Now I have told you. Before this lecture closes I shall hope to indicate enough niceties in the material, enough lines fine, yet profitable to follow, to stir in you some realization of the meaning of the telling. Just this last thing to end the exhortation: your instructors, many of them, have taught some cases ten or twenty times, and studied those cases over each time before they taught them. *Constantly*, they are finding new things, new light, new problems, in that same material. They have meanwhile increased their apperceptive mass. They sit triumphantly astride the beast!

One other point I wish to make in the same connection. Note-taking is well nigh essential. Writing helps memory. Writing records. What seems so easy to remember slips away. You need it, if you would consolidate. But note-taking, like briefing, is a treacherous tool. Notes that have any value are not *copied* down. Before the writing down goes a critique. Notes that have value are not what is said, they are a selection, a working over, a working up, of what is said—a preservation of the queries opened by the instructor, a preservation of the independent queries which occur to you. If you are actively—though silently—engaged in the discussion, your mind *must* open queries as the class proceeds. Those things belong in your notes. What the instructor gives as information then has some reference value. You can see its setting. You can judge whether it is holding or mere dictum.

It is much harder, it is much slower to take notes this way. It is much harder: reacting, rephrasing, you must *think* to take a note. Selecting in the light of the discussion the essential from the surrounding whirl of words, you have to give attention, to be using the stuff between your ears, throughout the whole discussion. So, too, it is much harder, much slower, to brief cases with intelligence. It is much harder, slower, to put in daily time upon consolidation of your notes. These things take guts, some mental and some moral. They are the conjugations and declensions and syntax of your study of the law; they are your plant, your engine, your machine. If they are grubbed through once, and grubbed through hard, if they are once put together and set moving—then you have them. The outlay on investment is complete. Within a month or two they pay out dividends. Within six months you find them a bonanza. Then your machine is oiled and running smoothly, while your neighbor who speeded blithely through the football season knocks and stalls. This is a wisdom hidden from the frog.

So, I have said my piece. Let us get on to something interesting.

{58} We looked yesterday at the art of matching cases to extract the rules from them. Today we go further. We take up what can be done with such an extract when you have it. We take up also some of the less systematized lore which lies in the cases if you have the wit to find it. The two types of study interlock. Both take us back to the cases themselves as the ore which we are to refine.

For the cases go some distance to show us what types of dispute arise. Here, as in the measuring of effects of rules, we must indeed recall that the facts assumed or adopted by an appellate court have gone through straining and distortion. We shall not attribute to them, therefore, any quality of accurate description of the events they purport to bring before us. Yet, as historians have learned, much can be pieced together from accounts which may be biased, partial, even propagandist. And, in my constant reference, for convenience, to "the facts" of cases, I trust that you will understand me as always assuming that the cases in this aspect of their "facts" are to be read and will be read by you as an historian would read a document— looking for evidence of bias, of omission, of distortion; and concluding to the facts not as one would conclude from laboratory evidence, but as one would conclude, say, from the "London letter" of a fairly skillful correspondent.

The cases, I say, give us an indication of what types of dispute arise. Being cases at law, however, they indicate in the first instance not disputes in life, but quarrels before the courts. Now I have already argued that quarrels before the courts are but a minor fraction of the quarrels of life. I can go further and argue that quarrels in life are a still lesser fraction of life's business. Both points need stressing as we seek to place the meaning of the cases. Are the facts typical? And typical of what?

You will find one great group of litigated cases which were predestined to be litigated. They bear the same relation as does homicidal mania or sleeping sickness, to our normal life. They are in court because they are so exceptional that the normal ways of society have afforded no solid basis for deciding them, or even because the ordinary machinery of adjusting cases in society has no teeth which fasten on them. The rules which arise out of such cases may be very useful. They may indeed to lawyers become of vast importance. The lawyer specializes in this flotsam of events as the doctor specializes in diseases of the eye and ear. What to him is the mine-run of his cases is to the ordinary man accident, misfortune, the event of a life-time. Indeed, such cases may be thus exceptional to the layman over whole groups or over whole communities. I strongly suspect that a great bulk of our rules will prove on study to touch only these pathological cases. Such rules have little touch with rules for living life. By hypothesis any cases which call them into play are in the living of life extraordinary, unforeseen. They enter into *calculation* at most as remote contingencies— against which, however, it may pay to seek protection or insurance. Such rules, then, are *rules* for {59} *decision*, rules for officials, rules for the most specialized of specialists. They interest you because you may become such specialists. They interest you also because to you they suggest contingencies which no ordinary man would think about, but which, when he comes to you for counsel, may well often give you the wherewithal to furnish him more adequate insurance service.

But much more important, much more vital, much more focal for your study and your understanding, are those cases in which the rules hit closer to the norms of living; those disputes which typify whole groups of interest-clashes commonly occurring. Here the rule laid down will be a rule whose application people may foresee; a rule whose application, even if they do not foresee it, threatens them. Here then is a rule to which men can and should and often do orient the action which they take *apart from* litigation. Most commonly you will find cases of this sort upon the growing fringe of institutions. A new type of contract, of market organization, of insurance, of corporate stock has been thought hopeful, has been tried out. As yet its outlines and its bearing are not certain. A dispute arises. The two parties each honestly regard as right the view which will be favorable to him. There can be doubt. The ways, the attitudes, of men who deal in the connection are not yet fixed. They fluctuate. They are conflicting. The issue may be compromised and no case reach the courts until the social process-es of trial and error and of imitation have worked out fairly definite re-sults. But quite as likely is that the dispute will come to litigation. Perhaps it is pushed as a test case, purposefully. Perhaps it comes by social acci-dent, and merely because one party proves to be stubborn. In either event, a test case it will be. The court will pass upon some feature of a half-formed institution. Such test cases, once they are decided, shape, limit, block its further growth. If, as is likely, the court in the future stands by the decision it has once made, that decision shapes not only the further growth of the law, but the further action of the community. So the decision may have been handed down two centuries ago and still be one which has made and left its mark upon the social organization of today. This is the one side, the power of courts over society. The other has been already intimated, the power of society over the courts. It is society and not the courts which gives rise to, which shapes in the first instance the emerging institution;

which kicks the courts into action. It is only from observation of society that the courts can pick their notions of what needs the new institution serves, what needs it baffles. Partly courts look directly at society. Partly they look at the deposit of their own work made in the past on similar occasions, that is, at the existing "ways" of law. In any event, if the needs press and recur, sooner or later recognition of them will work into the law. Either they will induce the courts to break through and depart from earlier molds, or the bar will find some way to put new wine into old bottles and to induce in the bottles that elasticity and {60} change of shape which, in the long run, marks all social institutions. Or, finally, if the courts stand fast themselves, and clamp down the lid, too, on the bar's experiments, then, if the need resurges long and hard enough, the change will be made by way of legislation.

Each case now which is not one purely pathological is an experiment in this great laboratory, and the problem is how to milk that experiment for your training.

The first thing, not only for this purpose, but indeed for any, is to *visualize* the initial transaction between the parties. Who were they? What did they look like? Above all, what did each one want, and why did he want it? If you can see the facts in their chronological order, one by one; if you can see them occurring one by one as particular people (be they well or ill advised) were moving to the accomplishment of their desires—if you can see these desires and feel them in the light of who the parties were and of their situation—then and then only will the case become real to you, will it stick in your head, will the words speak and set your mind to working. Call this, if you will, dramatizing. Call it, if you will, the writing of fiction. It resembles them at least in this: that to do it will require you to loose your imagination—but with discipline; will require you first to feel yourself into the situation as depicted and then to see, to feel the texture and the rough knobs of each fact.

So equally when the case arises out of an event. You will, I may say, find it very useful to take this distinction between *transaction* and *event*, to keep it in mind. We have a *transaction* when two or more parties get together to accomplish something. They bargain, they sell, they lease, they write insurance. Here, before the dispute, there is a deal. Here the possibility offers always of shaping the transaction in advance and with design to the ends of the two parties or of one. Here, therefore, there is room for all kinds of legal safeguard, room for the work of counsel in the office. But what I am calling *events* will rarely be intended by both parties, if by either. A man is killed. It may be purpose in the killer; it rarely is in the deceased. There is a brawl. True, in a sense, the two parties deal together, and now that the brawl is on they may be dealing with intent. Still, it is rare to have the brawl in mind beforehand. With events, equally, however, visualization helps. But their dramatic character leads commonly of itself to your doing what visualization you may need. Hence the facts of tort cases commonly are "easy". But in the facts of contract cases, or of property cases, you are more likely to have to drive yourself to the work. Drive, then, for it is needed.

There is more, however, to dramatize than merely what the parties wanted, or what they did. Especially in the transaction. There you have eternally the question, *what would you, had you been counsel, have advised* this man on this point, at each stage of the negotiation? How do you {61} analyze the facts thus far? What is their legal meaning? How will that legal meaning bear on this party's proper course?

If you can read facts thus the case is no longer flat. It foams as golden as Toronto ale. Fine bubbles rise: did the court read the facts as did the parties? Did the court see what the parties were driving at? To put the question in legal phrasing, was the court's interpretation of the facts sound?

This leads us into one of the most striking and useful discriminations that in your reading of the cases you must make, to wit, the difference between the *rule of law* laid down on a set of facts assumed, on the one hand, and on the other, the *way the court interpreted the facts* before it. I like to call these the two levels of the decision. In logic you will observe the interpretation of the facts comes first. There are some statements in the record as to evidence. You give a meaning to these statements. You decide precisely what they mean. Your application of a rule of law bears then on what you have already decided to be the meaning of the facts. It does not touch the raw evidence at all. It touches only the final product that remains after the evidence has been worked over.

Yet in life the operation may be the reverse; rule and decision may dictate the interpretation of the facts. For it is clear that if a later court, in pondering a case substantially equivalent, does not like the results achieved by the earlier court, then it may reach a contrary decision in either of two ways. Either it may reject the rule laid down by court number one; and this is not so likely. Or it may accept that rule as a verbal formula, may cite the prior case as authority, and yet interpret the raw evidence before it differently, saying that due to the difference in the facts, the rule does not apply. For example, it is conceded on all hands that if A makes B an offer, and B then writes a letter which purports to be an acceptance but which adds a new and different term to the proposed agreement and which further conditions acceptance upon the introduction of that term, then B has not accepted. This rule looks clear enough. Yet it means almost nothing until you get down to what I have called the first level, and see how the courts in their work interpret different kinds of letter as falling inside or outside the rule. A offers B, for example, a deed of his Greenwich

Village stable for $30,000 payable Tuesday. A is in New York, B in Philadelphia. That offer, by itself, means $30,000 payable in New York. B replies, "offer accepted money available girard national {bank} here send on your deed." Is this a new condition, or was it a mere suggestion that A shift the place of payment? Not all the universal agreement in the world as to "the rule" can give you light on this. From which I reason: until you study the first level of decision, the interpretation of the facts at hand, you do not *know* the rule. I do not care what you may know about its words, until you know what the words *stand for*. This is important in putting your cases together. It is important, too, in saving time. For it does not pay to quarrel with the {62} rule of law laid down by a court because you just do not like its way of interpreting the evidence. You can see and approve the rule of law announced and still reserve your quarrel upon the evidence. But to quarrel intelligently you must clarify the issues. On the other hand, when it comes to seeing the bearing of the rule on life, on actual disputes, on actual transactions, it is clear that the first level moves into the limelight of your mind.

This brings me now to a further point about the courts. Some courts in their work of interpretation you will discover very eager to find what the parties' situation really was; to read their words, to interpret the bits of evidence as the parties themselves would have regarded them. Such courts feel their way into the situation as you ought to. They take you with them. Other courts sit in what seems to be sublime indifference. They act not only in their laying down of rules of law, but even in their interpretation of the facts, as if life had been made for law. We find, I say, in the interpretation of the evidence divergencies in *attitude* among the courts.

And this concept of *attitude* carries further. I spoke in the last lecture of a common occurrence: that we turn up two cases which the two courts have put upon two inconsistent grounds: upon two different, two conflicting rules. I spoke of the possibility of framing a third rule which would, as the phrase goes, reconcile the cases—a rule perhaps which differs from that laid down in either case, but which would warrant and, indeed, require, both results. Commonly this is achieved by taking a *distinction*, by picking out some feature which differentiates the cases, but which neither court has stressed, and by insisting that this differentiating feature is what accounts for the results. The differentiating feature may be a point of fact; it may be a difference in the procedural set-up of the cases. In either event its striking aspect, from our angle, is that the distinction taken occupied no great amount of the attention of the two courts under discussion. Which brings us to the point of attitude. Granted that *if a court desires*, it will find the distinction sufficient to harmonize the cases—granted, that is to say that the distinction makes technically *possible* our proposed solution, remains the question, *will* a court do this? Will any court do this? Will either of the two courts under discussion do it? Or will they say, each one of them, or either, when facts do come before them like those in the apparently opposing case: "We cannot rule as the court there did because in our first case we settled the rule to the contrary."

Here, you observe, we have passed out of the realm of pure logic. We have indeed passed out of the realm of pure scientific observation and inference. Logic and science can tell us, and tell us with some certainty, what the doctrinal *possibilities* are. They can tell us whether without self-contradiction the results of the cases *can* be so settled as to stand together. They can even provide us with a tool for argument to a court that the cases *should* be made in this fashion to stand together. But they give us no certainty as {63} to *whether* the possibility embodied in the argument will be adopted by a given court.

But here is a situation in which the very aspects of the case which give us most trouble when we seek pure doctrine, come now to our help. The phrasing of the court, the points that it picks out for stress, the patience or impatience displayed in dealing with cases cited and with contentions of counsel, the interest or lack of interest shown (on the level of evidence-interpretation) in what the parties seem really to have had in mind, the bluntness or the delicacy of the logical tools with which the court has reasoned—these lay the foundation for a prediction, for a prediction not sure, but very helpful, as to how the particular court in a later case will respond.

Not the least helpful thing in reaching such a prediction, is the occasional presence of an extra opinion of some other judge. In the English courts of appeal it is the common practice for each judge successively to give his opinion on the case. He sometimes makes his own statement of the facts; he regularly puts forward his own reasoning and finally his conclusion. You will discover that the statements of the facts will often differ, and will differ peculiarly in their emphasis and their arrangement. You will discover, further, that the lines of legal argument which seem persuasive to the different judges also differ. Occasionally, too, but much less often, there is a divergence in result. Now this challenges attention. If, after seeing the same record and hearing the same arguments, different judges emphasize differently, even select differently, the facts which they assume to be "the case", it would seem to follow that the manner of selection and presentation of the facts may be a useful indication of the judges' thinking and reactions to the cases. If different judges, moreover, find different lines of argument persuasive in leading to a single result, then it would seem to follow that judges' reactions to the facts are more nearly alike, at least are more predictable, than are their reactions to the forms of words we know as legal rules. Surely it must give pause to any man who believes conclusions can be drawn out ineluctably from the words of general formulae, when he finds these English judges in the same case announcing different rules as the basis of the same decision. One result of the English practice where the rules in the individual opinions differ is that it often for a while remains in doubt as to which of the opinions represents (for later courts) "the rule of the case". There are a variety of rationes decidendi served up—and so to speak competing.

In the main—whether under pressure of business, since the court can do business faster if but one judge prepares an opinion for each case; or because it seemed wiser to avoid this trouble of leaving the bar often in the air as to what was the rule on which the court preferred to rest the case; or perhaps because our judges in the main are less trained in oral composition than the English, unwilling to prepare an opinion except in writing and therefore {64} led somewhat naturally to concentrate the labor—for whatever reason, our courts have in the main fallen into the practice of confining themselves to one opinion. That, however, has not wholly rooted out the ancient English practice. Extra opinions we find still. Sometimes concurring opinions, where the concurring judge finds it impossible to approve some portion of the reasoning of the final opinion of the court. Sometimes dissenting opinions, in which the judge feels so strongly the objectionable character of the decision that, not content with voting against it, he brings his views to print with the report. What is of interest here is that when such a dissenting opinion is found, it gives us, so to speak, a second point of observation from which to predict the action of that court in the future.

And I may add that while it is very hard to generalize about the effect of a dissenting opinion in the future, certain things seem probable. First, that in the court which decides the case a dissenting opinion proves that a fight has been had and is settled, and that the majority will almost certainly stay put, at least so long as the same personnel is on the bench. The great exceptions to this rule (and they are rare) are cases in which the dissent in the words of Cardozo "was the voice of a new day", too unfamiliar to have found as yet the acceptance that awaited it. Outside of the court which announced the decision the effect of a dissenting opinion is ambiguous. Always it somewhat weakens the authority of the case. Partly because it is by a divided court, partly because side by side with the reasoning of the majority and weakening its psychological effect appears another line of reasoning. Yet the argument is often met with, and seems sometimes to have weight, that the very fact of a dissent proves peculiarly careful consideration, and should therefore strengthen rather than weaken the case as an authority.

I think we are now ready to lock horns with the problem of *precedent* and make something out of it. I fear that I am going to have to be as unorthodox in what I say about this as in what I said about law. The one vagary is indeed a corollary of the other. For, whereas much or most of what is commonly written about precedent takes as its raw material what judges have *said* about precedent, I propose to take as mine, not so much what they have said as what they have *done* about it.

First, what is precedent? In the large, disregarding for the moment peculiarities of our law and of legal doctrine—in the large, precedent consists in an official doing over again under similar circumstances substantially what has been done by him or his predecessor before. The foundation, then, of precedent is the official analogue of what, in society at large, we know as folkways, or as institutions, and of what, in the individual, we know as habit. And the things which make for precedent in this broad sense are the same which make for habit and for institutions. It takes time and effort to solve problems. Once you have solved one it seems foolish to reopen it. Indeed, you are likely to be quite impatient with the notion of reopening it. {65} Both inertia and convenience speak for building further on what you have already built; for incorporating the decision once made, *the solution once worked out*, into your operating technique *without reexamination* of what *earlier went into* reaching your solution. From this side you will observe that the urge to precedent will be present in the action of any official, irrespective of whether he wants it, or not; irrespective likewise of whether he thinks it is there, or not. From this angle precedent is but a somewhat dignified name for the *practice* of the officer or of the office. And it should be clear that unless there were such practices it would be hard to know there was an office or an officer. It is further clear that with the institution of written records the background range of the practice of officers is likely to be considerably extended; and even more so is the possible outward range, the possibility of outside imitation. Finally, it is clear that if the written records both exist and are somewhat carefully and continuously consulted, the possibility of change creeping into the practices unannounced is greatly lessened. At this place on the law side the institution of the bar rises into significance. For whereas the courts might make records and keep them, but yet pay small attention to them; or might pay desultory attention; or might even deliberately neglect an inconvenient record if they should later change their minds about that type of case, the lawyer searches the records for convenient cases to support his point, presses upon the court what it has already done before, capitalizes the human drive toward repetition by finding, by making explicit, by urging, the prior cases.

At this point there enters into the picture an ethical element, the argument that courts (and other officials) not only do, but *should* continue what they have been doing. Here, again, the first analogue is in the folkway or the individual habit. I do not know why, nor do I know how, but I observe the fact that what one has been doing acquires in due course another flavor, another level of value than mere practice; a flavor on the level of policy, or ethics, or morality. What one has been doing becomes the "right" thing to do; not only the expected thing but the thing whose happening will be welcomed and whose failure to happen will be resented. This is true in individuals whose habits are interrupted; this is true in social intercourse when the expected event, when the expectation based upon the knowledge of other people's habits, materializes or fails to materialize. Indeed, in social matters in the large, there develops distinct group pressure to *force conformity* with the existing and expected social ways.

All of this, now, the lawyer brings to bear upon law itself. Here speaks the judicial conscience.

And apart from the unreasoned and unreasoning fact that oughtness attaches to practice, they are, particularly in the case of officials, and most particularly in the case of judges, reasons of policy to buttress this ethical element. To continue past practices is to provide a new official in his inexperience {66} with the accumulated experience of his predecessors. If he is ignorant, he can learn from them and profit by the knowledge of those who have gone before him. If he is idle he can have their action brought to his attention and profit by their industry. If he is foolish he can profit by their wisdom. If he is biased or corrupt the existence of past practices to compare his action with gives a public check upon his biases and his corruption, limits the frame in which he can indulge them unchallenged. Finally, even though his predecessors may themselves, as they set up the practice, have been idle, ignorant, foolish and biased, yet the knowledge that he will continue what they have done gives a basis from which men may predict the action of the courts; a basis to which they can adjust their expectations and their affairs in advance. To know the law is helpful, even when the law is bad. Hence it is readily understandable that in our system there has grown up first the habit of following precedent, and then the legal norm that precedent is to be followed. The main form that this principle takes we have seen. It is essentially the canon that each case must be decided as one instance under a general rule. This much is common to almost all systems of law. The other canons are to be regarded rather as subsidiary canons that have been built to facilitate working with and reasoning from our past decisions.

But it will have occurred to you that despite all that I have said in favor of precedent, there are objections. It may be the ignorance or folly, or idleness, or bias of the predecessor which chains a new strong judge. It may be, too, that conditions have changed, and that the precedent, good when it was made, has since become outworn. The rule laid down the first time that a case came up may have been badly phrased, may have failed to foresee the types of dispute which later came to plague the court. Our society is changing, and law, if it is to fit society, must also change. Our society is stable, else it would not be a society, and law which is to fit it must stay fixed. Both truths are true at once. Perhaps some reconciliation lies along this line; that the stability is needed most greatly in large things, that the change is needed most in matters of detail. At any rate, it now becomes our task to inquire into how the system of precedent which we actually have works out in fact, accomplishing at once stability and change.

We turn first to what I may call the orthodox doctrine of precedent, with which, in its essence, you are already familiar. Every case lays down a rule, the rule of the case. The express ratio decidendi is prima facie the rule of the case, since it is the ground upon which the court chose to rest its decision. But a later court can reexamine the case and can invoke the canon that no judge has power to decide what is not before him, can, through examination of the facts or of the procedural issue, narrow the picture of what was actually before the court and can hold that the ruling made requires to be understood as thus restricted. In the extreme form this results in what is known as expressly "confining the case to its particular facts." This rule {67} holds only of redheaded Walpoles in pale magenta Buick cars. And when you find this said of a past case you know that in effect it has been overruled. Only a convention, a somewhat absurd convention, prevents flat overruling in such instances. It seems to be felt as definitely improper to state that the court in a prior case was wrong, peculiarly so if that case was in the same court which is speaking now. It seems to be felt that this would undermine the dogma of the infallibility of courts. So lip service is done to that dogma, while the rule which the prior court laid down is disembowelled. The execution proceeds with due respect, with mandarin courtesy.

Now this orthodox view of the authority of precedent—which I shall call the *strict* view—is but *one of two views* which seem to me wholly contradictory to each other. It is in practice the dogma which is applied to *unwelcome* precedents. It is the recognized, legitimate, honorable technique for whittling precedents away, for making the lawyer, in his argument, and the court, in its decision, free of them. It is a surgeon's knife.

It is orthodox, I think, because it has been more discussed than is the other. Consider the situation. It is not easy thus to carve a case to pieces. It takes thought, it takes conscious thought, it takes analysis. There is no great art and no great difficulty in merely looking at a case, reading its language, and then applying some sentence which is there expressly stated. But there is difficulty in going underneath what is said, in making a keen reexamination of the case that stood before the court, in showing that the language used was quite beside the point, as the point is revealed under the lens of leisured microscopic refinement. Hence the technique of distinguishing cases has given rise to the closest of scrutiny. The technique of arguing for a distinction has become systematized. And when men start talking of authority, or of the doctrine of precedent, they turn naturally to that part of their minds which has been *consciously* devoted to the problem; they call up the cases, the analyses, the arguments, which have been made under such conditions. They put this together, and call this *"the doctrine"*. I suspect there is still another reason for the orthodoxy. That is that only finer minds, minds with sharp mental scalpels, can do this work, and that it is the finer minds—the minds with sharp cutting edge—which write about it and which thus set up the tradition of the books. To them it must seem that what blunt minds can do as well as they is poor; but that which they alone can do is good. They hit in this on a truth in part: you can pass with ease from this strict doctrine of precedent to the other. If you can handle this, then you can handle both. Not vice versa. The strict doctrine, then, is the technique to be learned. *But not to be mistaken for the whole.*

For when you turn to the actual operations of the courts, or, indeed, to the arguments of lawyers, you will find a totally different view of precedent at work beside this first one. That I shall call, to give it a name, the *loose view* of precedent. That is the view that a court has decided, and decided {68} authoritatively, *any* points or all points on which it chose to rest a case, or on which it chose, after due argument, to pass. No matter how broad the statement, no matter how unnecessary on the facts or the procedural issues, if that was the rule the court laid down, then that the court has held. Indeed, this view carries over often into dicta, and even into dicta which are grandly obiter. In its extreme form this results in thinking and arguing exclusively from *language* that is found in past opinions, and in citing and working with that language wholly without reference to the facts of the case which called the language forth.

Now it is obvious that this is a device not for cutting past opinions away from judges' feet, but for using them as a springboard when they are found convenient. This is a device for *capitalizing welcome precedents.* And both the lawyers and the judges use it so. And judged by the *practice* of the most respected courts, as of the courts of ordinary stature, this doctrine of precedent is like the other, recognized, legitimate, honorable.

What I wish to sink deep into your minds about the doctrine of precedent, therefore, is that it is two-headed. It is Janus-faced. That it is not one doctrine, nor one line of doctrine, but two, and two which, *applied at the same time to the same precedent, are contradictory of each other.* That there is one doctrine for getting rid of precedents deemed troublesome and one doctrine for making use of precedents that seem helpful. That these two doctrines exist side by side. That the same lawyer in the same brief, the same judge in the same opinion, may be using the one doctrine, the technically strict one, to cut down half the older cases that he deals with, and using the other doctrine, the loose one, for building with the other half. Until you realize this you do not see how it is possible for law to change and to develop, and yet to stand on the past. You do not see how it is possible to avoid the past mistakes of courts, and yet to make use of every happy insight for which a judge in writing may have found expression. Indeed it seems to me that here we may have part of the answer to the problem as to whether precedent is not as bad as good—supporting a weak judge with the labors of strong predecessors, but binding a strong judge by the errors of the weak. For look again at this matter of the *difficulty* of the doctrine. The strict view—that view that cuts the past away—is *hard* to use. An ignorant, an unskillful judge will find it hard to use: the past will bind him. But the skillful judge—he whom we would make free— *is* thus made free. He has the knife in hand; and he can free himself.

Nor, until you see this double aspect of the doctrine-in-action, do you appreciate how little, in detail, you can predict *out of the rules alone*; how much you must turn, for purposes of prediction, to the reactions of the judges to the facts and to the life around them. Think again in this connection of an English court, all the judges unanimous upon the conclusion, {69} all the judges in disagreement as to what rule the outcome should be rested on.

Applying this two-faced doctrine of precedent to your work in a case class you get, it seems to me, some such result as this: You read each case from the angle of its *maximum* value as a precedent, at least from the angle of its maximum value as a precedent *of the first water*. You will recall that I recommended taking down the ratio decidendi in substantially the court's own words. You see now what I had in mind. Contrariwise, you will also read each case for its *minimum* value as a precedent, to set against the maximum. In doing this you have your eyes out for the narrow issue in the case, the narrower the better. The first question is, how much can this case fairly be made to stand for by a later court to whom the precedent is welcome? You may well add—though this will be slightly flawed authority—the dicta which appear to have been well considered. The second question is, how much is there in this case that cannot be got around, even by a later court that wishes to avoid it?

You have now the tools for arguing from that case as counsel on *either* side of a new case. You turn them to the problem of prediction. Which view will this same court, on a later case on slightly different facts, take: will it choose the narrow or the loose? Which use will be made of this case by one of the other courts whose opinions are before you? Here you will call to your aid the matter of attitude that I have been discussing. Here you will use all that you know of individual judges, or of the trends in specific courts, or, indeed, of the trend in the line of business, or in the situation, or in the times at large—in anything which you may expect to become apparent and important to the court in later cases. But always and always, you will bear in mind that each precedent has not one value, but two, and that the two are wide apart, and that whichever value a later court assigns to it, such assignment will be respectable, traditionally sound, dogmatically correct. Above all, as you turn this information to your own training you will, I hope, come to see that in most doubtful cases the precedents *must* speak ambiguously until the court has made up its mind whether each one of them is welcome or unwelcome. And that the job of persuasion which falls upon you will call, therefore, not only for providing a technical ladder to reach on authority the result that you contend for, but even more, if you are to have *your* use of the precedents made as *you* propose it, the job calls for you, on the facts, to persuade the court your case is sound.

People—and they are curiously many—who think that precedent produces or ever did produce a certainty that did not involve matters of judgment and of persuasion, or who think that what I have described involves improper equivocation by the courts or departure from the court-ways of some golden age—such people simply do not know our system of precedent in which they live.

V · SHIPS AND SHOES
AND SEALING WAX

There is more to the law and to the study of law than the Case System. And now that that most pressing business is over, and you see at least something of what the study of cases is about, we can sit back more at our ease, give fancy freer rein, and loaf a little in such pastures of the law as the old nag will take us to. There is no end of pastures: logic, and legal history, and the Register of Writs; law on the Continent, law among the Cheyenne, juvenile courts; Hohfeldian analysis, the federal Constitution; Bracton and Blackstone, Mansfield, Coke and Bentham; how English law came to America; statutes, the judge in politics, legal research; admission to the bar, the bar itself; use of the library, codes, and the law's delay. Let us pick out a few of these, and stuff our pipes, touch a match, puff, and watch the pictures in the smoke.

I. Logic

Perhaps first as to the part that logic plays in law. For if you remember, I have been a little hard on logic. There was a view, and I suppose some hold it still, that law is made up of principles and rules. A master craftsman would be able to arrange them in one great hierarchical scheme. At the apex, ideally, stands a single major premise, the Grand Exalted Ruler of the Order. Under him Kleagles, Klaxons, Klaws, and so on down to the more ordinary rules of law. Under these ordinary rules, in turn, the cases range: the single sets of fact, each in its due appointed place, each one a term in a minor premise of which the major is the rule that holds its class. In less idealized and ambitious form such ordering has repeatedly been attempted for particular fields of law. Indeed, what I have urged upon you as the problem of putting a group of cases together comes in essence to the building of a tiny system of this nature for a tiny field.

Now such a logical system of propositions, however modest in scope, inevitably goes beyond the instances in hand. The essence of inductive construction is the building of a major premise which will include not only the observed phenomena, but all *like* phenomena as well. The most modest, the most purely descriptive logical arrangement of the rules of cases therefore always is broad enough to cover more cases than you start from.

73

As to such further cases, and when viewed still as a system of description, your logical set-up now remarks to you as follows: "*If* I am a correct description of the cases, then the future cases *a* and *b* will have the outcome *x*, as have past cases *a* and *b*; and cases *a'* and *b'* will also have that outcome; but the future cases *c* and *d* will like their predecessors have the outcome *y*; so will the cases *c'* and *d'*."

{71} But in law your logical system refuses to remain on the level of description, of arranging existing observation. Backed by the fact and doctrine of precedent, your logical system shifts *its content* to the level of Ought (this does not affect the logic). Its remarks change in tone and substance. Now they run: "*If I am a correct description of the accepted doctrine*, the future cases *a* and *b* *are* to have the outcome *x*—they *should* have that outcome, and if the judge is on the job he will see to it that they do." For your logical system has now incorporated into each of its initial data—into each decision from which it is built up—the Ought idea. No longer are these initial data statements *merely* of how courts have held on given facts. They have—thanks to the addition of precedent—become each one a statement simultaneously of how a court *has* held, and in addition of how future courts *ought* to hold. To describe the one is to announce the other, by describing an *authoritative* command to future officials given by the precedents.

The rules that you derive from putting cases together are therefore *rules not merely of description but of Ought*, major premises from which one concludes that if the rule is correct, a particular further case ought to be so decided and not otherwise; to which is added an implication in fact that the judge in the future case will be on his job.

Now on the level of *predicting* what will in fact come to pass, clearly there are three places to attack your rule as you thus set it up. One may attack it by challenging your logic: you have slipped in your reasoning; you have, let us say, indulged in the lawyer's most frequent logical blunder, ambiguous middle, using the same word-symbol in two different senses. Or, and here we recur to the level of observation, you may have so built your alleged rule that it fails to cover some of the cases before you, or covers some of them contrary to their holdings. Then not your logical *de*duction, but the adequacy of your *in*duction is in question. Or, and finally, one may attack you on your implication about future judges; you may have picked a premise perfectly all right as covering your material, you may have deduced soundly the conclusion which follows—and yet your future judge may kick over the traces. To use the language of my last lecture, his *attitude* may not admit acceptance of your reasoning. And, since we have seen that *every single precedent, according to what may be the attitude of future judges, is ambiguous*, is wide or narrow at need, it is clear that your original induction must either run in terms of the future judge's attitude in this, or else fail to jibe with what he will do.

Seen in these terms it becomes clear that whereas the deductive aspects of your *application* of a rule once made may be, ideally, perfectly certain, your induction, which precedes, is one which *begins* not with definite, but with indefinite material: one therefore into which elements of judgment, hunches, prediction enter as you freeze it into definite arbitrary form to make possible its logical manipulation; and it is clear that in choosing the definite {72} form you give it, you must be guided by the desire that your conclusion may work out in fact, in life. You must therefore cut the raw material of your single case according to your *expectation* about how courts will handle each one of them as a precedent. So far, in your role as a non-participant, a business adviser, a man figuring what courts *will* do, in order to arrange his affairs to suit.

But as an advocate, as one about to argue to a court, the matter is somewhat different. There, the rule which you derive by induction is a rule which has one striking characteristic absent in the observer's work. In addition to the cases which are given in the books it must cover the case which you have in hand, and must cover it cogently, and must decide it as you need it decided. Here your job of induction has a predetermined goal. And the inductive reasoning you now put forward is less in terms of what the present court's attitude *is* than of what you desire it to be, and of what you hope you can induce it to be. This does not change the job of making a logically perfect structure—of making what I have called a sound technical ladder to reach the result. But it affects the way in which you deal with the ambiguous raw material of the prior cases. And, since your ladder must be persuasive on the deductive side as well, it affects the way in which you emphasize, arrange, classify the facts of the case in hand, to drive home as significant those aspects of the facts which fit conveniently into the premise you have erected, which nail *this* case down "within the rule."

Indeed, it is time now to challenge what I have thus far assumed: to wit, that on the purely deductive side of these logical structures, a *certainty* of conclusion is to be found when you move into the world of fact. Remember again the infinite diversity of fact-situations in life. Remember again, in the court's decision, the level of "interpreting the raw evidence." Remember, finally, that even when the evidence has been interpreted as to what it means—in *fact*—there remains the job of seeing what it means in *law*: of putting the individual facts or groups of facts into those legal abstract categories which are the terms of legal rules: "motor-car" or "vehicle"; "road" or "public highway"—and the rest. What shall we do with a scooter in a private park? There is judgment to be exercised, then, first, in selection of raw evidence; second, in interpreting or transforming what has been selected; third, in classifying for legal significance the material after its *fact*-meaning has been assured. And for the advocate there is persuading to be done not only on the side of induction from ambiguous precedents, but also on the side of deduction, of classifying any concrete facts into the abstract fact-categories which are all that rules at law can hope to deal with. Of a truth the logic of law, however indebted it may be to formal logic for method, however nice it may be in its middle reaches, loses all sharp precision, all firm footing, in the two battlegrounds in which the two feet of the ladder stand.

{73} Is this an excuse for sloppiness of logic? It is not. To slip in logic is to curse your case. Even if otherwise good, it then is bad. But to mistake your logic for persuasion is an error as great. Where the material on each end speaks with a forked tongue there rises against you a ladder of logic as impeccable as yours. And there remains to you the problem of *persuasion* —in your initial building of your ladder; and in your argument.

So far we have looked at the relation of logic to the law from the angle of the observer, or adviser, and from the angle of the advocate. We have seen how the counselor must add to his logic his understanding of the attitude of the judge; and how the advocate must add not only that, but also the wherewithal to persuade the judge to accept a major premise from which the advocate's conclusion flows. *What now of the judge himself?* Is he a machine, merely with a set, an attitude, which goes on mechanically, and which an observer requires only to discover? Is he a weather-vane which the advocate can blow this way or that? Is he a despot, free of all control, thanks to the leeway offered by the ambiguities of his material, and able at will, or as a favor, or in caprice, or for a price, to throw the decision this way or that? As to this last question, within limits, yes; but much more truly, no. He *can* throw the decision this way or that. *But not freely.* For to him the logical ladder, or the several logical ladders, are ways of keeping himself in touch with the decisions of the past. This, as a judge, he wishes to do. This, as a judge, he would have to do even if he did not wish. This is the public's check upon his work. This is his own check on his own work. For while it is possible to build a number of divergent logical ladders up out of the same cases and down again to the same dispute, *there are not so many that can be built defensibly.* And of these few there are some, or there is one, toward which the prior cases pretty definitely press. Already you see the walls closing in around the judge. Finally, when all is done, he does remain free to choose—in a sense. But not free in another—for he is a judge. As a human being, his "attitude"—the resultant of his life—conditions him. As a judge—and a potent factor in his attitude—his conscience conditions him. It is his job to decide which ladder leads to the *just* conclusion, or to the *wise* conclusion—when he sees two clear possibilities. He does that job, and in the main he does it well. Often indeed he will not get that far. Often the prior cases push so strongly toward one line-up that he will not even see the chance we here point out to line them up differently. Then, unless the result raises the hair (*his* hair, not yours!), and forces a different outcome to speak at the muzzle of a gun, the judge will never get as far as inquiring into justice. He will decide "by law" and let it go at that. Particularly, to come back to a point made earlier, will this be true of the weaker, the less skillful judge. Advance upon him with a ladder sound in logic, and he grows uncomfortable: his duty calls for application of the law; his skill does not suffice to find the alternative ladder which a {74} more able or sophisticated mind might find. Again we see wisdom made institutional, caught up and crystallized into a working system: by way of logic the weak judge is penned within the walls his predecessors built; by way of logic the strong judge can scale those walls when in his judgment that is needed. And either phase, and both, promote the common weal.

Now this ad hoc approach to logic, this building of major premises out of a group of cases not so much to find what is in them as to decide a case in hand—this is of the essence of our case-law system. It is not so of every legal system, even of every system built on case law. The classical jurists of Rome seem, though they worked case by case, to have built up a strangely systematic whole; the French and German writers before the Codes had gone a great distance further on that road. *Elegantia juris* is the Latin for it: *form* in the law, in whole and in each part. Our sin is lack of elegance and even taste; our virtue is a sturdy, earthy common-sense.

From this angle I think you will understand the attitude of some of your instructors. They show so little interest in the deductive consequences of a proposition. They show no patience in following deductive reasoning through. Put them an inconvenient case within their rule; there is no thrill of battle. The minute they see the inconvenience they will junk the rule, restate it to avoid the bother, and go on. They do not seem depressed. Students who have had rigorous deductive training are amazed—and often are disgusted. I think, with no great reason. Here is a man whose training is ad hoc, who knows our courts to work as he is working. His search is not for a rule which holds, at large, but for a rule which holds good *for the matter in hand*. His interest is in *forming premises* in consonance with the authorities, and premises which decide according to need the case before him. One is as good as another, ad hoc—apart from the question of persuasion. That he is there to teach you. And one thing he can teach you which is worth learning. That is, resilience in *choosing* major premises. This is a pragmatic world. Most major premises still are dictated by a conclusion needed and already fixed.

Not that I would have your training stop at this. You must have exercise in deduction as well. Fortunately, you have other instructors who lay down major premises and work with them. Though they tend to be as weak in logic as the others. They, too, are products of their training ground, our law. And our law has had no love for definitions—except ad hoc. The more careful of our statutes do include some definitions. But for the law at large? Not at all. "In this act", is as far as they purport to go. And even there, they lack (and lack for reason) the touch of Puritan courage of conviction. The definitions follow weasel words: "except when the context or subject-matter otherwise requires" x shall mean a or b or c. Now deduction without definition of terms is a game of cop and robber: you can have anything you catch. You will find, too, in this academic deductive exercise— {75} as with the legal writers—that what we have seen as a most difficult, ambiguous task is regularly slurred over: to wit, the allocation of the raw facts among the generalized "significant" categories of the law.

In short, on the side of logic, our law has much to learn, and we, your instructors, not a little. But, as I hope I have indicated, that does not mean that *you* can get along without it. It means that you have a chance to improve on the techniques now current—if you will season your logic *at each end* with knowledge of the cases, and with common sense.

From this angle, moreover, you will observe another value in the study of the cases. Each opinion is an example of legal reasoning—with and from prior cases. Each opinion is an example of what some court has thought persuasive. Both as to the legal use of logic and as to persuasion there is something here to learn. And please note that there is as much, almost, to learn from the poor reasoning as from the good. A fine opinion is a model piece of work. But an execrable opinion gives an example of a type of mind you have to deal with, too.

In this connection, too, I should like to ask you to observe the difference between logical argument and argumentative statement, between showing a given logical relation between two matters, and *persuading* someone else that it exists by *attributing* the relationship to them in your discussion or description. This appears nowhere more strikingly than in the presentation of the facts with an eye to the rule you are trying to bring them under. Allied in technique, but different logically, is the use of *emotive* words in your argument, which are designed to induce the attitude toward the result your argument requires. The crass case, as you already must have seen, is in old-fashioned pleadings. Watch for these things in the judges' opinions. Not always, but often, they mean that defective logic is being covered up.

II. Rules, Practices, Policy, Statutes

Now, having raised the question of rules of law as rules of Ought, rules which tell judges and other officials what to do, and having in my first lecture argued that the law really was not so much rules as what the officials did, I fear I must wrestle with the relation between the two. And at the same time with the place in all this scheme of statute-law.

Perhaps the best approach to an answer will be to back-track a little on the assertion in my introduction, and to assert instead (so to speak as a corrected hypothesis) that law must embrace in its very heart and core what the officials do, and that rules take on meaning in life only as they aid one either to predict what officials will do, or to get them to do something. Or, if you prefer to state the dispute aspect of law broadly enough to include the most primitive forms of law within the group, and the still primitive forms of law between the great groups we call states: that a heart and core {76} of living law is how disputes are in fact settled, and that rules take on live meaning only as they bear on that. But whether you go with me in this opinion or not, you will surely agree that rules and results both will need attention. That is one thing. And that the two must never be confused, if you are to see what you are talking about, or where you are going. That is another.

It will pay you to observe here and to sever off one by one what we may call the *levels of discussion* about law, especially in a case class. Cross-level discussion is *never* profitable. One must be conscious, always, of which level he is talking on, and which level the other person is talking on, and see to it that differences in level are corrected. One must, moreover, know and signal his shifting from one level to another. Else false issues, cross-purposes, and general footlessness ensue.

1) (a) There is first the question of what the court *actually decided* in a given case: judgment reversed, and new trial ordered. And the question of what express ratio decidendi it announced. These are facts of observation. They are the starting point of all discussion. Until you have them there is no use doing any arguing about anything.

1) (b) There is the question of *what the rule of the case is,* as derived from its comparison with a number of other cases. This is not so simple, but the technical procedures for determining it are clear. Skilled observers should rather regularly be able to agree on two points: (i) the reasonably safe maximum rule the case can be used for; (ii) the reasonably certain minimum rule the case must be admitted to contain.

2) As against both of these, there is the question of the manner, attitude and accuracy of the court's *interpretation* or transformation of the raw evidence. Here judgment factors enter, and you and I may not agree about it. But at least we can keep the level of discussion separate from the levels just above. There we *presuppose* facts as they *result* from this interpretation we are here discussing; and we look to the rule laid down upon the facts already transformed.

3) There is the question of what the *probable* precedent value of the case is, in a given court or in general. Here, too, judgment factors enter very largely, and objective agreement is not to be expected; for we must draw into our thinking the results of our work on the second level, and must draw further things as well. Yet here, too, as to the *level* of discourse all can agree: it is a question of predicting what some court will in fact do. You can phrase this, if you will, in terms of Ought: what some court will understand this case to tell it to do. I think this latter phrasing slightly misleading, and certainly cumbersome; but defensible it surely is. {77}

4) There is the question of *estimating what consequences the case* (and its effects on other cases) will have to laymen: the relation between the *ways* of the court and the *ways* of those affected by the court. This I take again to be purely on the level of description or prediction, but to be a very complicated matter, and one which involves even more information from outside the cases than does problem 3. The consequences may turn, for instance, on the persons concerned making quite inaccurate prediction of how later cases will eventuate—on their quite misinterpreting the case, on their readjusting their own ways not to their actual environment, but to an *imaginary* environment of court ways.

5) (a) There is the question of *evaluating* the court's action in the case—of concluding how desirable it is. And this is of course the most complicated of all, because it includes all the foregoing, and various premises also as to what values are to be taken as the baseline and the goal. What is utterly vital to see at least is that you cannot begin on this *until you have settled* the matters in the first and second problems, and grappled with those in the third and fourth. And, finally, that this matter of evaluation, while it presupposes the others, in no way touches the *level* on which they are discussed.

5) (b) There is the evaluation of the court's decision or ratio from the angle of *doctrine*. Here some premise or concept is *assumed*, as authoritatively given, and the court's action is tested for whether it is or is not dogmatically *correct*, when compared with that premise. Less dogmatically minded thinkers use the same technique, on the same *logical* level, to see not whether the case is "correct", but whether it *squares* with a given hypothesis (either of doctrine or of prediction) —i.e., to test its consistency with some formulation of a "rule" derived inductively from other cases. It should be clear that this touches neither 3, nor 4, nor (really) even 5a.

Now it would be a case-hardened theorist who proposed to exclude any of these problems from the field of law. Yet I think it equally clear that central to them all is the question of what the courts will do. I think it also clear that after study of a group of cases and estimates of just how far

courts do follow what prior courts have done, one can set about constructing generalized statements, generalized predictions of their action. I have
no hesitancy in calling these predictions rules; they are, however, thus far
only rules *of* the court's action; they are statements of the practices of the
court. Thanks to the doctrine of precedent the courts themselves regard
them also and simultaneously as rules *for* the court's action, *precepts* for
the court. So far, the two phases of prediction and of Ought cover identical
territory. Yet the moment that you forsake the relatively solid rock of
attempted prediction, you run into difficulty, and for this reason: that
when you are told {78} by anyone that a given rule is *the proper rule* (not
"an accurate prediction") you are dealing with his value judgment, based
on no man knows what. *If* you will keep that fact in mind, and your own
feet on the cases, and *if* you will remember especially that the only test of
whether and how far a rule *authoritatively prevails as a rule of Ought* is:
how far will courts follow it—then you will be safe, whatever language is
employed.

How shall I reconcile this position with the fact of statutes? We live
under a regime of theoretical separation of powers. So far, at least, that
theory holds true in fact, that courts and legislatures agree that when
legislatures properly pass statutes, the courts are bound by them. But
statutes are rules, they are forms of words on books.

Now the essential differences between statutes and the law of case decisions are these. A judge makes his rule in and around a specific case, and
looking backward. The case shapes the rule; the judge's feet are firmly on
the particular instance; his rule is commonly good sense, and very narrow.
And any innovation is confined regularly within rather narrow limits—
partly by the practice of trying hard to square the new decision with old
law; it is hard to keep daring innovations even verbally consistent with old
rules. And partly innovation is confined through conscious policy: case law
rules (though new) are applied *as if* they had always been the law; this
derives from our convention that "judges only declare and do not make the
law". Knowing that the effect of their ruling will be retroactive, and unable
to foresee how many men's calculations a new ruling may upset, the judges
move very cautiously into new ground. Then, when a case has been decided, it enters into the sea of common law—available to any court within the
Anglo-American world, and peculiarly, within this country. Finally, and
important here, case law is flexible around the edges; the rules are commonly somewhat uncertain in their wording, and not too easy to make
definite. Else why your study?

But statutes are made relatively in the large, to cover wider sweeps,
and looking forward. They apply only to events and transactions occurring
after they have come into force; that element of caution disappears. They
are, moreover, a recognized machinery for readjustment of the law. They

represent not single disputes, but whole classes of disputes. They are political, not judicial in their nature, represent readjustments along the lines of balance of power, decide not single cases by a tiny shift of rule, but the rearrangement of a great mass of clashing interests. Statute-making, too, is confined within what in relation to society at large is a straitened margin of free movement; but in comparison to courts the legislature is a horse without a halter. Finally, statutes have a wording fixed and firm. And their effect is local for the single state. You cannot reason from a statute to the common law. The statute of one state affords no ground for urging a like conclusion in another with no similar statute. If anything, the contrary. The presence {79} of a statute argues rather that the common law was otherwise in the state of the statute—and hence everywhere.

Well, say you, these statutory rules with their fixed words take us wholly out of the prediction problem. Here is Ought, naked. That, I fear, I must doubt. For the very basis of this statute is its generality. Made without any particular case in mind—or in some instances, with a single particular case too much in mind, and without the caution drilled by experience into the judges—the language is faced now with a succession of particular cases. And as with the problem of deduction raised above, the question is that of classifying these new ambiguous concrete facts: do they or do they not fit into the statutory boxes? The meaning of the statute in life, like the meaning of a case-law rule, turns on the answer. We must turn to prediction, then, of what the courts will do, if we would read the statute. We turn, if we can, to what the judges have already done, to make our prediction sound.

I am not touching here the Constitution, the power of the judges to set constitution above legislation, and to deny that a given statute has validity. I am dealing with the meaning of a statute which by the judges' announcement and practice they hold to bind themselves, and which they set out merely to "apply".

Much of the situation I describe is inherent in the nature of the case. We meet it abroad, where statutes have been drawn with prayer and skill, and judges deemed themselves for years to be almost mechanical interpreters. Even there, we find that it is to decisions we must turn, much of the time, to make out what the statute means, and that the Continentals have awakened to that fact. But in our system there are further reasons. First (to get it out of the way) we have so many statutes which are drawn so poorly that it seems doubtful whether the draftsman knew what he wanted, much less what meaning he has put into his words. This evil lessens as the practice of official legislative drafting service grows. But second, we have with us still the relics of a sort of feud between the courts and the legislature, a pride of office, a pride in prestige, a jealousy of skill, technique, of trade. Courts once saw the common law as a coherent system, filling the whole universe of possible disputes with sound solutions. But statutes were single innovations, intrusions upon this system; warts on the body of the common law. Systematic, complete, exclusive codification of the law is strange to us; though the Continentals know it. We see single statutes—warts; we treat them thus. Partly, with reason. Statutes surely require to be fitted in. They cannot stand alone. No language stands alone. It draws life from its background. Technical terms used in a statute, undefined, must draw their meaning from the law which brought them forth. Only the background of the case teaches what the law was which the statute-maker sought to clarify or change. Against that background, then, his meaning must be sought. If you have doubt of this, turn to some clarifying statute, such as the Sales {80} Act, excellent legislation, about a subject, sales of goods, with which you might suppose any business man familiar. Read over ten or twenty sections, in ignorance of the cases, and see how little they tell you. Finally, the statute must, as I said, be fitted into something. The fitting can be accomplished only by bringing the two together. The necessary accommodation must in part be mutual; the legislature can hardly be deemed, with its single aim in mind, to have willed the wrenching and ruin of all neighboring existing law it did not mention.

But in another aspect this antagonism to the statute has far less point. Statutes are passed precisely to the end of change. Then they should be given scope. Filling a statute out with meaning from the common law is one thing; emasculating it by artificial construction is another. I suspect, as I have indicated, that pride of skill and jealousy had some part in producing that great maxim that statutes in derogation of the common law are to be strictly construed—which means: are to be made to mean as little as they can be made to mean. Some other part is almost surely due to the training of the judges in reading any writing: first, as property lawyers, holding a conveyance down to the closest confine of its terms (what man would grant away more than he need to?); second, as skilled special pleaders, trained to construe the papers with all cunning against the party who had put them out. It is hardly needful to point out that most of the wordiness of our older statutes reflects this duel of wits against unwilling courts.

On the other hand, we have another maxim of more recent importance: remedial statutes are to be liberally construed. This represents a better insight. But observe here, as in the case of precedents, as throughout the law, the two-faced premise legal technique offers to the judge. At his need, as the case before him urges, he can construe the statute strictly (as "in derogation of the common law") when it would seem to work hardship, or liberally (as "remedial") if that seems indicated.

One more thing I must mention before I leave these statutes: if they are local, territorial in their effect, if they afford no ground for reasoning to the reservoir of law, then when you meet a statute in a case, you can skate over it? It has no *general* bearing? It need not be remembered? As *pure information*, it may be you will not need it, unless like statutes show signs of appearing elsewhere. But as a problem in legal technique, a statute in your case book deserves more intensive study than a common law decision. For whatever the concrete content it may have, it presents to the court a problem: how to interpret—what to do about it? As to that problem, the court's approach and solution are typical of all our courts, typical of a *process* you must know. And of a process which you cannot follow except in its abominable detail. You cannot read a statute like a case. There is no pleasant repetition of the same thought in different forms. Each word stands there. You get {81} it, or you miss the whole. There is nothing that one dares to scant. There is little indeed of dictum in a statute. Eyes out, then, for *each word* of each statute that you meet!

III. Rightness, Rights, Hohfeld

Looking back, I see that I have spoken about how courts *ought* to construe statutes. I doubt not that on several occasions I may have skidded into remarking on what courts *ought* to do. Law has so long been dealt with as a question *exclusively* of Ought that it is hard going to run one's thinking onto the level of description and to keep it there. Yet it will not do, either, to remain exclusively upon that level. So far as law officials order the affairs of men we must take account, too, of how we wish that ordering done. Some of us, more ambitious, will insist on having the ordering done "right". Others may wonder who knows what is "right", and how he can tell it; yet will insist no less vigorously for that on their own best judgment as to how the ordering ought to be.

This level, which I shall call that of social values, has always centered the attention of outsiders who thought about the law—the man in the street or the philosopher, the political scientist or the reformer. Partly this has been a matter of mistaken economy in thinking. Rules are easier to see than their effects; it is easier to seem to get ahead if you take will for deed, rule on the books as equal to activity. Partly it has been due to the nature of the subject: what we want from law is results, if we are laymen. Results in social ordering. It is the business of the law-men to produce results. The citizens' business is merely to instruct them *what* to do. Lastly, the lawmen themselves have through the ages lent themselves stature as the priests of what is right; it suits the dignity of the law to pitch discussion upon the moral plane. I find a nobler dignity in digging ditches. I find planes high as they result in action, in effective action on a level each day a little higher than the day before. This, however, is a personal vagary. It interests laymen little, and most law-men less.

So I return to what is of common interest, the right way of law, the legal right. And here at once you will find great confusion. *Right* as applied to law, as used by some, will mean *just* or *correct, morally sound,* or *socially desirable.* Right law in this sense is justice. As such, it is a matter of debate. People do not agree on what is just. We can limit the disagreement somewhat by distinguishing between *social* justice, justice in the whole set-up of society, and what I shall call *legal* justice, justice so far as it is possible within the framework which society at any given time has set. Any one man's views on the two will be related, yet his demands on the second must be more modest than on the first. On the side of social justice he will criticize the law entire, and indeed the other institutions of society. He will attribute to them much evil that is in them; he will attribute also to them {82} much misery which nature, not society, must answer for. His appeal will be for legislation, or constitutional amendment, or for revolution. But on the side of *legal* justice, he must address and criticize the courts. And if he has sense, he will see that the courts must move within the framework of the given rules. The rules, however socially unjust they seem to him or others, still are there. The court is in part their mouthpiece. What it can do, all it can do, is to soften a little here and there in a detail the rigor of the general scheme. Here, too, there will be room for dispute. Those who voice criticism of the general scheme, in gross or in a fraction, will call for the court to move to the full limit of its powers—or beyond. Others will cry wolf if the court seems to budge a hair. But most, on both sides, will *lack* what I have spoken of as sense. They will take no distinction between legal justice and social. They will demand all of both kinds, and in their own desired shape, and at once, and from all law officials, courts as well as others. If they fail to get it, they will curse "the law". In one way it is well that this is so. A fighting sense of injustice in "the law" will unchain forces for reform which a dispassionate weighing well might leave quiescent. On the other hand, he who sees clearly how the manner lies will, if *he* moves into battle, do more effective and more lasting work.

All of which touches us here because almost everyone who deals with law introduces at some stage of the discussion his notion of the justice or correctness of the courts' actions and the rules laid down. And because in so doing he rarely distinguishes, and still more rarely makes express, which kind of justice he is talking of—legal or social. And because he even more rarely makes explicit what the assumptions, the premises of value, are, from which he argues to the justice or injustice of particular cases; which means that he gives you no idea of whether it is wise to follow him. And, finally—this applying peculiarly to legal writers—because his judgment once made on justice or injustice, he becomes commonly imbued with a valor to defend his view which keeps him from seeing, or discussing, or duly weighing, the cases and authorities which tell against it. We could forgive him for omitting the arguments of policy against his view. But it is harder to forgive him when he misrepresents what courts are really doing, in his zeal to persuade them to do something else. And few indeed are the writers who can be acquitted of this charge.

The question of justice and legal right requires to be opened up for another bearing it has, a bearing even more directly practical. Legal rightness leads to the question of *legal rights*, and legal rights to rights at large; and rights is a phrase that drips confusion. In the first place, as between law and non-law, as between matters having to do with courts and matters not concerning courts at all. For *rights* are in common language, often indeed in court opinions, aspects of action or relation which are desirable and are socially approved. "Now don't you think I am within my rights?" {83} "All I want is my rights." These have to do with what I want, or do, and with a social approval of my want or action. I have a right in this sense to what people think I ought to have. Yet it is clear that these matters may not touch the court, may indeed bring the court to act against me. I may be socially approved when I insist on the deal passing to the left, or stop you as you lead from the wrong hand. I may be socially approved when I chase and beat up the man who threw an onion in my eye. The one the court will not notice; the other it will fine me for. So that in *legal* discussion one must start early, and be vigorous, in limiting the word *right* to matters *purely legal*. We have another term apt enough to denote the things you *want* or need irrespective of the law: an interest.

This, however, is not all. *Rights*, in law, are (as in non-legal usage) beneficial. And, as in non-legal usage, they are thought of as pertaining *to an individual. He* has rights. The law, in this sphere of thinking, is conceived as made up of rules. Out of the rules flow the individual's rights. The rules which breed rights are peculiarly the *substantive* rules, the rules which are conceived to direct the course of action in society. If a right is infringed, you then have, as a remedy, a different kind of right, a "right of action", a "secondary right", a "right to recover damages". You will see that the *contents* of the primary right and the remedy-right are different. As a primary right my right is to have you perform your agreement, or keep off my land, or refrain from striking me. But in all these cases my secondary right is likely to be merely one to *damages* at law.

At this point you come upon a division of opinion among those whom you may call the happy idealists and the black-visaged cynics. The idealists (and they, by the way, are orthodox and powerful, and have in this matter controlled the legal thinking of the past) see primary rights—my right, e.g., that you perform your agreement with me—almost as things. Almost, these primary rights are real. They are the *substance* of that insubstantial thing, the law. The idealists therefore have no great difficulty in thinking of you as having a perfectly good right which—simply because your only witness dies—is unenforceable. It is only the secondary thing, the remedy, which has failed. The right remains, to comfort you. Remedies—secondary rights—even in the absence of such misfortunes, may be so set up that they are inadequate: you cannot net at law the full value of your primary right. That, too, to the idealist, is unfortunate—but it is non-essential to the right.

> *The lunatic, the lawyer, and the lover*
> *Are of imagination all compact.*

The quotation is spurious, but Shakespeare wrote before this theory of rights was born to write of.

The cynic, on the other hand, says: a right is best measured by effects in life. Absence of remedy is absence of right. Defect of remedy is defect {84} of right. A right is as big, precisely, as what the courts will do. The differentiation between substantive law and adjective {procedural} law is an illusion, although the prevalence of this illusion (as of any other) has results in human behavior, and must be taken account of. What the idealist calls substantive rights are not things, not even shadowy things; they are *purposes* the legal officials have set themselves: to get you to perform your agreement, to keep you off my land. But the law can be seen only in its *effects*. Surely it is useful to measure the effects by the purposes, to see the effects, to line them up for seeing, in terms of purposes; but once more, let us not mistake words for results. Words—rules of substantive law—concepts of rights derived from them—these may be a good first step; they may be necessary to the goal. They are both. But they do not get us there alone. Let us go on.

You will have observed that I hold with the cynics. Yet even if you go with me there, you will have to become intimate with the other point of view. For it is a point of view which has repeatedly shaped court decisions as well as legal writing.

In addition to this quarrel between the idealists and the cynics, or the orthodox and the realists—give them what names you will—there is another quarrel which centers about rights, that over {Walter N.} Hohfeld's analysis, as further developed by {Arthur L.} Corbin and {Walter Wheeler} Cook. Space is too short here to do justice to the row. I shall present the thing, or a part of it, in briefest outline. I am of those who think it has great merit for your legal study.

In essence the matter is this: legal usage of technical words has sinned, and does still, in two respects; it is involved in ambiguity of two kinds: multiple senses of the same term, and terms too broad to be precise in application to the details of single disputes. First, it does not use terms in single senses, but uses the same term in several senses; and in several senses, indiscriminately, without awareness. This invites confusion, it makes bad logic, almost inevitable, it makes clear statement of clear thought difficult, it makes clear thought itself improbable. No logician worth his salt would stand for it; no scientist would stand for it. But law is rooted in tradition, and legal terms of art are in large measure borrowed from lay speech: trust, agency, sale, contract, offer, revocation, negligence. Some of the lay flavor clings still to the terms—and sometimes more, sometimes less, sometimes the nutmeg, sometimes the salt. Even as to terms purely legal, a similar ambiguous usage prevails: a system which moves ad hoc owns no academy to refine and make precise its terms. First, then, ambiguous terms. And second, terms too broad: contract, trust, agency, sale, property: each term comprises hosts of connotations. They are unusable, said Hohfeld, as common salt and quartz to chemistry. Surely one can find smaller common *elements* whose varied combinations make up these larger complexes. He found a number, described them, defined them, showed their interrelations, {85} gave them unambiguous names. And these smaller common elements, in essence, prove to be subdivisions of the concept *right*, as found in common legal use. I should say here that I shall now present Hohfeld from the standpoint of the cynic whose views I have described above. I am not sure that Hohfeld would approve. But I must labor to improve upon my teacher as you, I trust, will labor to improve upon yours.

Vital for use here are three of Hohfeld's major groupings: *right* or claim, in the narrow sense he chose; *privilege* or liberty; *power*. Very briefly, as Corbin puts it, a *duty* (the other end of a right) is what I *must* do; a *privilege* is what I *may* do; a power is what I *can* do. A *right*, then is what some other person *must* do for me. Now in this set-up the *must* and the *may* and the *can* all have reference only to what the *courts* are likely to do in the situation. *Must* do, or have the court on your neck; *may* do, and not be bothered by the court; *can* do, and so affect what the court will do. Let us take up these narrow concepts one by one.

A man has a *right* only in regard to another man. All of these legal relations are relations between persons, and only between persons. There is a person on *each* end, always. A has a right that B shall do something, I repeat, when, should B fail to do it, A can get the court to make trouble for B. But the right has B on the other end. *The right is indeed the duty*, a duty seen other end to. The relation is identical; the only difference is in the point of observation. If you look at the man whom the court may smite, you see it as a duty. If you look at the man who may call upon the court to smite the other, you see it as a right. You see the same elephant, in either case, whether he look like a wall or like a tree. If B has a *duty* to A to do something, that means that, should he fail to do it, A can get the court to make trouble for B.

Now observe what this means to the cynic. "Performance" of the so-called duty (be it to paint a house, as I agreed; or to refrain from calling you a thief; or to fence my cattle in from your garden) is to the cynic but *a certain line of action or abstention which will keep the court off the duty-bearer's neck.* There is, to the cynic, no content *to the duty* as such at all, nor any moral force. To him it is a matter of pure prediction about the court. *Unless* I paint the house, the court may climb my frame. The *measure* of the duty, on the other hand, is very clear. It is twofold: how hard will the court climb, if it climbs at all? How likely is the climbing? With decrease in either vigor or probability of climbing, the duty dwindles. Which is to say also, the right dwindles. For practical purposes it may sometimes be convenient to talk *as if* the probability were a certainty; and *as if* the frame climbing were precisely as uncomfortable as the conduct necessary to prevent it. But it never pays to lose track of the fact that for *any individual duty bearer* the degree of probability, and the extent of the climbing, are of the essence of the situation. Just one last thing. There is one, and {86} only one, *certain* test of whether a duty existed, on the facts assumed. That is: a judgment by the court in favor of the claimant and *against the defendant* on the claim in question. This, you observe, by definition.

A judgment *for the defendant* is ambiguous in regard to duty. It may mean: there never was a duty—e.g., the defendant never made the promise, or the promise was without consideration, and so of no interest in law. Or it may mean: although there was a duty, the defendant has done all he had to: "performance". Or it may mean: the plaintiff has on his part failed to do what was necessary in order to make the defendant's duty become *immediate*; e.g., the plaintiff insists on getting the goods without offering the price. Or it may mean: the plaintiff has slipped in his procedure—and it becomes unnecessary to determine whether there was really any duty on the defendant or not. But a judgment *for the plaintiff* always indicates a duty. As does a judgment for the defendant *on a cross-action* in which he acts in substance as a plaintiff, and the procedure simply allows two cross-claims to be tried at once, for convenience, because both are based on pretty much the same transaction.

So far for the right-duty. And Hohfeld would remind you to always look for the *duty* before you use the term *right*. *Who* is the particular duty-bearer you have in mind? Can you phrase the conduct expected of him to correspond point for point and line for line with the conduct to which you say the other party has a right? If not, says Hohfeld, you are not talking about what I call a right. Have you a *right* to use your watch as you wish? Then who bears the duty on the other end? Everybody—each one with a duty to let you alone, or not to interfere? Does not-interfering by X correspond with and cover your using your watch? Something is out of kilter here. What is it?

Hohfeld would answer by turning to his second grouping: *privilege*. Using your watch as you wish, says he, is not a "right" at all, but a privilege. It is not a case where you *can* kick if the other party fails to do something; it is a case where the other party *cannot* kick if *you do* something. The situation differs wholly from the right-duty. It is not one measured by the prediction that *unless* something happens the courts *can* be spurred to action. It is one measured by the prediction that *even if* something happens the courts *cannot* be spurred to action. *When I can act, and be safe from courts, I have a privilege.* But a privilege, too, has a definite person at its other end. The privilege, seen other end to, Hohfeld called a *no-right*. When A has a privilege to smash A's own watch, B has a no-right about the smashing. I think you will see this more clearly if you substitute the term *no-kick*. It is not elegant; but it is useful. It brings out graphically Hohfeld's other point: that privileges (like rights in tort) commonly come in huge bunches, all alike in content, all different only as to the persons at the other end. I have a vast bundle of privileges to destroy my watch, one as against any {87} person you can name—each person you can name has no-kick if I do. But I might contract with B in particular to sell him that watch. Thereafter, though I retained my prior privileges as against you and C, and an infinity of others, I should have lost it as *against this one prospective buyer B*. Now you begin to see the utility of Hohfeld's thinking. It looks very cumbersome to conceive yourself as dragging a thousand bundles of a million privileges each as you pass through the daily round of tying up shoe laces, eating lunch, and smoking cigarettes. But Hohfeld, for all his theorizing, was a practical man. His mind was on the cases which come before the courts: in each case one plaintiff, one defendant, one issue: one privilege or one right is all that needs examination: the one relation between these two people. And here, surely, thinking is greatly clarified when one limits A's *right* to the other squint along B's *duty*; and makes A's *privilege* the other squint along B's *no-kick*.

Privilege becomes of immediate interest in your work in torts. A strikes B. He had a duty not to, prima facie. But B was assaulting A; A struck in self defense: then he was privileged to strike B. B has no-kick. The court gives judgment for A, the defendant. The cataloguing of your cases will be clearer than if you say A had a *right* to strike B, but can find no damages for A to get. The analysis of your cases, too, will be clearer. For if a judgment *for the defendant* is based not on a procedural slip by the plaintiff, but on particular facts, then *something* in the facts assumed is *held* to have created a privilege in the defendant—whereas it cannot possibly be *held*, under the strict doctrine of precedent, to have created any *right* in anybody.

In contracts, on the other hand, you meet especially Hohfeld's third category of relations. It differs greatly from these other two. Right-duty and privilege-no-kick are, so to speak, the elements of the existing legal status. They deal with a world which can for a moment be deemed at rest. *Power-liability*, the third category, deals with a dynamic world, with a change of the legal situation by men's actions. Power-liability looks ultimately toward the *creation* of the conditions we know as right-duty or privilege-no-right between two people. But as yet that anticipated creation has not occurred. For the purpose of considering *powers*, then, we depart from our cynic's point of view. We assume, for the moment and for convenience, that rights and privileges *are* something—in order more conveniently to mark off the different steps which lead to our predictions about what courts will do. In regard to your thinking and talking this is perilous business. I hope, however, that we may weather the storm.

Power, says Hohfeld, is the situation when A *can* in some significant manner *change* some one of B's legal relations, any one of B's legal relations. Power, therefore, is a prediction *two* steps removed from the action of the court. Most powers, like most privileges, are unimportant. We can conceive {88} them if we will, but there is no point in willing. It makes very little difference that I may be said to have a power to create in you, by assaulting you, an immediate right to damages against me which you did not have before. What is important is the duty aspect of the situation, not the power aspect. Yet when the question is whether I have a power to break my contract with you, and thus not only give you an immediate right to damages, but *limit* you to damages as of a given date, the power concept serves to bring out much more clearly what the so-called right to performance really was.

And in many fields the power concept is extremely valuable. Thus when I make you an offer I create in you a *power to accept*, and the whole negotiation between us gains clarity if we think of it in terms of what you now, by your sole act *independent of me*, are able to accomplish in changing our relations with each other. But it will not do to forget the power, seen from the other end: that of the man whose legal relations may *be* affected by the other; the *passive* party in the situation. He is said to have or be under a *liability* that the change in relations (say acceptance of the offer) will occur. The term is stripped of its unpleasant business connotation; I may want sorely to have you accept my offer. The term liability here looks to be one thing only: that some act of one man, of his own motion, will change some legal relation of another; the man thus exposed is under a legal liability.

Now as to the utility of these strange terms to you. The cases are complex, hard to compare, so many facts, so much talk. It is hard to get at the nub of each. It is even harder to get them schematized so as to get their mutual bearings clear. But in *each* one of your cases, if you look closely, you will find the issue centering about some *one* of these Hohfeldian categories between two distinct people. Was there a given duty, or was there not, to the plaintiff—and has there been failure by the defendant in "performance" of its content? Was there a given privilege, or was there not, in the defendant to do what he did, as against the plaintiff? Was there a given power, or was there not—and if there was, was it duly exercised? Some *one* of these is in the center of the fight. And thinking thus, in nicer terms, with nicer tools of thought, you pull the issue into clarity. Thinking thus, you pull a series of issues into clarity for comparison—you see sharply how each decision bears upon the others. Unambiguously, because your terms are not ambiguous. Precisely, because your terms are very narrow.

Then when it comes to putting larger chunks of law together, instead of slithering hither and yon with general terms whose content changes under every context, you build your general concepts up out of these unambiguous bricks—and have a clearcut whole. A whole with which you can work, because you know its parts, you know its structure. "Contract" is a duty of A to B or B to A (more normally both at once) which arises out of some kind of agreement. But observe, first, that even if both duties should be {89} present (as in an agreement to buy and sell) *only one* is likely to be in litigation in any given case. And how do you know that the court will not let A recover from B, while refusing a recovery by B from A on the same facts? You will have to deal with the duties *one by one*, to find out. Moreover, your "contract" you will observe to have been formed, ordinarily, by a series of remarks exchanged by the parties. The courts talk of these in terms of offer and acceptance. But you will see the situation much more clearly if you watch for what situations give B (on his *own* motion) the *power* to do something to A's legal set-up; and then ask precisely *what* effect B can have on A's legal set-up, and precisely *how* he must act to have it. For you then discover that even after "acceptance" B *still* has powers with respect to A—for all the world like the power to accept; save only in this, that they mostly are *not* revocable at A's will. A has lost the power to revoke; yet we may be still far from any *immediate* right of B that A shall do anything. "Contract" under this analysis loses its vague simultaneous attempted application to a hundred cases. It grows definite because you see its constituent elements. You must make it grow definite because it is these constituent elements, one by one, and not "contract" in block, which appear in, which are the turning point of, the individual cases that make up the law—and which will make up your work.

IV. Trial Courts? People?

There is one more matter to take up before we cease our talk of sealing wax and cabbages and kings; it is the most important matter in all this odd-lot jumble of importances. It has to do at once with the apperceptive mass, and with what law is, and with what lies behind the case, and with the relation of adjective to substantive law, and with the relation of your study to your practice, and of both to the world at large. That matter is the almost hopeless bias of all present and past discussion about law. *We talk of legislatures and of courts of last resort. We talk of almost nothing else.* You find me trying at great length to make you see what lies behind the case. For its own sake? Not at all; *only to make you understand the opinion in the appellate courts.* You find me trying to analyze the work of "courts" and "judges"—criticizing here, moved there to admiration. What judges? *Judges of appellate courts.* You find me dealing with "the law" and what it is and does. I say its center is the action of officials, *all* law officials—and no sooner say it than I slip off my own platform to land for lecture after lecture in discussion purely of these courts of high review: what *they* do.

Surely it is clear that I am damned out of my own mouth. If, as I claim, what appellate judges *do* is vastly more important than what appellate judges say, that can be only because importance to *other* people, to the laymen, to the poor devils *to whom* they do it, appears to me the primary {90} measure of importance. And on that basis surely you should ask me: how *many* people do appellate courts affect? For a thousand cases appealed to the court of last resort there are ten thousand which stop at the intermediate court of review. For a thousand which reach the intermediate court there are ten or twenty thousand which go wholly unappealed. More; for a thousand cases on trial in the higher courts of trial—the County Court, or Circuit, or Supreme—there are again ten or twenty thousand settled *finally* in some lesser court of trial: a small claims court, a municipal court, the court of a magistrate or justice of the peace. Here in this moving mountain of the cases *un*appealed, is the impact of the officials on society—even within the realm of litigation. Beyond, there is the massive impact of the administrative machine. By my own showing, on my own premises, these are what count. I pass them by. Out of my own mouth, damned.

Yet what can I do? I am a prey, as is every man who tries to work with law, to the apperceptive mass. I see best what I have learned to see. I am a prey, too—as are the others—to the old truth that the *available* limits vision, the available bulks as if it were the whole. What records have I of the work of magistrates? How shall I get them? Are there any? And if there are, must I search them out myself? But the appellate courts make access to their work convenient. They issue reports, printed, bound, to be had all gathered for me in the libraries. The *convenient* source of information lures. Men work with it, first, because it is there; and because they have worked with it, men build it into ideology. The ideology grows and spreads and gains acceptance, acquires a force and an existence of its own, becomes a thing to conjure with: the rules and concepts *of the courts of last resort*. And there is more to the matter than this. It does remain true that if a case is appealed, it is the appellate court whose word is the last word, the word that counts. We cannot then neglect it. In large matters (which will pay appeal) we can and must work with the high court in the forefront of our minds. Even in small matters, we have seen that the rules of appellate courts are good to press upon the lower, that the lower court attempts to give heed to them, that with them we may bring the lower court to see our way. There is excuse, then, there is reason, for fixing attention on these upper courts. But is that either reason or excuse for *stopping* with them?

What warrant have we for assuming that even the judicial system alone (I say nothing of the administrative) works with any unity? We look at our highest courts and find their *words* a long way from their *doing*. In their own work we find that we can trust their rules part way, but part way only. In their own work the drive-belt slips between rules and results. Must we not then assume a further slipping as the distance grows, and as we move down the line? At each stage less exalted judges, at each stage more of them: are we not to guess that the average of ability is lower, too? Are we {91} not to guess that other factors join in giving the wheels their drive, as the factor of high court rules slips more and more into ineffectiveness; that the interplay of belt and gearing turns the machine in strange, unsuspected ways? Ignorance, prejudice, accidents of experience, favor, indolence, even corruption: how much, how often, when, and where? How far, too, does the set-up of the procedural system stand between the rules and the result? Yet *by their fruits shall ye know them.* Law *is*, to the community, what law *does*. What picture of the doing can you find in all this study of appellate courts alone?

Again, as so often, I have no remedy. One thing of *great* importance we can offer: the wherewithal to discover the official version of the rules, and some experience in how the highest of judicial officials work with them. Some practice, too, and some information, as to what they mean to laymen whose affairs are big enough to call for taking thought about the officials. We can, too, call attention, now and again, to the limitations of the picture thus set up. But we cannot keep the picture from distortion, as you go more and more deeply into a single part of it, neglecting all the others. We cannot take you into the other parts. We have neither the wit nor the knowledge—neither we, nor any man. A first beginning has been made, is being made, at getting the necessary knowledge. No more: a first beginning. We have achieved in this the first stage on the road to wisdom: some few of us have begun to guess how limited the knowledge of any of us is. For you, meanwhile, the task of setting yourself so far as in you lies to question always, as you go, what lies beyond; to *whom* does this rule mean anything at all? And *how much*, even to that man, does it mean?

VI • AND LAW SCHOOL OFFERS WHAT?

{92}

We have had enough of technical stuff which you are supposed to need, or at least to hear of, in order to make your case class go. It is time to go back to where we began, and to take bearings once again on what it is all about. I propose to take observations with you along three different lines. First, what is the orientation of the school with regard to the profession? What does it offer that you need? Why does it offer some things and not others? What do you need for your practice which it does not offer? To which the answer is: almost everything you will need for your practice. And, as inescapable, I shall have something to say on how to stay in the school. Tomorrow, a second line of observation: what of the law in reference to our civilization? What is it worth? How did it get that way? What does it add? In part derived from the first two, there is a third line worth pursuing as we close these lectures: what are the possibilities in studying law? To what end? What is there in the study worth the having?

Now to the school, and first, to the curriculum. What is its aim? We have already seen that it has two aims at least. One is to equip you for the practice, the other to equip you for itself. Let me begin with equipping you for practice.

And there, I suppose, the first thing which occurs to you, as the first which would normally occur to any man, is that you need to "learn the law". That you need information, knowledge; that you become the repository of the rules. *I am Sir Oracle—and when I ope my mouth let no dog bark.* Would, gentlemen, that we could make you so! But between us and the making stretches, looms, a bulk of learning which three years can never compass, which, I think fair to say, no life-time is enough to compass. Any system of law bulks large enough. The law of a high civilization bulks out of all understanding. Our own law is the regulation of the clashes of interest in a society so complex we gasp before it. Even then, there might be some hope of learning much of it—for rules are all abstract. Even if one has to wrestle with a dozen cases for each rule, to see its meaning, the abstraction reduces the ground "to be covered". The rules, laid end to end, no longer stretch so many miles. And so, in France or Germany, where great portions of the rules have been reduced to systematic codes, law study gallops desperately across these stretches, endeavoring to heel the aspirant on *All* the law. The task is made relatively easy by the fact that the codes are cleanly thought out, well-ordered books, neatly enough phrased in the main, and wide in their scope. The task is made relatively easy, also, by there being in substance but a single system of law for Germany, a single system for France. One legislature, one supreme court. And despite this, the instructors throw up their hands and pant at the impossibility of what {93} they try. Despite this the worry grows at the hopeless overabstraction of what they teach. So much so that in Germany, for instance, a sort of legal internship three years in length follows upon the three or four years' academic study before the young man is allowed to take up practice.

We have three years, save in a few States no internship at all, and even there it runs both loose and short. What is more, and worse (from this angle), we have no code. Statutes we have, mostly irregular heaps of what happens to have seemed worth legislating on. They are no ordered body, still less are they an attempt to cover the whole of law complete. And save for the statutes, our law is found in cases: hard therefore to find, hard to dig out, difficult to phrase, unwieldy, cumbersome. Nor is there one legislature, one supreme court, but fifty-one, each speaking its own last word and adding its pronouncements to the mass. Go down to the shelves and count the shelf-feet of repositories of our law! Ask the librarian how many shelf-feet per year are added. No, the nature of our system of multiple jurisdictions, the accidental constellation of our statutes, the inductive concrete method of our case-materials—these make the learning of our law entire, AS INFORMATION, hopeless.

Then what to do? We can pick out some fields of information which look peculiarly useful. Some we feel that *every* lawyer needs to know, as such. These are very few indeed. I personally should count nothing in but *some* procedure and *some* evidence. Other bodies of knowledge we feel sure are, in our system, working and thinking tools of such basic character that one must have some familiarity with them to think like a lawyer, to size up a situation, to orient himself among the branches of the law. Also, lawyers will need some part of these bodies of information directly in their practice. So: some contracts, some torts, some trusts, some corporations, some property, some equity. From here on the question of information becomes more incidental. The chances of any particular student being able to use *directly* the amount or anything like the amount of information he acquires even in these courses is very slight. The information becomes rather a *vehicle for study*. Without the information, no understanding. Therefore the information must be insisted on. *But it does not* from the angle of professional use have peculiar value in itself. One could make twenty courses which we have not, and no school has, and substitute them for twenty that we give, and no great difference would be made in grand utility. Again, go to the books, with your school catalog in hand. Get down the table of the major articles in Corpus Juris and compare them with the catalog. Moreover, any live instructor could build several courses, good courses, too, and useful, on material which Corpus Juris has not yet become aware of. Or could build three out of any "one" we "give."

So that we turn on the side of information, after exhausting the little odds and ends most men will surely need, to doing with you what your {94} college instructors attempted: equipping you to *find what you want* when you know what it is; and to knowing what it will be. And on both matters the job we do is lamentable. It is hardly an exaggeration to say that we let the job alone. Note then your first extracurricular task: to find out how to know what you want in the way of law; to find out how to get it when you want it. That is not of peculiar importance this first year. *It is your main job next year!*

And another main job, next year and the year after, will be filling in information, reading for yourselves. Information which you need because you are you, not because you are a member of a class. Information that has to do with *your* prospective practice, or *your* interest, or the deficiencies in *your* present stock-in-trade. Information, therefore, which cannot be poured on just and unjust alike as is the rain, but must be cut and fitted to *your* needs. In three matters particularly. The *cases* of the state in which you intend to practice. It is not enough to know a "prevailing" American view. If the case is up in Chicago, you need to know the law of Illinois; it may be peculiar to itself. It is never too early to start in on your notes and independent reading in this regard. Not that the law of your own state is the only thing that counts, even where it is settled. I have been wasting breath if you have not come to see that *method* is everywhere alike, and that you cannot learn method except by grubbing with the same details which occupied the court whose method you are studying. Moreover, transactions make no bones about crossing state borders, nor does the mail. You need an extensive awareness of what law lies beyond. And holes in your own settled law will be filled with an eye on what lies beyond. But that is no reason for not accumulating a growing body of clean-cut notes on your own local law.

Which leads to the second point: the text of your local *statutes*. It helps amazingly little in fighting a case to know the fine old rules of the common law if the local legislature has been busy making that fine rule over. What subjects has your state got statutes on? And what is in them? Then back to the cases: what have the courts done with them? Little enough you will find of this in your curricular classes.

Finally, there are *fields of law* you will not have time to take courses in. Indeed there are fields in which no courses will be offered. Now there you have a just grievance. You are Americans. And Americans know, as of right, that education comes in packages. Like perfume: content is immaterial; the package must attract; when you buy it, you have it. No course, no

education. If no instructor drives, let there be darkness. You have a grievance. But your grievance will not help you. There is no justice, social or
legal, in the matter. There are, of course, books.—An interesting thought.
Might it be part of one's legal education to peruse a book? Might it be part
of a legal education, even to accumulate some books? I wonder sometimes
what students think a legal education looked like before there was a {95}
law school.—This you can tie to: if you are after *information*, it can be had
from books at something like a tenth the cost in time per cubic inch that
you will pay out in a case-"course". And this, too, you can tie to: no so-
called course has ever *covered* a subject on the information side. The first
job in course or case-book building is to decide what parts of the subject to
leave out, to never mention. It is important that you realize this. Even the
"courses", I repeat, do not begin to *cover* the respective "fields" which go
by the same names. From which it follows, first, that a *whole* view of a
subject comes *always* better from a book than from a course: and second,
that there is no virtue in an instructor's "covering" the whole case-book—
much more important things have commonly been left out of the case-
book by the editor than are left in it for the instructor to leave out. And it
follows, third, that even if you have bartered your soul to the package
theory of education, you will be in trouble: your "pounds" are 9 ounces,
your "dozens" run from seven down to three.

So that on the side of "getting the rules", to sum up, the answer is: to
cover the ground is impossible, but half or so of the curriculum touches
material which has much value for most lawyers. We do not purport to
teach you the rules you need to know. We run on the theory that we are a
full-time school. That theory means that students are to get not courses,
but an education, and that they are to put in fifty hours a week in getting
it.

On the other hand, we labor diligently and not without skill at getting
you to *handle* cases when you find them. This is the matter of case-law
technique. I shall not repeat what I have said about it; I shall note only
that there again we do not teach—you learn. *If* you learn, then we may be
said to teach; but our part is like the sowing of the wheat: it must be sown,
it must be fertile, but the sowing is soon done; time, soil and weather make
the crop. Moreover, you will notice that any *wide* synthesis of the subject-
matter of a case class is left to you. Piece-wise, we help. As to any whole,
our wiser members still leave you largely to yourselves. A second reason
for review. The first—daily and weekly review—is to build firm footing
under technical work. The second reason is the reason for the grand review: to see the subject whole—to gain perspective; in a word, to get stuff
so filed in your head that you can quickly find your way about, and also
have a guide on whither to drive, for your whole training.

One other piece of technique we start you on: the *argument* from cases. But here again, class training reaches only to argument on the narrowest of points. Argument on the grand scale—that is left to you. And see what goes into it: first, the analysis of the situation, the picking of the pertinent questions, the *framing* of the questions to be presented. Here is a double job of synthesis. You begin by putting together law that bears on the question. When Hines or Harris takes cigar in hand to stab the aces in his narrative to you, his case does not come labeled "I am a case in torts". It {96} is more likely that the situation involves elements of torts, of trial practice, of corporations (which you may indeed have had, but had each one *separately*) and also some phase of public regulations which you have hardly heard of. All to be sorted out. All to be seen. All to be put together. Here then goes along with analysis a new synthesis of law from different "fields" *around the situation.* Seeing possibilities; reading, to discover other possibilities; finding the case or statutes and discovering their bearing; seeing how they fit together and affect each other; *weighing* their relative importance. A next job of effective synthesis: framing the argument. Giving it a beginning and a middle and an end. Making the middle grow out of the beginning, and the end an inescapable development of both. Meditating on the tactics of persuasion: which point to center on, which facts to stress. And shall you put the strong point first, to make a strong impression, or put it last to leave a strong impression, or discard all but the crowning point and gamble on the clarity and force of concentration? Such matters are the meat of our profession but have as yet no place in class. You can begin a training on these lines in the extra-curricular *moot court*—the play-court before which students argue pretended cases. And moot court work will head you, too, into the library, and into the first attack on *finding* law. Moot court work will bring you into quick contact with a group. And in *groups* of students lies your hope of education.

I pause in exposition to exhort. What I am trying to write in fire on the wall is that the task before you is immense, is overwhelming, and that the official courses of the school are not enough to compass it. "Tekel: thou art weighed in the balance, and found wanting." To do the work is not: to do the classes. Rather must you immerse yourself for all your hours in the law. Eat law, talk law, think law, drink law, babble of law and judgments in your sleep. Pickle yourselves in law—it is your only hope. And to do this you need more than your classes and your case-books, and yourselves. You need your fellows. You need your neighbor on the right. Grapple him to thy soul with hooks of steel—with boarding hooks, if needs must: the devil drives, indeed. In group work lies the deepening of thought. In group work lie ideas, cross-lights; dispute, and practice in dispute; cooperative thinking and practice in consultation; spur for the weary, pleasure for the strong. A threefold cord is not quickly broken: in group-work lies salvation.

All of this becomes fairly obvious if you but glance at some of the things which go to make up the practice of the law. The trial of cases. Your curriculum affords some background here: first year procedure, second year procedure, evidence. But what does it say on getting the facts out of your client—those inconvenient facts on which he keeps an inconvenient thumb? What does it say of what to do when on the witness-stand, on cross-examination, he blasts your case with facts you had not heard of? What does it say of weighing evidence for its effect upon a jury? Or of the art of {97} summing up? Or even of the initial analysis of a case, before trial, not for its "law," but for whether it can persuade the tribunal? Some first conception your curriculum gives you of the ways and means of bringing on your cases; some first conception of the task of making your record proof against reversal, or of attacking the other fellow's record. The rest is a question, in first instance, of going into court, of watching men at work, of putting yourself their problems and working at your own solutions, of gleaning their methods and seeing how far they help you think your way in.

Or take appellate practice. Most of your "cases" are appellate cases. But do you know how to build a brief? Do you see a record? Do you get practice in going through the record to size up what case can be best made on an appeal (or, equally instructive, to size up how the erring counsel below should, on the trial, have steered his course to bar out the objection you are making)? Granted this first most vital operation, your moot court gives you some practice in the rest. Your moot court—*not your courses.*

Or take the phase of business counseling. Some training, thanks to the new ferment in legal education, you do acquire in seeing the business bearing of the rules. Some training, even, in sizing up a *situation* from all its legal angles. But how much training in sizing the same situation up according to your client's needs? How much in the art of negotiating with the other party or his counsel? Negotiating: when to insist on all the strength of your case, and when to yield, how much to concede. When it is better to lay out the cards—when it is better to add to your claim a dozen points you are content to let the other fellow win, in order to force him finally—as his one concession—to let you have the only point you want. The value of being alone in your own negotiating, but dealing with a number of the others, playing each one into discussion, and sweetly assuming the most favorable position any of them takes to be the standpoint of them all. And so on down. What tells you of your dangers with your client—that he will ask advice upon a partial state of facts—that if you give it to him, he will act—that if the thing goes wrong he will regard you as responsible—and that you *are*, because as a lawyer you should know enough to suspect more facts, to suspect what they are, to get them out, whether he wants to bring them out or not. Who tells you that "a" corporation client means half the time one of the officers consulting you, not for advice, but to have someone to whom the buck will pass if his own judgment misses? Who tells you that a cautious lawyer never gives advice upon a situation in the loose, but carefully rehearses in his opinion the facts given to him, fully, and gives advice expressly and only upon *that* state of facts?

Or there is drafting. Most of you have not learned to write lay English. You cannot frame a clean-cut argument for beer and ale—or one against them. You cannot do a decent narrative, much less a quick, incisive piece of exposition. There is one way to cure this, and that is practice. But you {98} do not practice. And even if it were cured, there would remain the task of legal composition. Drafting: I know no art more difficult. I know no art more fascinating. The law is given; we will presuppose you understand it. The situation, too, is given. We will presuppose you understand that, too. Not only what your client *wants*, but what he *can get*. Now, with these things in mind, to turn them into action; to find them words, to make the words clean-cut, precise in outline; to steer the words around the legal dangers; to keep them self-consistent as between the first paragraph and the fourth; to read them with an eye not only to where you want to get, but keenly, from opposing counsel's outlook, with an eye to what they will seem to have said if fifteen unanticipated troubles happen to arise—this, gentlemen, is drafting. I commend it to you. As yet the proper slogan still is: *Tekel!*

I have said nothing as to that other hugely growing phase of practice, the work not with courts, but with the tax officials, the building commissioner, the workmen's compensation people, the legislative committees, and the rest. I have said nothing of office management. I have said nothing of a host of other phases of the practice. One thing, however, I must touch upon: the schooling of your *hunching-power* as to the outcome of a case, as to the way a court will jump. If I am right in what I have argued as to the uncertainty of the law in *any one detail*, if I am right about the leeway open to the court on facts and precedent, if I am right about the huge importance of court-attitude—then hunching must be vital to your practice. Your client pays you to hunch right. Of course, he pays you too, if you hunch wrong. Once.

Now this hunching is not a matter of mere guesswork. Haul Johnson off the street: his hunch is worthless. Good hunching-power is a resultant of good sense, imagination, and *much* knowledge. The *more* knowledge of what courts have done, the more skillful the hunch. The *better quality* the knowledge has, the more open-eyed the reading of the cases, the more skillful will be the hunch. So that your case-work here builds a foundation in another way, for all your practice. Only this: that the foundation from the classes is *not broad enough*. You need more cases, more cases, more and more and more. It is not so important that you remember their details, their holdings, where they can be found again. What is important is their constant, careful reading—seeing and following and *understanding* court's reactions, over and over again. As you get the facts in the case, hunch first, *before* you meet the outcome. Then go back over. If you were right, were your bases those the court displays? If you were wrong, wherein did you go wrong? The bad with the good you want, the blind with the keen, the stupid with the wise. For you will have to hunch as to *all* kinds of judges. Now in the main your casebooks give you better cases rather than worse. For a fair sampling you must turn to the advance sheets. Moreover, in the main {99} your casebooks give you doubtful cases rather than the better settled. Again, for perspective you must turn to the current grist of the advance-sheets. And I say once more, it does not make so very much difference whether you remember the specific rules. Good, if you do. But even if you do not, there remains a deposit, formless, curious—but one which informs your hunches in the future. *Authorities* can in the main be found. An outcome that will go, a theory that will *carry*—these are the goal.

I am left with the question of your staying in the school. There is the matter of handling your cases, of briefing, of review. On these I have said enough—except perhaps this word: eyes are saved, and time is saved, on review, if appropriate passages in your notes are duly underscored in bright red ink.

But examinations call for some remark. We have two kinds. The essay type is made up of problems. A did this and B did that and C absconded and whose is the doughnut? The first problem with a problem is to read it. The wise man reads it chronologically, taking the facts one by one as they occurred, and getting clear the bearing of *each one*, as it occurred. He then has only one new, changing fact to wrestle with at once. He has, then, by the time he has finished reading, *analyzed* the case. He may, if he finds it complicated, have made scratch-notes to prevent forgetting, and have put into them the points of law he intends to make. When he turns to his answer, he is supposed to build an argument. An argument, as I have already suggested, *begins with a conclusion.* If you do not know where you are going, it is damnably hard to get there. It is even harder for the instructor to see how you got there. If there is no end, there is no beginning, and there certainly is no middle. I insist upon this. I insist upon it because students so regularly cut into the matter wrong-end to. They come in nervous. They read the whole problem at once, like a commuter eating breakfast. They are left with so many conflicting impressions that they are even more nervous than before. They chew a half inch off their fountain pens, while the impressions swirl. A sudden glance at the watch shows that the time is already half gone. They dash into a discussion, write half a page, get a new idea between the eyes, reverse their position, acquire a further doubt, and close their answer with "Unfinished. Pressed for time". But if you know where you are going, you can get there. What time is left can be devoted to tidying up. You have a chance, in essay questions, to wander curiously around the problem, indicating all the things that would have been if things were other than they are. Do that, *if* you have time. But do the other *first*.

One last point: if the case calls for a succession of decisions, on fact *or* law, make each one as you come to it, and make it *explicit* that you have determined a doubt, and how you have determined it. And if your way of determining the doubt removes all further difficulty, say so. But do not stop! Your instructor wants those other difficulties discussed, which you have so {100} successfully removed. So you go on: "If, on the other hand, this doubt is resolved the other way, then..." Essay questions, in a word, are built to test your skill at analysis, judgment, and argument. Also your judgment as to policy where rules conflict. But they are also intended to look into your knowledge of the subject. The rest, as teachers go, is useless without this; but this is never enough without the rest. *Some information* we require, even in case-classes. *Put it down*, first. *Then* you build on it, and with it.

Another type of examination is the true-false. What that consists of is a large number of statements to be marked either true or false. Its great value lies in the amount of ground that can be covered in a relatively short time, first by directing your attention to specific points and second by saving you the physical work of writing. You are not to regard the true-false examination as a mere exercise in memory, nor as merely testing information. It is possible to frame questions and series of questions which test your powers of synthesis in a way which is difficult on essay questions, and it is possible to put a set of facts and then frame true-false questions about that set of facts which tests your powers of analysis almost as well as an essay question can. But the true-false—or multiple-choice— question does not normally test your powers of constructing an argument. And for that reason we supplement it somewhat regularly by the essay.

Now true-false questions can be tricky things. To begin with, there is always some unmentioned standard of truth or falsity. It is commonly safe to pick your instructor and his attitude as the standard. And one of the jobs of taking a course consists in sizing up what your instructor wants on an examination. On an essay question this is advisable. Some instructors like to be flattered with their own ideas. Some prefer contradiction. Some insist that the dope which you bring into play shall be the precise dope which they most approve. Some have no such preference. Some are highly interested in policy argument—though even these, I repeat, insist upon your stating the holdings of the cases *before* you indulge in flights of policy. Whereas some are interested almost exclusively in the outcome, as indicated by the cases. Some expect from you only the material of the course. Some, on the other hand, undertake to examine on the subject as a whole, irrespective of how much of it has been covered in the course. Such are the stripes and spots of the instructor which need your attention, and diagnosing the instructor is as important, even in the essay, as diagnosing a judge will later be. But in the true-false examination these things become vital, become matters of continued existence in the school; and you must operate accordingly.

As to the bar examinations, which we do not control, I have little to say. They do play a part in our curriculum. The part they play is this: since we know that you will, during the third year and immediately after, be reading with an eye on the bar examinations, be widening out your information and {101} deepening knowledge of law in a particular state, we have thus far felt we can afford to count on these examinations to accomplish this aspect of your education. Our hand is freer to work toward giving you techniques that you may need, instead of dope. As to the bar examinations themselves, I think we can be sure that any man who does the work of the school and survives in it has skill enough to pass them. What more he needs is information as to the statutes, as to the procedure and as to the cases of the state concerned. And for these, as I remarked before, there is the library.

But there remain, before we have placed the curriculum in its relation to the practice, some observations as to the arrangement of the work in the three years. The first year, I have already stated, aims to drill into you the more essential techniques of handling cases. It lays a foundation simultaneously for law school and law practice. It aims, in the old phrase, to get you to "thinking like a lawyer". The hardest job of the first year is to lop off your common sense, to knock your ethics into temporary anesthesia. Your view of social policy, your sense of justice—to knock these out of you along with woozy thinking, along with ideas all fuzzed along their edges. You are to acquire ability to think precisely, to analyze coldly, to work within a body of materials that is given, to see, and see only, and manipulate, the machinery of the law. It is not easy thus to turn human beings into lawyers. Neither is it safe. For a mere legal machine is a social danger. Indeed, a mere legal machine is not even a good lawyer. It lacks insight and judgment. It lacks the power to draw into hunching that body of intangibles that lie in social experience. None the less, it is an almost impossible process to achieve the technique without sacrificing some humanity first. Hence, as rapidly as we may, we shall first cut under all attributes of *homo*, though the *sapiens* we shall then duly endeavor to develop will, we hope, regain the *homo*.

The most immediately essential part of the first year work is that in procedure, because it alone provides an adequate wherewithal to work out the procedural aspects of the *narrow* issue of all the cases in all the courses. The subject matter of contracts is supposed to be the general theory of the law of agreement and to build a foundation for a body of other materials you meet later, such as sales, insurance, partnership, mortgages, etc. The torts course has its importance less as a foundation for specific materials than as a cleaning up of the ground outside of the field of transactions, a cleaning up of it early so that the transaction side of law may not wholly obscure the picture in the future. Development of Legal Institutions, as well as some parts of torts and some parts of procedure, are all intended to open up a most important phenomenon in law: the conditioning of legal growth and legal action not merely by the specific precedents of the immediate past, but by the whole course of legal history. These historical aspects will seem to you in good part strange and dead and useless. But however strange, they are neither dead nor useless. They are not dead because their hand controls {102} present developments. They are not useless, because through them, and through them only, can you understand what the present developments are, how present developments hang together, why they are not more efficient and adequate tools of society than they are. It is not enough to study legal institutions as they stand. I have already referred to the snobbery of existing institutions. Nowhere is it more striking than in the law. Nowhere, either, are there more thin-blooded parasitic scions of past peers among the snobs. Piece after piece of law stands as a survival which is valueless or worse, and still goes on unchallenged. Piece after piece which has some value has its value as an old-fashioned bucket will have value in a neighborhood where every other outfit is using an electric pump. Now to study these law-things in their present shape and only in their present shape is almost inevitably to come to take them for granted, as curious but as present, as things which are, and which merely because they are require no criticism. Perspective comes only through the perception of difference. To perceive difference differences must be presented. To see such survivals set in the time which they fitted and out of which they arose is to gain insight not only as to what they are, but as to how much they are worth today. We cannot hope to achieve this as to every legal institution. There is not time. But the point of view can be developed and can be brought to bear upon enough concrete material to drive it home, and to be worthwhile as to that concrete material in itself.

Your history will have, too, another bearing. As in geology, the forces that changed the past are at work today. Case-law changes from year to year. But when you read modern cases, almost inevitably you lose the sense of change, and the perception of the ways of change, over the job of fitting holdings together. Unless, that is, sweeping through long stretches, you have become alive, awake, sensitive to change, and its ways, and its meaning.

In the second half of the first year you get your first dose of the law of property. By that time you have come to see contracts, the law of commercial transactions, as a thing depending very largely upon the shaping of the parties. The law of torts you have seen as a field in constant flux as the affairs of men produce one clash and then another. Procedure, which appears at first fairly rigid, has come to seem the lawyer's special ritual. Then you meet property and you discover that there is a whole body of law in which the molds are cast with a firmness torts and contracts never dreamed of. This is of peculiar value when later you meet such bodies of law as leases and mortgages, and expect, at first blush, to see them handled like business transactions, only to discover that they are compounded not only of commercial law and concepts but of the property point of view as well. The procedure work, meanwhile, goes on, and takes you into that more elastic field of procedure and law that we call equity, the body of law that grew up in the chancery courts, outside of and beyond the {103} common law of that time, which had succumbed to the eternal tendency of institutions to grow too rigid for their changing purposes; or better, for their purposes amid changing conditions. Here again you meet a new point of view, which informs great bodies of the law you will later have to meet: reformation of instruments, trusts, redemption of mortgage, injunctive relief, and the specific performance of contracts for the sale of land. You meet further in the second half of the first year, and for the first time, a systematic approach not to the cases, but to legislation. Until then legislation has been looming in the background somewhat ghost-like, more guessed at than even glimpsed. It has become high time to bring it forward as one of the vital processes of law today, as the device which, by one sweep, can accomplish more than fifty cases. Finally, you meet the criminal law. I have already indicated that this is not for most of you a course in any way related to your bread and butter. It is the first entry on the scene of what I shall call mind-opening, or background, or cultural, courses in your professional training. It is put into the first year because at least this piece of background is deemed essential to your appreciation of the law's place in the community.

When you come to the second year you enter into a regime of electives. Meanwhile, the fundamental tools, the most fundamental background, these have been provided. What you know will of course need practice and more practice still. Both range and skill will badly need development. Yet the most basic stuff you will have met. Still, the case method has passed its peak return per hour. Your commonsense has gone. It is time now to seek to regain it; to reshape it. It is time, too, to bring your ethics out from under ether. This time, however, in a better guise, a commonsense, a body of ethics no longer at war with law or preventing you from seeing the legal question, but informing law, helping you solve and criticize; no longer impeding your techniques, but furthering them. This I think best achieved by turning forthwith to one or more of the background courses. Family law, in which you see law wrestling with well nigh the oldest of our institutions, as that institution itself changes and shifts in response to the growth of cities and the break-up tendencies among the older social groupings. Industrial relations, in which you see law in the first instance stamping out all moves for social change; and then, more gradually, helping them along. Constitutional law, the apex of so-called judicial government, in which you find nine judges in Washington giving their final voice as to how far the legislature may or may not revamp the machinery of American society. Comparative law, or Roman law, in which a challenge to reexamination of our own institutions is presented more vigorously if possible even than by history.

Or the work you have done in statutes is picked up and merged with case-work in bills and notes or sales, where a whole "field" of law has been brought into a code and the code lies before you to be *construed* word by word, and section by section, and as a whole. Intensively construed, and {104} your construction checked against the cases over a whole half year. And the work in procedure is picked up and carried down to date through the more intricate proceedings in our modern courts. Or the commercial side is picked up and carried on in the course in business organization, which sets the picture of the modern business unit, or in creditors' rights, the law of debt collection, or in security.

Two things are clear as you move through the second year. One is that your range of choice extends beyond what you can do in *courses*. The other is that the time has come and come with a vengeance for independent work outside of class.—I add a last: graduation already impends, and the time is passing when you have a chance to take work that has some chance of opening out your minds. The second year is a good time to use such chances as are open there. There begins, too, in the second year a regime of papers, the production of your own research, in the course of which you must make some acquaintance with the library and with the art of writing.

What has been said of the second year must do as well for the third. There is then only one new problem there, and it should not be new: the problem of preparing for the bars. Any man with an atom of intelligence begins that as soon as he has first learned how to handle cases. That is so obvious that it does not need repeating.

There are, however, three things more that I should mention. First, in addition to what I have said of choosing courses, the question of instructors. You will find some you like and some you don't. You will find some whose vaudevillian arts "bring the stuff" to you with little effort on your part to keep awake, and others who put on no song and dance. The thing that is vital to remember in all this is that technique in keeping a class awake is no indicium of brains or of deep thinking, and even more, that the absence of such technique is no indicium of the absence of the brains. There is no man on the faculty who has not much you need to learn. But the most adventitious of his qualities is his skill in putting on a show. If you have an eye out to your own education you will indeed distrust the man whose class proves too enjoyable. He may be sound. Indeed he is, or we would never let him get before you. *But what you will get out of him need not be sound.* The more pleasing his performance, the more the enjoyment of the performance, between your ears, will substitute for thought. Your chance of education, I repeat, is vastly greater with the performer whom the cheaper minded would think wet. To milk his classes you must keep yourselves awake. To keep yourselves awake—well, you must milk his classes. Have you ever considered the *cost* to *you* of these so-called "effective" teachers—the cost in the dulling of your own initiative, and in the loss of fruits from other classes?

Another aspect of this faculty business is that there is no one of us who is not good. And at the same time there is no one of us who is not bad. {105} We are lopsided, very, each of us. And our teaching is even more lopsided than ourselves. Partly this is the way we grow. Partly it is deliberate. We feel it well that you should be exposed to a series of lopsided men, to the end that you learn from each his virtues and see in each his defects. For you the balance, for you the rounding out, for you the building of a legal equipment better than that of any one of us.

Now this you jeopardize if you play favorites strongly. You jeopardize the very balance which the faculty has put years in trying to achieve, both by placing all instructors in courses that give opportunities to their peculiar qualities, and by picking out instructors with most peculiar qualities to place.

The second matter is that of informal instruction. If there be those among you who do well, and who desire to get loose from classroom work, to throw themselves into more intensive work in smaller groups, the opportunity is open in the second year and after. What I think upon the wisdom of seizing that opportunity should need no further statement.

Third, there is the matter of the law review. We have in law schools an aristocracy of a peculiar kind. We may almost say it is a perfect aristocracy. One achieves membership exclusively in terms of his performance. Membership carries honor, but the honor that it carries is the duty to work and slave and drive oneself as no other student is expected to. A perfect aristocracy, then, *because* continued membership is based on higher performance than is demanded of non-members. Now this law review is a scientific publication, on which in good part the reputation of the school depends. Here is a thing American. Here is a thing Americans may well be proud of. There is not so far as I know in the world an academic faculty which pins its reputation before the public upon the work of undergraduate students—there is none, that is, except in the American law reviews. Such an institution it is a privilege to serve. Such an institution it is an honor to belong to. And by virtue of the terms of tenure of office, of this you may be sure: to earn that honor is to *earn* an education. I hold out before you, then, as the goal of highest achievement in your first year, this chance to enter on real training in your second.

Here then we are. Two men's work, for six years, at double-time, might turn any one of you out equipped to do quite well. The medics take six years, for one man at single time, and feel the public to be poorly served. I have not seen that their task is in any way more difficult than yours. It seems to be simply that the public's pocket is to the public less precious than its health.

So, gentlemen, the prospect: the thicket of thorns. The subtleties of the case method to disentangle, and a half-year course in Procedure to master before you can bring to disentangle them. Yet you are to begin the disentanglement forthwith. Logic across your path, and history, and the social bearings of the rules, Hohfeld's analysis, and clashing schools of jurisprudence. {106} Details, unnumbered, shifting, sharp, disordered, unchartable, jagged. And all of this that goes on in class but an excuse to start you on a wilderness of other matters that you need. The thicket presses in, the great hooked spikes rip clothes and hide and eyes. High sun, no path, no light, thirst and the thorns.—I fear there is no cure. No cure for law but more law. No vision save at the cost of plunging deeper. But men do say that if you stand these thousand vicious gaffs, if you fight through to the next bush, the gashing there brings sight.

THE OTHER ONE

VII • LAW AND CIVILIZATION*

{107}

When one turns his eyes from law outward, the first effect is to make law shrink into seeming insignificance. There is so much outside. And it so obviously bears in upon and changes and remodels law itself. After a further while—so to speak as the eyes grow adjusted to the glare—one attains a truer picture. One perceives an interplay of causation between law and the world outside. One begins to suspect something of the nature of the interplay. It may have value for you, it may shorten the period of refocusing, it may indeed stir you to break the surface tension of the law and take a slow look around, if I sketch here some outline of what I think one comes to see when he sets out to survey law's relation to civilization.

By *civilization* I mean what anthropologists call *culture*, the whole set-up of society, including the ways in which we act and the ways in which we are organized, including our material and intellectual equipment and our ways of using both. As to law, you know roughly what I mean. But it is not workable to tie to a single meaning when dealing with primitive times and with our own as well. You would not have me deny the presence of law in a society merely because there were no state officials. There was an international law before League {of Nations} or U. N. Both law and state have grown, and grown gradually, and at times quite independently of each other. If we are to watch law's relation to civilization we must therefore watch law's development in civilization—and what we watch will be a different thing from time to time and place to place. The sole inescapable common element is dealing with disputes. The sole inescapable common focus is the relation between the *ways* of dealing with disputes and the other ways of living. Hence, when I am talking of a ruder culture, before the state and the state's courts, I shall be thinking in the first instance of established ways for settling disputes without resort to violence by the contending parties, or even for settling them by violence, but by violence bridled and curb-bitted. As the state of culture concerned grows more advanced I shall be introducing other ideas commonly associated with this

---

* Today this chapter seems to me richly unripe; but unripe. See Afterword.

113

symbol *law*: e.g., the regular tribunal. As soon as a state appears upon the scene, the idea of action about disputes by the officials of the state will of course appear, and will be contrasted, say with the settlement of a strike by the mediation of a prominent citizen. And that other aspect of law, regulation by officials for greater convenience and safety and prevention of disputes, will play a part. And there will come in {108} from the beginning the notion of some considerable regularity in anything that is done, some recurrence and predictability, and some conception that there ought to be recurrence and predictability: the ideas of precedent and rules—for these are aspects of any institution, legal or other.

If, then, I am treating law as a part of government, and especially as the dispute-adjusting machinery of government, and civilization as the *whole* of the ways in which we live together, and of the things that we do while we are living together, it would seem to be clear that law becomes for me a *part* of civilization, and the question of law's relation to civilization becomes a question like that of the relation of the nervous system to the human body. It is not a matter of something from outside being turned over to or compared with civilization. It is a question of what role law plays in the same civilization of which law is itself one of the vital parts.

I think we make the best approach to that if we distinguish first *law* from *order*. Without order there is no group life, there is no group. If the members of a group do not in some manner manage to live together, if their respective conduct is not to some degree oriented with reference to each other, if there is not some cooperation, some self-restraint, some specialization, and some predictability for each one as to how the others will act when they cross his path, you have no group. And a "group" becomes more a group and less an accidental accumulation of several individuals in one spot precisely as this *order* becomes increasingly definite, increasingly certain, increasingly extensive. But it is not clear that to the exact extent that order does exist in the actions of the group, members' disputes are non-existent. Disputes mean, precisely to the extent that they occur, an *absence* of achieved order. *Settlement* of disputes, in any fashion, means reestablishment of the old order, or as the case may be, a new establishment of a somewhat different order in the group. And order is, to ninety-five or ninety-nine percent, a question of the existence of *ways* or patterns of action among the members of the group, and of the *organization* of those ways into the interlocking complex sets of ways we know as institutions—ways common to all, and ways of some complementary to ways of others. And settlement of disputes is, too, a question primarily of ways: ways called into play when the more normal ways of doing hit a snag.

Now between civilization and order the main relations seem to be these. Order is a part of civilization, if only because civilization is a method of group life, and group life without order is inconceivable. Moreover, it seems to be fairly clear that what we call a *high* degree of civilization, a *complex* structure of cooperation, an effective way of coping with the environment which gives some high assurance of survival to the group, is possible only on the basis of a very considerable degree of order. We could not run our present specialized economic life, relying on the West or the Argentine for meat, the East and South for coal, Brazil for coffee and {109} Detroit for automobiles, wondering whether we are troubled by grain sales from Russia, unless there existed as *part of our civilization* a fairly predictable set of ways that somewhat assured the specialized producer of a market, and assured the consumer that he can, without undue trouble, find someone to supply most of what he wants. And it would seem to be a fairly safe assumption that if any man with magnetism and skill enough to gather a gang of gunmen were wholly free to disregard our expectations, to take what he could seize, then savings, investments and trade would undergo what we should think of as degeneration, and the resulting picture would increasingly approach the situation in such a country as Albania, where life is much simpler, wealth less, and a semi-feudal system of contending chiefs maintain what we think of as an irregular and half warlike existence. So that it would appear some order, indeed a high degree of order, is a necessary basis for a complex civilization; a conclusion buttressed somewhat further by the fact that we know of no complex civilization which has arisen or survived without such order. The Italian cities at the time of the condottieri and various phases of life in China are the extreme cases that I happen to know of. They suggest strongly, as I read the evidence, the limits of the growth available. Industrialism in any modern sense halts and staggers under the shock of upset traffic, of repeated forced loans and levies. Especially is sustained trade in low-priced commodities embarrassed. Commerce is possible, but the heavy commerce runs to the luxury field, to quick turnover rather than to long investments, except within the relatively smaller units where a single war-chief monopolizes for a while the privilege of exactions. Who he is makes less difference than that he shall not be displaced too often. Art can flourish—indeed the war-chief's spending may encourage it. The common man finds life a sorry business. Famine, given low transport facilities, is inevitable locally as crops fail from time to time. Consider how this holds for present China, even with the constant tapping of the reservoir of the better ordered peoples. (Written in 1930.)

On the other hand, *too high* a degree of order seems to paralyze change, to freeze a society into inability to cope with emergencies. This statement may of course be merely a repetition in one half of the sentence of what is already contained in the other. "Too high a degree of order" may mean nothing more than a situation in which change cannot be coped with. But I think there is more to the matter than that. I think that in a regime of almost *total* predictability, men are likely to lose the elasticity of mind which is necessary to work out new adjustments. Without the unexpected to deal with, it is not easy to keep fit to meet the unexpected. So that I take it we want order enough to get on with, but free play and unpredictability enough to keep at least some minds in the community elastic. To which I suspect that most modern men (and certainly I) would add, free play enough, too, to keep life interesting.

{110} It is the presence of this free play in society which makes one great need for law. *For in the realm of free play disputes arise.*

Before I come to that phase of disputes, I wish to look at one other. There is one type of dispute which arises, not because the social scheme admits of free individual action, but because some individual or group refuses to abide by the social scheme where it does not admit free action. By and large the *basic order* in our society, and for that matter in any society, *is not produced by law.* And one of the most misleading claims that has ever been put forward for law's contribution to civilization is the notion that it is law from which the basic order flows. The basic order grows, I repeat, not from law, but (at least every generation) *from the process of education.* With that process law may have much to do. But the much is not too much. Official Law may have its due part in the institution of public schools. The presence of policemen on the beat may have some part in keeping small boys from breaking windows and taking apples, in getting them into the habit of refraining from breaking and taking other things. Indeed, the activities of the police may have some important part in keeping bad examples from being constantly before the boy, in turning bad examples into horrible examples instead. But all that taken together amounts to very little, when compared with education as a whole. Law plays mostly upon the fringes.

But how big a part education plays in *producing order* in the group one can only realize, I think, by close observation of young children. Certainly the child is born into the world a squalling wild man, a small bundle of barbarity; outlandish, unformed, as is no barbarian our records give us knowledge of. But from the beginning that small bundle is put through a learning process which turns him out as early as the age of five, a fairly civilized human being—and this, you will note, before the process of organized education has begun to take hold at all. The education, the learning goes on partly by the child's observation and imitation of what goes on around him; partly by way of careful and patient urging (learning to *speak* in the approved manner of his household); partly by an interminable series of checks (not always so patient) on the child's experiments in action. His resourcefulness in finding things to do, or break, or upset, or to make noises with, is boundless, is inexhaustible. But over the years his experiments along these lines result in a series of don'ts and slaps on the one hand, and a series of praises and pats on the other, bring him into holding himself back from conduct not approved, and let his energies loose along lines of conduct that find approval. And it is the group-ways, the order of his group, which make for approval or for disapproval of his experiments in speaking or striking or manipulating. At the same time, he learns what he may expect, and what is expected of him. In a word, he becomes an {111} ordered part of the order of his group—an American, not a Frenchman, a city and not a country boy, equipped with subgroup and status.

But we know that for one reason or another, this learning process is imperfect in some individuals; in some individuals, various native desires, whether or not stirred by particular chance contacts that we can trace, break through the accepted mold. While the child is in the home, this goes by the name of naughtiness. When he gets out of the home it goes by the name of badness, or queerness, and in due course delinquency—or brilliance. When he becomes an adult, we call it criminality on the one hand and greatness on the other. And one thing to which I should like to recur is that much crime is one price we pay for greatness. For the same imperfections in our scheme of teaching which keep the spirit of the great from being broken are those which keep other lads of energy, resourcefulness or peculiar self-will running counter to the law. We do not beat and starve and torture youth into perfect receptivity as do the old men of so many simpler cultures. Our stamp upon youth is neither as firm nor as sharp as theirs; we do not shape youth *wholly* to our Order. Youth can experiment. But no means has yet been devised for giving play to experiment which does not result in trouble quite as well as in advance, in experiments that bother us quite as much as in those that we rejoice in. One type of trouble and dispute, then, with which law must deal, will be the experiment of the moron, the psychopath, or the pirate, in ways and places which the group as a whole wishes most distinctly let alone.

To sum up what I have said thus far: I conceive civilization as based upon and containing a wide core of established order (which we are the less conscious of because we breathe it like the air), and a much smaller field of relatively free play. Here and there some man, for some reason, attempts to break through the established core of order. Moreover, within the field of free movement interests of different individuals are in constant flux and clash. One man can run free in that field, but two men, each running free, may bump. *In the field of free play disputes arise.* Law did not create the order, but law attempts to guarantee its continuance. Law does not create the sphere of free movement, nor control very much of it, but the office of law is to make sure as far as may be *that the clashes of interest within that sphere run off without disturbing* the great core of order, and in cases where the ordinary processes of bargain, competition, wearing down, economic and social pressure, fail to produce a workable result or offer machinery to settle particular disputes and give us all a new foundation for getting on. Disputes between single individuals and between organized corporations (those business groups that are so tightly organized that we can treat them as units), law settles, chiefly through *courts*, when it is called upon. Disputes between wider, less organized groups or classes (such as the beet sugar growers and the consumers, between factory workmen {112} at large and employers at large, between lumbermen and conservationists) law is more likely to settle by sweeping regulation through the legislature. Administrative officials—commissioners, mayors, police captains—serve now in the one capacity, now in the other, today passing on an individual case, tomorrow laying down a regulation in advance as to the method of assessing property taxes, or the rates that shall be charged for telephone services, or whether the traffic lights are to be enforced against pedestrians.

Seen thus, perhaps, law appears to be a tiny thing, an infinitesimal part of civilization. In a similar way, medicine may perhaps appear to be a tiny thing. Few of us are interested in the doctor while we are well, or until an epidemic threatens. But like medicine, law is needed desperately when it is needed at all. It operates upon the fringe. But that fringe is a fringe of high necessity. And also, as is the case with medicine, intelligent use of law is often capable of so arranging matters that this climax of need has no occasion to occur. Or, if I may have resort to another image, it is a safety-valve—a minor and unimportant feature of an engine, *most* of the time.

But how important this safety-valve law is, one finds it difficult to realize until one sets himself to studying societies which are attempting to get on without it. I do not mean societies which had looked at the possibility of law and had deliberately rejected it. I know of no case in which that has occurred. I mean societies which had not yet *invented* the machinery with which we are so familiar, or to whom the inventions were novel playthings, toys as yet, of a few, and no integral part of the makeup of the whole civilization. In our culture and many others, before law, we find the blood feud. A man's strength is in his kin. And for a man his kin must share responsibility. If A kills B, clan war ensues. B's kin are not particularly interested in killing A. Their honor will be satisfied in killing any of the A's, and in the process of satisfying it they may kill several. But even if they kill A himself the A's will not regard that as closing the affair. Their honor was involved in protection of their kinsman, in his protection even when he was wrong. His death, though in one sense an expiation, is in another a challenge to reprisals. In logic always, and in practice often, there is no end until one blood or the other is wiped out.

Into such a situation law in its crudest form has cut along three lines.

I will mention them all to show how various the approach may be, but even more to show through that variety how difficult the invention of a good system of non-violent adjustment is. One road is through regulation of the fighting. Before attack, it becomes accepted practice to serve notice that the war is on, with perhaps a period of waiting, and perhaps fixed times of truce; or perhaps (as once in Iceland) it is a breach of fighting manners to surround and burn a house instead of calling the inhabitants out into the open for the fight. Or perhaps, as in ancient Israel, note is taken of {113} the fact that sometimes killings may be done in accident, and should then stand on a different footing from killings done intentionally. There the rule was that the killer might flee to a city of refuge. If the avenger of blood caught him on the way, a vengeance-killing was in order. But if the killer reached the city, then he was to be brought back for trial before the congregation to see whether he had killed with intent; if he had, he was delivered over to the avenger of blood. But if not, he remained safe, but in exile, in the city of refuge. You will observe the great care taken to avoid provoking the avenger by letting the killer of his kinsmen stay within his sight. All this may seem to you exceedingly crude. But stop and consider how big the gap is between brute sudden attack, and requiring a declaration of the feud; and again how big the gap between merely requiring a declaration of war and inventing a city of refuge.

A second angle of cutting into the same problem is to avoid continuance of the feud, the constant roll-up of killing following killing, by laying down a rule of like for like: an eye for an eye and a tooth for a tooth. Again this may seem crude, but consider what a sacrifice of fighting propensities was required on the part of the avengers, what a sacrifice of pride on the part of the offender's kinsmen.

Still a third line into the problem is found in the practice of composition, by buying off vengeance for a price, and on the other hand, of preventing war by insisting on acceptance of an offer of a price. This is a system out of which our own law grew. Its echoes still run through the civil suit for damages for injury to person or to property, or for breach of contract. A most modern innovation (not, I think, an echo, but a parallel development) is found in the schedules of a workmen's compensation act in which the amount that an injured workman's employer must pay him is fixed according to whether he has lost a finger or a hand, the sight of one eye or of both. It will not do to think of the price-list for injuries as the outworn crudity of barbarians when we find ourselves returning to something closely like it in one of the most modern of our laws. Modern and ancient, the problem is the same: Modern and ancient, each painful partial solution makes a *little* broader, a *little* more secure, the foundation on which all of civilization has to rest. Always the same problem: to find some means of adjusting disputes, some means of regulating the conflict of interests—without disturbing other people, without endangering the peace of the non-disputants, without threatening the strength of the society or the solid core of order on which society must rest. For the fighting out of quarrels affects more than the participants. The commerce of the western cattle towns could gain no solid footing until the quarrels and feuds of rival cattle men were kept from being fought out on the streets. When gang war gets too heavy today, we find either that shop keepers shut up shop and move, or else that the military are called in for policing.

{114} Perhaps, however, I have stressed too much the criminal side of law, the adjustment of the graver breaches of the peace. The mind moves too readily to the criminal court as the type of all law. We must not let it rest there. The work of most lawyers, of most courts and most legislatures, and most of the ordinary individual's contacts with the law, lie, as we have seen, in a wholly different field, not on the criminal but on the *civil* side; in the adjustment of disputes and conflicts between individuals and groups which have no connection with the jails. Here, too, in the regulation of business, in the enforcement of contracts, in the division of property, law plays a vital part in stiffening the order of society. Peculiarly with property and contract we find this stiffening. The taboo on touching others' goods breaks down in unfamiliar circumstances; the farmer's dogwood blossoms travel off in city cars. The lure of the rising market can become too great, and cashiers borrow from the till. And squatters squat, tenants refuse to move or to pay rent, mortgagors fail to pay and still hold their land, the gentleman still sporting at the Ritz ignores his tailor. There is no question of the stiffening.

But in the civil field the law does more. No longer is the question exclusively: "this you must not do, and that you must!" "You must not kill, except in time of war. In time of war you must enlist, to kill." Ordering and forbidding has been the burden of the criminal law. But in the civil law, the law of *transactions*, the law of *business*, there is another aspect. Law there picks up and shapes and hardens, or sometimes even creates out of itself, a host of *devices for accomplishing* one's purposes. If a man wishes to dispose of his goods and land after death, he can do it by a will. If a man wishes to invest some assets in an enterprise without endangering the balance of his fortune, he can do it by way of a corporation. If a man wishes to make a loan for twenty years, and be sure that in spite of death and change of management he will retain a prospect of repayment, he can do it by means of mortgage. If he wishes to procure use of land for five years without taking all the permanent hazards of its change in value, he can do it by a lease. The civil law is full of these devices to make it easier for people to accomplish what they want in their relations with other people; to make it easier for people to deal at long range, or over long time periods, and still have some moderate guaranty that the arrangements made will stand.

Nowhere in the field of contract does the law make arrangements *wholly* certain, or the guaranty of performance *wholly* solid. Law is no substitute for sense. Your bond may be a legal bond, but will be worthless if the corporation whose bond it is falls prey to footless management, or is engaged in footless enterprise. Your mortgage on a boom plot may be good in law and yet a piece of paper. But if the *thing* goes well, then law assures you that no mere change of management, no loss of your trusted {115} friend by death, no severance of social relations by an intervening quarrel, will kill off your prospect of repayment. So that, through these devices to get men's purposes accomplished, law and legal rights serve the property system and the business structure of the community as a framework. Bones are not flesh. They are not blood. They are not, it may be, very much alive, but they serve to *hold up* (and to limit!) what is both flesh and blood and very much alive.

Thus far I have spoken chiefly of the law that *is* at any given time, taken in relation to the life of that time. I have referred to the fact that disputes arose out of the fact that some one man kicked over the traces. I might refer equally to those other disputes which arise because two parties disagree about the facts. Did you make the promise I claim you made, or did you not? Have you performed as you agreed? We are likely to differ on that. The bank has been robbed. Did John Smith do it? You and he will have different views on that. These are questions which must be settled. But they can be settled on the basis of the order of society *as it is*. It is important that they be settled right. But let me insist upon a thing too often overlooked. *It is more important still that they be settled.* Indeed, the settling of disputes of fact *right* instead of *merely settling them* is both a sign and a responsibility of the presence in society of enough surplus energy to spend some of it on more than the mere struggle for existence. Like the radio, silk stockings and the motor, it is a luxury which grows into a necessity—though fewer people are alive to its necessity.

One other phase of this difficulty of social invention I must get before you. It is common to all legal institutions, it is common indeed to all social institutions, but it shows up with peculiar clarity in the machinery for settling disputes. One machine will be constantly put to and used for several purposes—but the needs of the various purposes are not the same, and to accomplish one is to defeat another. If I have a just claim against you, it needs collection. Speed is the need. If I have a dispute upon the facts with you, it needs a hearing. Settlement is needed; but fairness counts for more than speed. If fairness is to be judged by a standard from the community and not by the special ritualists, a lay tribunal is called for. But if I have a dispute with you about the ritual, only a ritual expert can decide it, and it may call for an appeal to the most expert of them all. Now all of these types of case tend constantly to be drawn into the same tribunal, and no man knows *in advance* which type of case is up. Then sham disputes about fact and sham disputes about ritual defeat speed in the just collection. And the lay tribunal handling the facts works at cross-purposes with the official handling the rules. And the complex machinery makes possible the eternal dragging out of unjust claims. All of this, in the courts as in other social institutions, calls for conscious readjustment: to diagnose the various purposes a given piece of machinery serves; to refine and specialize {116} the machinery to accomplish *each* of them, to devise a *sieve* to throw each type of problem to its proper specialized machine. This is one lesson of industrial technique, of factory management, for law. Some of the lesson we have learned, as when we specialize our courts, set up commissions, even set a jury off to try the facts. Yet we are far from adequacy here. This is an instance where the planning aspect of the law has lagged behind the folkways of self-maintenance, of industry, of machine-design.

There are, now, other disputes which arise within the fringe of free movement and which *cannot* be *settled* on the basis of society as it exists. Dairymen are threatened by the manufacture of a new filled cheese or milk in cans. It may be healthful; it is cheap. The filled cheese maker profits. The dairyman suffers—yet he claims that only he makes filled cheese possible—and he wants profits. Or the apple tree is killed by cedar rust. The only known protection is to cut down cedar trees. Apple growers want the cedar trees cut down. Those who have and love cedar trees do not. Someone is bound to suffer. Shall we do nothing and let the apple growers howl? Shall we cut down the cedar trees? Shall we have war? In the moving fringes of conflict of interest have we no machinery for adjustment? Again I wish to insist that the machinery we have, to wit, the *legislature*, and the use of that machinery for the purpose, is *not* a thing which can be taken for granted, is not a thing which every society has known. On the contrary, it has been by the slowest and most painful growth that we have moved an increasing body of disputes over into that field of orderly adjustment. I need only to remind you that in 15th century England, and in a Rome more highly civilized by far, they fought their elections out by arms. Within the memory of living man the privilege of stuffing the ballot box in New York City was the prize of combat between gangs of thugs. Rhode Island, Texas and Oklahoma have witnessed reminders of such practices within five years. And what of the revolutions in South America and Europe? Still, more often than not, a strike means violence on one side or the other or on both. This shifting of *readjustments in the order* of society to the sphere of order and of peace means a tremendous alteration in civilization. It means the growth as *part of the great core of order* in civilization, of machinery for working out the remodeling of the core itself. It represents the addition to the nervous system and the skeleton of the body politic, of the cortex of the brain. A machinery for taking in new conditions, and for finding new means of action, and of regulating action which will keep the whole from disintegration. Like the work of the cortex, the work of the legislature is partially stupid, partially disregardful of the facts, highly irrational too much of the time. Like the work of the cortex, however, the work of the legislature, with all its blundering, does manage to keep matters bearable. And if we {117} can claim no more than that for our individual persons, it is not surprising that that should be the limit of the performance of all of us together.

If we try now to put together all of this, what does it come to? Law in any form is an achievement of painful, slow invention—and probably, like most inventions, dependent in first instance upon accident. Its more developed forms are the product of whole series of inventions—yet lag and lag far behind the technique of physical production. Law consumes energy in its creation, consumes energy in its operation. What does it offer in return? At first sight, nothing. Order exists without law. Order continues. Yet maintenance, upkeep, is also one problem of a plant; and law seems to be the maintenance department of this order which is in turn a precondition to civilization itself. As to tools, law has borrowed copiously from the rest of culture: language, logic, writing; and for the subject matter of its thinking it borrows the whole stock of practices, standards, ethics that make up the social, economic and religious phases of society. What is dominant in society, then, is dominant in law. If oppression is the keynote of society, then so of law. But even as to the oppressor, law accomplishes something that other phases of order may not. Law makes order *express*. It thus sets limits, some limits, even on oppression. Stop and consider: it is no slight thing to be sure that the oppression you are open to extends only to the more *established* forms. And law has through the years gone far to guarantee you that; to guarantee you against the free play of ingenuity in your tyrant. Law, then, maintains the order as it is. Yet "as it is" means with its play of change. And here we find law at work on change. It offers, in its machinery for dispute-adjustment—courts, legislatures, and administrators—simultaneously a machinery for authoritative *choice* among experiments. Thus limiting experiment; but concentrating it, within the fields thus limited. Thus, too, guaranteeing the continuance of such experiments as it accepts. Here then is a positive contribution to our civilization.

One other possible contribution of law to civilization I should like to mention, although as to it I must speak with great hesitancy, and with the feeling that I am guessing rather than talking of what we have some reasonable assurance of. I refer to law's part in the intellectual developments of our society. I strongly suspect that the conception of order in the universe to which we still refer as law of nature is derived in great part from the conception of law as the fundamental order of society; that old grand-father law, who survives today as perhaps the least scientific of important disciplines, is yet to be credited with having had an important part (in his youth) in bringing the natural sciences into the world. More. *Disputes arise when differences are perceived.* And *when* disputes arise, differences *are* perceived. And the urge to deal with like things alike, which pervades law from the earliest times, forces men to *generalizing* about *likenesses* {118} and *differences.* And while I am here on the most uncertain of ground, I am also strongly inclined to believe that one of the earliest and most persistent stimuli to the growth of generalization, and classification, and so of rational thought, especially that branch of rational thought which we call formal logic, is attributable more to law than to any other phase of civilization except perhaps language.

I should argue that later students of logic and language might do well to make contact, again, with such a wellspring.

Finally, I think it is to law that we owe the conception of *justice.* I am not wholly sure of this. There is a very remote chance that the matter runs the other way, that we owe law to the concept of justice. There is a greater chance that both are shoots of the same root. Still, I think law as a disci-pline may claim the concept. It should, if it can, for the concept marks a noble achievement. As legislation offers the wherewithal for readjusting that same order which brought forth the device of legislation, so justice and the law. Recall what I have said before of social justice, and of the confusion of social injustice with the workings of the law. Here law, at the point of pressure, by its own weight calls its own concept to its own perfec-tion. There are few social institutions that can boast of self-sanation. Indeed this idea of self-sanation, the proof of its possibility, the provision and testing of machinery for its accomplishment: these may be not the least of law's contributions.

VIII • BEYOND BREAD AND BUTTER[*]

To me there is more joy than pain, by a good deal, in the thorns of such a thicket as that through which I have just dragged you. And as the tonic iodine burns in the wounds and beneath the skin the whole body tingles with that curious bubbling sense of muscle pleasure, there comes again the thought: for too much law, more law will be the cure. If law makes blind, more law will make you see.

But more law of what kind? More of the bread and butter kind, of the straight trade dope? That turns, I fancy, on how you conceive your trade. There is a bony structure of technique without which you will be a feckless artisan—worthless, and unsuccessful. Those hard bones you must have. You must assemble them into a whole, each in its place, each one articulated with the rest. When that is done you can refine somewhat on the articulation, get joints to working neatly. But I do not know that extra bones will bring much vision to the eye-sockets of a skull.

It all depends on what you want of law, what law can offer you. That turns, in turn, on what you want of life.

There is a brand of lawyer for whom law is the making of a livelihood, a competence, a fortune. Law offers means to live, to get ahead. It is so viewed. Such men give their whole selves to it, in this aspect. Coin is their reward. Coin makes it possible to live. Coin is success, coin is prestige, and coin is power. Such lawyers, I take it, reflect rather adequately the standards of our civilization. They have perceived the mainspring of a money economy. They follow single-heartedly on their perception. Coin *is*, in this society, the measure of a man.

I have no quarrel to fight out with this way of life. No quarrel to fight out with it, even as a way of *life*. It is as satisfactory, doubtless, as any; it may be more so. Single-heartedness simplifies choices; choices are most uncomfortable business. And if the coin-chaser does achieve his goal at forty-five, he has achieved a happiness that few can rival. Happiness after all is a balance between desires and fulfillment. He whose desires have shrunk to meat and drink and income tax evasion, to bowing butlers and the bejeweling of his wife—he has his happiness if he can gain the coin. I

---

[*] This lecture, and X, use a rhetoric assuming an initially adverse hearer which I should not use today.

would not say that "more law" had brought him vision. But neither do I see that he desires vision, or could use it.

One thing does trouble me about a man like this, and about you, if you make this your ideal of the law. I shall say nothing here of service to society. As society stands, its own institutions warrant any man in holding that he best serves the whole who gathers purchasing power to {120} himself. I shall say nothing, either, of any ethical duty to make those institutions work out a bit more decently. As things stand I perceive no basis for assuming such a duty, *except as to men who can themselves perceive it.* I shall say nothing of a possible conflict in this way of practice between a lawyer's own interests and his client's, or between his client's and the common welfare. That presupposes that a lawyer's business is to serve his client rather than to use him—within the limits laid down by business-getting policy; it presupposes, too, that a lawyer's function includes some service to the community, to his own disadvantage. And I think our lawyer might pungently ask me whence I purport to derive such presuppositions, except from my own head, and tell me that the measure of an institution's purpose is not what any man or group of men have said of it, nor any sweet dream of philosophers and schools, but is, and is only, what the institution is.

What troubles me about a man like this is something else. It may seem far-fetched to you—a matter of a foolish distant future. To me, an educator, it seems pressing to you even now. What troubles me about this man is his children. How is this single-minded lawyer to get the resiliency without which he will stand blank and helpless before the new generation that he raises up—on which, in keeping with his way of life, he pins more hopes and more ambitions than on his own career? I have watched many of these simple, hardheaded, single-hearted men, with those grown sons and daughters who were *never* like themselves. I have watched the complete satisfaction of achievement fade and give place to hopeless emptiness. If this is your aim, you may do better not to marry. It seems to be possible to be a husband, comfortably, along these lines; although it is not easy on the wife. But being a father calls for human qualities which will get in your way. It will destroy the virtue of the single heart.

There are men to whom this choice of life is barred by an eager, uneasy temperament. We find them making another current in the bar. They have ideals of another sort; they, like academicians, are prey to queer feelings that a profession—or even a trade—should carry an obligation of some weight to a community it purports (they think it does purport) to serve. They see specialization of effort less in terms of an accidental growth which is good for the favored of specialists, than in terms of a view of the whole which only the specialist's thought for the whole can bring to its finer fruiting. They have, too, restless desires. The grind of the law they accept. A man must keep alive. Indeed, a man must get ahead—to keep in with the intellectual set, to follow the theatre, to be abreast of music and art, to have the adequate residence address and freedom of movement that metropolitan living requires.

These men do not sink themselves in the trade as do the others. Yet often, for that very reason, they outgeneral the others. Even cobbling gains {121} something from perspective, and in a trade devoted as yours is to battle, perspective is a generous addition to your fighting plant. Perspective, however, is not gained by losing yourself among the trees. It takes detachment, it takes standing off, it takes the seeing of other things to give ideas and standards of comparison. So these men outgeneral the legal cobblers—and they outsell them. There is another reason why they have success: they have brains, and they are eager. And they work. For, observing the facts of life, they see that the road to coin is the road to freedom. Freedom is their desire.

Neither with these men have I any quarrel. Their work I welcome. They find time and interest, again and again, to do things which the others will not do, and which need doing. They give service to new causes, whether popular or not. They have, as I said, ideals. And they are good companions.

Yet happy they are not. A good way of life they have not found. The cartoons in the New Yorker give them a pleasant moment; a lovely distortion by Brancusi in the living room brings comfort for a while; there is a fine superior feeling at spreading abroad the inside dope on this and that, at being one of the first to take up the tabloids, tom thumb golf, what have you next; at wisecracking over the Yahoos in the sticks. But it is a nervous, a sickish business, to be disgusted at your work. Calm cynicism counsels: you need the money; you can do this as well as the next man, and better; at times you give some service that he would not give. Yet of two things one: either the man finds himself not man enough to carry his two lives separately, either he goes under in the surge of the law-factory, to be thrown up after five years upon the beach, a dry, smooth, shining pebble with the others of our first, our hard-boiled group; so with the vast bulk of the men who try this road.—Or else, or else, carrying on—as so few can—after ten years of it or twenty the man looks out on the world with the sensation: part of my soul, though it has shrunk and warped, I still have saved, but at the cost of all my working hours. It is more than a feeling of wastage in his work; it is a feeling of unremittent compromising and soiling of the very ideals that the coin was meant to salvage.

As to this course of life at the bar I have only this to say: do not fool yourselves into thinking it is easy. Most who try it fail. And those who succeed are far from finding ease.

As at the bar, so in your schooling. You can do nothing but the law, and of that content yourself with bones. Grubbing of rules today, grubbing of dollars tomorrow. Or you can divide your time into the dirt and the delight; do what you must with law, and do it well, but leave the real hours of living for your reading, for social contacts, and for Toscanini.

There is a third course I would put before you: to wed the unity of the one way with the perspective of the other. To make of your law a {122} study of the way and the working and the wonder of this curious higher primate known as Man. That will not hamper your learning of the trade. On the contrary, if you know anything of Man you will know that only perfect mastery of the details of his institutions will give you any key to what he is or how he works; but, you will know also that only study of his ways and drives will give you insight into these his institutions. You will study the details, the techniques, the otherwise dull and remote intricacies of procedure, as records of how ape-like creatures have gone gropingly about their ends, of how inertia and blindness and self-interest and child-like pride of skill have played through the centuries a multipartite game of chess against intelligence and energy and further self-interest and arrogance and ambition—and against ideals. You cannot *see* this, without seeing also the details, without seeing also how to move when it comes your turn. You will see your own move vastly better for the study. For now there will be against you not merely a lawyer, but one of the creatures whose workings with this structure you have watched—and you will watch him as you watched them, and diagnose his attitude as you did theirs, and play the game against him with more skill *and with more interest* for it.

So, too, and so only, if you are one of those queer souls who dream dreams of something, somehow, sometime better, can you be proof against disgust. There can be no disgust at what you understand. Each one of us is what his life has made him. See that, and look to the causes. That will leave regrets. But it will remove the sticky, queasy feeling. It will leave you free to observe, and understand, and act, and learn. Of course, if you grow jaded, this is no help for long: If this "is just another case of an injured workman" your contact with living life will have been lost.

Nor do I know how to forestall the jading. I can say only this. That human drama, for all that it runs in types, is never twice the same. Our typification, our setting up of types—and so our jading—I take to be chiefly due to a pair of factors. The first, intellectual. To cope with situations one must think. To get out of them their common elements, and thus to arrange one's thinking, one's tools for dealing with new situations like them, is, while the work goes on, a pleasant process. So, for a while, is the check-up process which follows, the testing of one's prior thinking, the trying out of one's tools and skill. When that is over, when one is sure that he is right, this stimulus ceases. There comes no further titillation of the wish for novelty.

The second factor I take to be emotional. Life is so full of pain, so instinct with {i.e., infused with} trouble, that in a mere effort to keep going we have either to shut ourselves in from suffering, to keep from seeing it, or else to dull our sensitivity. The latter is the rule when we are called upon to do our work with social pain. To give oneself wholly to one's case is to burn {123} oneself up. But to condition oneself against the burning is to set the ruts for jading.

These tendencies are present and eternal. Nor does one man know the answer, for another's temperament. But it should be possible to retain as live an interest in the *differences* of situations as in their similarities. It should be possible to see in types of situation not merely a technical tool, but a device for ordering, arranging, deepening his knowledge of his fellows, a device whereby the similarities of situations are employed to throw their unfailing differences into relief. And on the emotional side, it should be possible to dampen burning, consuming, useless sympathy, to dampen down expectation of results as well, without destroying all one's urge to learn and do—or help.

This last I would turn to first. It is close to me. I rebel against some of the fiercer tricks old nature plays our passions. Love and begetting—and children where there are no means to keep a child in health, alive. That is one trick that I rebel against. To reach for one thing—to be blinded into reaching—and then see crouching costs creep forth from cover. To find your poor self *used*, without your knowledge or against your will. So with this other trick, that unleashes action only by leaving men prey to dreams sure-fated for despair. Is there no other way? Must we forever be the fops of blind illusion? Is youth to have energy only because it has not yet discovered the yard-thick jutting wall before its head? Is urge to *do* to be conditioned always on will o' the wisps, on flickering visions of achieving the impossible? It has been so. It has been so throughout the ages. But I rebel. I find it hard to believe in the necessity. I find it hard to believe that this is not another force of nature man can partly tame. I know here no obscenity legislation to combat the taming.

The problem, I say, touches me closely. It cuts into the marrow of my work. For you come to us disillusioned as few other generations have been disillusioned. I meet and talk with you. I have, I think, learned to see and discount pose. Yet with all such allowance, I find you, great numbers of you, curiously bleak. You are the post-war inheritors. "The war to end war" is for you an exploded slogan. Our economic system you find neither the best of all possible worlds, with captains of industry to gape at in admiration, nor yet a crying injustice to be fought. Nay—at the captains you lift your eyebrows with a sneer compound of envy and contempt: servants of the commonwealth? Tell that to Adam Smith! Great men? Twaddle! Yet not in revolt: you know the revolters for the beaten at the game. Religion, too many of you, for all I see, have none. Governmental corruption does not shock—it is an interesting item like {the sensational 1926 murder trial of the} Hall-Mills case. The culture of the hinterland you scorn, its voiced ideals you turn off as mere prating. I do not share such views on any of these matters. I am aware, too, that you are not all alike. I meet in you also a homeless, forlorn idealism that is {124} ill at ease among the disillusioned thoughts it lives among. Yet with most of you the process has gone far, with some so far that not far is left to go. Let me then put my case as would a lawyer, upon demurrer to the plea. Conceding the worst, the most, I still ask judgment. It then will matter little that here and there in you is still an enthusiasm that has not yet discovered its futility. I can then take it that each futility, as it comes to discovery, will kill off one enthusiasm more. And still deny that this must mean defeat.

But the case looks bad, against me. For observe wherein you are peculiar. In most generations of the past this damping of illusion indeed has come, but it has come *late*. It has come after *ways of life* were formed. A good part of the basic *working* ethics of life had been already taken over from the world as it was found given, and disillusion worked out only as to individual pieces of that world. But yours comes early. Yours cuts to the whole.

You come then to us. Whatever has gone, the law is yet left to you. Left to you as the fixed sure order of society. Left to you as that which controls the judges, which clothes the judge with a certain majesty even while and indeed because it does control him, which lifts him and his work to a level he could not attain alone. Left to you as the million of sonorous sentences that in a million cases expound the inescapable logic under which the judgment is dictated by the law. And we? These fabrics we seize and tear as idle cobweb. These mirrors of old dear-held truth we shatter. The law itself dissolves before our acids. Right and justice come to figure as pretty names for very human acts done on often the less human of human motivations. I have said before that this tendency of our teaching has caused me worry, in its aspect as developing the technician at the cost of the whole man. It gives me double pause in this connection—in its effect on young men already disillusioned beyond the portion of young men.

In the first place, iconoclasm can be a sport as well as a condition; even when not so viewed, the fact of smashing calls disproportionate attention to the broken pieces; revolt is seldom characterized by balanced judgment. We of the teaching world are still as full of our discovery as once was tortured Galileo: move, move it *does*, the law. And if to make you see the movement we must shout down the pious words with which courts have pretended that no change occurred—then we must shout, shout disbelief. We must blaspheme the legal oracles. Well, then, we do. We strip the trappings, verbal and other, off the courts. We turn the spotlight on the places where the tinsel gaps, where you see cheap cotton, or see sweaty skin beneath. These are the crucial cases for the argument—but are they type or caricature of the run of legal work? The tendency of the teaching has its worry. To get across a vital lesson one must risk distortion.

{125} The sight of falling tinsel, too, may seem to argue falling dignity. It is a vicious seeming. It is as false as the ill superstition that the tinsel is the measure of a man. Rather are measures and dignity of man and office to be found when folderol and claptrap are stripped off; when, free of pomp, on the record and the naked fact, they stand four-square. So must we strip the courts; so must we test them. The stripping is a tribute. An institution we could not honor naked we should not dare to strip. You are to remember, too, the dignity and measure of a critic: they lie in that he sees the record whole; in that his judgment and his tone of judgment weigh the accomplishment against the difficulty, weigh partial flaws against the fullness of what has been done. Seen thus, judged as you would judge a man upon his life, law and the courts stand up. It may be that as your knowledge grows your disillusion will be tinged with wonder, as has mine. The heaped-up cases through the centuries; the heaped-up wisdom. As I watch the succession of the cases—moving, rising, taking form eternally—as I see the sweep of them entire, I find old formulae of tribute rising to my tongue: "the full perfection of right reason"! The closer I can come to seeing law whole, the more nearly do I, of the skeptic's clan, find myself bordering on mysticism. There is such balance and such beauty and such consummate skill in this whole—seen whole; balance and beauty and skill beyond the little powers of the individual judges. It is the little powers you are watching in the individual cases. Loose logic, or even bad, lies open to your sight; the wisdom of the holding when set in the rhythm of the pillaring years—to see that is not so simple.

Single case after single case there is that irks me, that I would pluck out. Yet take them: what is it that offends? Here is the case whose reasoning is wretched, grotesque. Yet how of the outcome, on the *facts*—was it not rather sane? Systematizing conclusions is after all the business of the second or the fourth case in a series, not of the first; our law has grown by trial, and then correction. This same court which has mangled the authorities: may it not when the need comes mangle this one, too—and reach another sane result? Here is another case; it seems outrageous. Yet stay— why so outrageous? Because it cuts across *my* precious prejudices; because it does not square with *my* opinions. But how many are there here beside the judges who do not square with my opinions? These judges may judge social values differently from me: no sign that they are fools; opinions differ. A third type of case: a technical problem; a crazy decision; the court has utterly failed to see the point. Look to the counsel: has a Root misled the court? Yet even so, that would be but an excuse. But now the question rises of perspective. *How often does it happen, in the large?* How often, too, in the light of the maze of matters that in a year are brought before a court? Criticize such a decision, attack it—yes; attack it with all vigor that is in us, as we attack the others that we doubt. {126} *The courts need such attacks.* The court requires attack on its *decisions*, because the *court* is strong. The law requires detailed surgery, the law can stand up under major operations, because the law is strong to stand the shock. Foursquare it stands, upon its whole performance. He who helps cut out error gives it strength.

Yet the effect of our teaching cannot but be to make the courts, for a while, seem vaporers, uttering falsehood as to what they do, ignorant, misguided, blind. This will not last—but while it lasts it devastates the little there is left in you undevastated.

> "A thousand cases, many of them upon trifling or transitory matters, to represent half a lifetime! A thousand cases, when one would have liked to study to the bottom and to say his say on every question which the law has ever presented, and then to go on and invent new problems which should be the test of doctrine, and then to generalize it all and write it in continuous, logical, philosophic exposition, setting forth the whole corpus with its roots in history and its justifications of expedience real or supposed! ... We cannot live our dreams. We are lucky enough if we can give a sample of our best, and if in our hearts we can feel that it has been nobly done." {Oliver Wendell Holmes, Jr., 1900}

Now here is a thought spun pure of faith and beauty. But it is the thought and phrasing of an older generation. It will not do for you and me. Not for us the gesture of high resignation, made in the fullness of a ripe experience. Ours is a more pedestrian, prosaic business. On us the blow of disillusion has crashed in the flush of youth. What noble doing is to comfort us is still undone.

Yet I say again, I see no help. I see no way to train you but to give you the light your teachers think they have, whatever it may cost in shattering. I see no way but to risk all upon it. I see no way but to pass you through this further fire.

If nature is ineluctable, then we are beaten. Then you go forth, hard-eyed, hard-minded, with one end in life. If we are beaten, then since life is bunk, and law is bunk, and ideals of the softer sort are folly, a single-mindedness for the bank account will be in order, and God help any who are in the way! (You will excuse an "archaistic" phrasing.) I have seen this result in many, and I have beat my breast to have contributed to the schooling of the wolves.

But I cannot believe that nature has us thus in the stranglehold. I cannot believe that analysis and observation leave us helpless. There is a will to do, *apart* from expectation of result, a will to do that gives heart even to the disillusioned. There is in Gauguin's painting an expression of what I am trying to say that dwarfs poor words, and dwarfs the half way artist. Look on the faces of his South Sea women. There is no expectation there, from life. Desire is empty, effort is illusion. Do what one will, there {127} will come disappointment. Yet look again, and see the power of living, the vigor, the exuberance of life, driving on gloriously—while expecting nothing. There is the answer to our disillusion, in that old truth that neither rainbow nor the pot of gold can be attained, nor would be worth the having if it were. But the search is good.

If I knew ways of making this seem real I should be troubled at your disillusion not at all. Nay, I should welcome it. Freedom from butted aching heads, freedom from sacrifices to the empty idols, freedom for action fitted to your ends, straight-cut, hard-hitting. These, if you grasp them, are the fruits of shattered dreams. These—if you grasp them.

For I see in disillusion no dampening of interest. Rather I see all interest gaining height and depth. All that is lost is expectation of the unattainable. And the attainable becomes the more worthwhile, the more enthralling. Two things, and two things only, are the need: a will to understand, and a certain patience.

No, gentlemen, for the disillusioned there are three roads, unless they are to rack themselves to bits. The first, a whole-souled selfishness, in any form: self-seeking, self-consistent, self-contained. The second, mysticism —which your very turning to the law well nigh negates, for you.—The third, an act of faith in the worthwhileness of doing, accepting in advance a failure to achieve the ultimate end.

Such faith in the worthwhileness of doing as such, and grounds for such faith, I personally can conceive only in terms of interest in people, in Man, in men; and for a lawyer I can conceive them only in terms of grafting upon his law that interest, of working out a unity between law and his living life.

I have hinted before at what can be gotten even from the cases. I know no more fascinating record of the human tribe if you have the wit to read it. The wit to read it! Within a hair we have lost the art of reading. There was a time when men read by putting all of themselves and their experience into what they have read. Reading was active, reading was creation. There is one book on which that has been proved. See what the Bible meant to Puritan culture. Read over Pilgrim's Progress once again, and see what John Bunyan put into his Bible. Each terse, sharp story, each pregnant word, became a focus for experience, as the theme of the Annunciation became to a medieval artist the vehicle to work out all the message and miracle of impending motherhood.

Now, reading is different. Pay by the word. More words, more pay. The author does your thinking for you—as your instructors, you sometimes hope, will do your thinking for you. A pleasant evening with the Satevepost {magazine}, each thought sprawled out at length and twice repeated.—And what you read there as much as three months ago, is washed away. Why, indeed, should it stick? You cannot read the Bible so. Either it bores you, and you {128} drop it; or it stays with you. Either you get nothing, or you do the bulk of the work yourself.

So of the cases. Put yourself into them; dig beneath the surface, make your experience count, bring out the story, and you have dramatic tales that stir, that make the cases stick, that weld your law into the whole of culture. There are the parties. There are, as well, the judges: working at shaping the law to human needs. In every case the drama of society unrolls before you—in all its grandeur, in all its humor, in all its futility, in the eternal wonder of the coral-reef. The clash of ideals, the courage of high hope—and man's purblind inadequacy with man's problems. This, for the seeing. Humanity and law—not two, but one. Not veneer-coating of a so-called culture, cracking, discolored as the body of you grows or shrinks. But culture that keeps pace with, that *is* your human sympathy and understanding; human sympathy and understanding which *are* your law.

The drama of society: each opinion a human document; each case a human struggle, warm with life; each changing rule a motion of the giant whose hands control your destiny and mine. Mansfield, a Scot, and once a Jacobite, ascending to the Lord Chief Justiceship of the King's Bench. Mansfield remaking the commercial law of England. Mansfield a judge for thirty solid years, and twice in thirty solid years, reversed. Mansfield in terror at a city mob. Mansfield struck white, speechless, quaking, in the House of Lords at Chatham's invective—and on a point of law, Cardozo, remaking the judicial theory of the country. Not alone, but effective as have been few others, Cardozo, through fifteen years, shaping, reshaping the attitude of the whole court of which he was a member, and of the other members of that court, leading it slowly, surely, to the position of our greatest court today.[*]

Holmes, in the Abrams Case, with pressure in the court and out to bring him to withdraw dissent, because "the country was in danger," Holmes, at what may be well the summit of a life lived among the peaks, firm in conviction that some things cannot be yielded—voicing that dissent that stands among the papers of our statesmen beside the Gettysburg address.

---

[*] This was written in 1930. And in 1960 the Cardozo tradition in that court can still be seen.

I say in these things there is poetry, in these things there is lie, in these things there is beauty. If this be not culture, I do not know where to find it. Nor do poetry, drama, culture, play alone among the kings. Lesser judges, lesser cases in their struggle shape not the destinies of peoples; but they have no lesser interest; they offer no less to learn.

Go, then, and read—in the law and out. By all means read. Work at your art, your science, your philosophy—work even at your {H.L.} Mencken, if you must, or {journalist} Heywood Broun. But bring the work home again, and merge it {129} with your law. Read, too, from your own law out. This, in your law—in school and practice—is the one part of wisdom: trade, culture and profession all in one.

The old-time lawyer of the finer sort, the counselor of his community—he needed no such telling. He grew that way. In these more hectic days the path is not so clear to see. One searches for it. What one thinks to have found he puts before you. That is your right.

And will you, then, if you tread my path find there what I have found? Of course you will not. One man, one path; one path and a hundred endings; expectation is illusion. Yet in one thing I find that I have faith: set out upon that path, and what you find, however wide apart from my own findings, will be a something just as good; or better.

Go, then, and read. Go, then, and look, and *see*. I cannot say that that way fortune lies. I cannot tempt you on with words to conquer, nor yet with words to save. Must you have the moon? I find this plain match enough, that flares for its tiny moment. Surely a nothing—tossed, it may be, for sport into the gutter. Yet a pitiful, brave flame. Some warmth, some light, some touch of burning courage. What have you more to ask—or to ask to be?

IX • THE SECOND YEAR

{130}

When I met you at this time a year back you were apple green. The green, as I look over your expectant faces now, seems somewhat to have paled. And you seem larger. If one should bite you now, he would expect to find some signs of juice. Sour, quite sour, doubtless; but still, juice. Clearly, you hold some promise. But with that gain in size and juiciness under the benignant sunshine of the faculty have come responsibilities, and these responsibilities I would recall to your attention. Last year it was a question of what you had a right to expect from the second year class and of how to go about realizing those expectations. This year it is a question of what the first year class has a right to expect from you, and of your job in making real those expectations, whether or not these new cubs have the sense to run you up a tree and bay for information.

I want to remind you that a school is not made up of faculty, and that a legal education is nine-tenths and upwards a product of the student body. I want to remind you the incoming class is, if possible, even greener than yourselves were once. I want to remind you of the strangeness with which you gazed upon a casebook and wondered what in hell a brief might be, or what you were to *do* with the cases; of your utter lack of knowledge of the meaning of the law library, or of how to take the first step in its utilization; of the days when {Arthur} Corbin was only a name and a law review an unknown concept; when Law Examination was a stark specter, vastly terrible because it had not been experienced. I want to remind you, too, of the comfort that came when you did get some advice from somewhere in one of your perplexities, and of how much easier the first four weeks would have been if that advice had been frequent and ready.

In a word, I want to call upon you to pick up your burden and to take your part in making the school for the incoming class a school and not a prison, a road to education and not a road to despair. There is nothing to make you do it. But if you do, this much at least I promise: that what you set about making clear to another man you will know vastly better yourself when you are through; that the time you spend on him will deepen your own understanding of the law, and that only in the measure that the practice of cooperation is built up or kept up, will the first year class or you yourselves, or the classes to follow, have a *school* which has a reason for existence.

There is another reason why you must perform upon the first year class. They come into these sacred halls of which you have become the yearling priests. They stink of laity. They must be cleansed, they must be quickly cleansed, or all of us will be profaned. Gird up your loins, then, my beloved, and descend into the pools; in each left hand a pot of legal germicidal soap, each right fist brandishing a foot-long brush of dialectic. Seize these new {131} woolly lambs and scrub them for the law. Scrub them with love—but above all things, scrub them. Then raise them as the young things should be raised.

But apart from this plea on behalf of the neophytes—and of our order—there are things to meditate upon in regard to your own work in this your second year.

The experience in all the law schools in the country runs clean and sharp to this: that the first semester of the second year is a slough of despond and a swamp of disaster.

For most of you the edge has been taken off ambition. For one thing, the job is no longer new and strange. That is more comfortable, but it spells less drive. You will no longer be running like mad in pure fear that you may be getting nowhere. Examinations may worry, but they no longer terrify. You know what they are like. You relegate the thought of them to certain hectic weeks which still lie far ahead. Nor is there heavy pressure on your back from day to day. You have learned the more elementary workings of the ropes. Not that you have learned all there is to know of reading cases; by no means that. But you have learned enough to lodge a fine fat cushion between yourselves and any effort to induce you to learn more. Even those of you who have not learned to read cases have learned at least the art of stalling through a recitation. You have acquired the technique, let us say, of breezing through the cases in the assignment, underlining the statement of a fact or two, marking "Question" in the margin at an appropriate passage, and spotting the three lines in the opinion which look as if they would do for a statement of the so-called rule. Thus fortified, and calm in your knowledge that instructors, too, are pressed for time, you can take on, if called upon, what may with charity be deemed a statement of the case—eyes shooting rapidly from line to line for further facts and scraps of argument, yet without altering the friendly flavors of your bedside manner. The wiser of you have learned to pay attention, strict attention, in the classroom, to take careful notes, learned to suck up each last drop of a summary. O, parched throat in the desert! O, oasis! That all saves time—for bridge, for petting, or for penny pitching. Demands have meanwhile come, upon your time. If you are here from out-of-town, you have local connections now. And there may even be a girl. If you belong locally you are now dropping back into the good old whirl from which you set your jaw to break away this time last year. So comes the pressure to reduce the working week. To the legal limit of hours for industry, say fifty-four. The union hours, down to forty-five. To the stenographer's delight, and down to forty. And down to thirty, down to twenty-five. Down to a Tarkington, at seventeen. The job, I say, becomes no longer new and strange. Nor is it still as interesting as it was. You know the motions now. If you are really good, you know them well. What once was high excitement, an intellectual game, is turning to routine. What {132} once was a search for a new light has become a squirrel-job—the gathering of nuts against the days in June. The instructor still summarizes, bless him. There is still good ink in the fountain pen. So less time on the cases, more on the instructor. Less interest in law, and more in what *he* is likely to expect on the exam. You are caught, my friends, in the *machine* of legal "education". Your eyes dull to its pounding. You lose perspective. You have forgotten what the game is all about. So the machine will dump you shortly —in the swamp.

Far be it from me to decry the study of machinery. Watch your instructor, note his weaknesses, his hobbies, diagnose his legal and non-legal prejudices, predict his questions, play him for an A. That is good sense. That is good realism. That, too, is training in the law. So must you one day diagnose a court. Study the technique of case method, build up your short cuts, economize your work, save all the time you can. Naught could be better. So must you some day organize an office and a job. *But do not let these matters rob you of your education.* You are about to throw another year of time upon the counter. Do you want nothing for it but a stick of Wrigley's or a good cigar?

You have now left behind the only period in which there was excuse for automatic, for machine-like teaching. You have graduated from the awkward squad, from the fixed drill of a first year that was needed to instill techniques no man can get along in law without. That grind is over. Now, education can begin. And I am talking to you because we find so seldom, we of the teaching staff—we find so seldom that education *does* begin.

Come with me to the mountain top—look out over the kingdoms of this world—and let me tempt you.

What are you here for? Where are you going? Wherein does this year differ from the last? The benefits of case method study you have seen, you have absorbed. Much is to be absorbed still, but more slowly now—more repetition, less new income from your work. The point of maximum return has passed. Partly the benefits have turned upon the concrete case, the driving home of every rule, every distinction in the meaning of every rule and every distinction, in terms of hard, sharp fact. Partly they go to intense, sustained analysis of finer points, and to nice reading. There you have much to do still—but the techniques you know; you need there chiefly *practice*. Meantime, however, two things should be growing clear to you.

139

Knowledge, brute knowledge, is bought in case classes at a huge expense in time. Are you going to take on no knowledge cargo, except at that expense? Are you going to rest for two more full years upon the case book and the instructor's summary? Will you let the library lie fallow and twiddle idle thumbs among the daisies?

Out of the deeps we cry our *"Culpa mea; culpa maxima mea"*—our guilt, our very guilt it is that tempts you to the twiddling. We have learned {133} so relatively well how to do one kind of teaching that we sit Narcissuslike before the pool. We go on teaching cases—and do too little teaching else. Well, then, so be it. But is your instructor's blindness to obscure your vision?

There is this other fact about case teaching which should be growing clear to you: intensive, sustained analysis in group-discussion *must* presuppose a narrow, a very narrow, common subject-matter. Narrow, and common: and hence of necessity, assigned. Thus the very precondition of case discussion lames initiative. Thus, in acquiring this best of techniques, you fall into the worst of study habits. You find yourselves already knee-deep in the swamp.

That, it is time to change. Now is the time to change it. Case teaching is graduate teaching in its training in analysis. It calls for ripe powers, it calls for a ripe attention-span, it calls for ripe depth of thought. But it is grade school teaching in its method of assigning stuff. You have your training for professional careers at stake. It is time to begin to act accordingly.

I am suspicious of comparison between the disciplines, more especially so of those I have most often met with, those between law and social science. There are so many men, so many books, so many theories loose in each. Each in itself is so bewilderingly uneven. If you are conservative, then you look to the fine peaks on your own side of the border, and challenge the plains across the way to a comparison. If you are fond for new things you see the peaks across the way, and conclude from them to mighty tablelands. So here. The best of graduate students, say in economics, learn in three years an independence of investigation, a hunger for wide reading in their fields, which few of our men find. Yet for the ruck, our case teaching seems to me a vastly better teaching engine than their lectures. But to judge their study by the lectures is to miss the real meat of their training. To judge our study by our case-classes—can you say the same?

The matter comes down, then, to this: do you propose to be bound by the limitations of our method and of your own sweet urge for ease? And if not—I shall assume not, I shall assume you have interest in what optimists would know as your career. I shall assume that independent effort is beyond neither your powers nor your desires. I am not content to take for granted that you are children who must eternally be handed out a daily task. Indeed, to my mind, I have a duty to make these assumptions. For of all professions surely there is none of which responsibility is more strikingly characteristic than it is of the law. You are to go out to handle business, not of your own, but of your clients. You are to go out equipped to stand on your own two feet, and then to shoulder others' burdens. You are to go out fit to be trusted by men who do not themselves know what they want. A schooling which takes responsibility off your shoulders is no schooling for that job. If sloth and dalliance are too much for you now unless the schoolmaster's {134} whip is snapping on your neck, then turn to something you can do well, while there is time. If foremen are your need, get under one.

What, then, do you need that we do not offer you, and how can you set about getting it? It is hard to answer that question. It is hard, first, because my own eyes are still muffled in tradition. On case teaching I was raised, and by it I have earned my living these twelve years. It is hard, second, because we still know so little of what constitutes the practice of the law today. How much of the old-time practice has been taken over by trust and title companies, and how many lawyers do they use? How much of their "law" is in the cases, on the statute books, how much is based upon their own practices and understandings? How much of law practice lies in trial of cases, and with what differences between New York and Wichita and Cedar Forks? How does trial practice in the city court differ from trial practice before the federal courts or the supreme? Where does appeal work fit into the picture? How much of practice lies in interviews with the dock commissioner or the tax commissioner, or the claim agent for the New York Central? Is there a special workman's compensation bar? How much of law practice lies in drafting contracts, how much in closing titles, how much lies in dispossessing tenants? How much in business strategy? How much in journeying to Albany or Washington to lobby; how much of the lobbying occurs when the committee has adjourned? How much of practice lies in getting business, and whose business, and how is it got? How much of practice lies in marrying the senior partner's niece, and which of them—and again, how? To these and to some hundred other questions we can answer: for some men, more or wholly; for some, less or not at all; for how many, or how much for any, we can only guess. And which of these questions is later to concern particular ones of you, that is not worth guessing at.

So that it is hard to answer the question: what do you need? Still harder, because different ones of you have different needs, even if you were all to come out at the same place. The best I can do is to put before you some of the things that every lawyer, or almost every lawyer, is sure to need, but which case study does not offer. I have picked very few, and those few I have chosen conservatively, practically. I have chosen them on the technical side. There will still be more of them than any individual can hope to do much with. But it is time you did some conscious choosing about your training for a profession for which no school I have yet learned of offers *in its curriculum* more than a first-aid-in-case-of-sun-stroke sort of training.

In three points you can profit by the example of the Law Review. I have said this to you before; it bears repeating. The Law Review is, to an insignificant degree, a mark of merit for the editor. It shows, to a quite insignificant degree, that some one thinks him good. But in its essence, law review editorship is an opportunity, and not a badge. (In its essence law review editorship has value not for what it took to get on, but for what the editor {135} learns because he has got on.) What the law review offers, and the only thing it offers, is a machine, geared, set up, waiting, into whose maw the editor is cast—and which we know that we can trust to educate him. And the advantage of law review men in getting jobs comes not because they come certified as having made the grade initially, but because they come certified as having had, and been capable of using, the best education that the school has thus far offered. (That education, in the qualities which make it best, lie, as you know, outside of the curriculum entirely.) The law review men, in a word, have set themselves to do their job—despite the faculty. The law review men have met the challenge of their education fairly: they undertake their training for themselves.

The training lies first in the group-spirit, the group work, the group-discussion, about law, about law school, about review problems, about class problems, which are the essence of the law review. Interchange of ideas, fertilization of ideas, self-clarification by attempting to make clear to someone else, training by having a point to fight and by fighting it. And these are aspects which *any* man can have, on the review or off, who gets together consistently over the law with a body of his fellows, who gets together with them not alone before exams but regularly, weekly, daily— *who will set up his own machine.* (A lone wolf in law school is either a genius or an idiot.) The pickle solution that turns watermelon rind into an ornament to any table can turn a seeming dud into a useful lawyer—but the process of soaking must be continuous, and it must last. Nor does the value of group work lie in the presence of the soi-disant {self-proclaimed} superior minds. If your neighbor is dumb, you learn in teaching him. If he is slow, you think your problems through more deeply. If he is fast, he stretches you to keep pace, but you may find flaws in his thought which he has overlooked.

The second advantage of law review education lies in the editor's learning to do research on his own, to diagnose a problem, to size it up, to locate relevant material, to analyze it, to *reject* the worse of what he finds in favor of the better (and that is hard, that scrapping of hard labor)—and then to put together again; to criticize and then to build. It is not enough to know how to find relevant data, one must gain patience to find *all* the relevant data, then to discard the less relevant. It is not enough to find them, one must work them over, weave them into a whole. It is not enough to make a pile; there is a building to be made. This is of the essence of any analysis or solution of a *problem* in the office. It is not all of such analysis, much less all of such solution. But it is a vital part. And it is a part which case-class study *never* gives, *per se*. Even if you really put your notes together, and gain some skill in synthesis, you miss the learning from research.

And the third aspect of the law review education is that the editor learns to write. He becomes, gentlemen, legally literate. I beg your attention to this fact. For if we had a legal army Alpha test, most of you would not {136} now rate as eligible to *take* it. For you the Beta test—the test for men who hardly read and do not write. Yet half of a lawyer's work consists in writing. There is the writing which leaps into your mind, the writing of an argument. Where do you learn that, now? In the examination you are too hurried to think how to write an argument. In your oral speech you give no thought to form, little to order. In your moot court brief you have no pressure toward economy of words. The essence of learning to write an argument is the limitation that the law review imposes: you *have* to be brief, therefore if you are to get anything across, you must clarify the *course* of argument. Each point must prepare the point to follow. The fourth point must follow of itself from the first three. You have to be brief; therefore you must clarify the presuppositions of your argument. You have to be brief; therefore you must find the one word that does the work of ten.

And the law review man learns, too, that most useful of lawyer's arts, argumentative exposition. The statement of a case, the arrangement of facts, the stress in presentation, which argues, without argument, the desired conclusion.

Two other types of lawyer's writing, to be sure, he does not learn. The one is drafting—whether it be lease or contract, testament or statute. The art, *given* the law, *given* the situation, *given* the prejudices, desires, needs of one party or of two, of planning and wording a document which charts a safe course and steers it cleanly then as charted. The other is the negotiating letter, that combination of drafting and persuasion, in which you save and strengthen your position while trying at the same time to sell your own desires to your adversary.

I go into these aspects of education on the law review in such detail because I am sick to nausea of the gutlessness that second year classes have displayed these many years. Some, who had hoped election, peeved, sneering, childishly aloof from law review and school and work and all—to comfort an injured vanity by scorn of the work their own careers will need. More, many more, the most, lined up and bowing. Stooping a supple back to slide onto the review men all leadership in class discussion. Supine, assuming that since theirs is not the Greatness, neither is it theirs to break in upon the close monopoly of better education. Taking as a sign of greatness, as a stamp of leadership, the accident of opportunity. To the review men this idolization doubtless does no heavy harm. The swelled head is no serious danger so long as review tradition and the revising editor will put on the screws, will keep up the speed; so long as prestige means sweat, means steady sweating. But for the class at large, I say it is abominable. What these review men get in education is yours, too, for the taking. They have indeed the numbered places at the trough, reserved and waiting. But there is trough enough for all. The trough is free. Let the review men profit by it, while you go without, and editorship indeed means "he is better": a {137} fatter pig, a bigger pig, a stronger pig, a quicker. Better indeed. Better, because he has *become* so, because he *has made* himself so. But not if you turn to now to keep the balance even. There are twenty men in the class who can hold their own with most of the review; there are fifty others who stand fair chances of still reaching the first group; there is not one whose education will not double or treble in its value if he breaks loose from following in the wake of constituted authority; if he knocks the halo off the class room, and sets about to get some training on his own.

You are a queer lot, in your intellectual inconsistencies. Our gods you scorn; you turn bold eyes into the green-white light of disillusion. You learn and accept from us some disillusion in the law. So far, the image-breakers, the scornful of idols, the sophisticates. Yet at the same time you labor building new images, walking in awe and self-abasement round before their sightless eyes. You have stripped the pedagog of his glory; he is a naked insect under your glass; you view him realistically, a problem in examination-setting to be reckoned with. I do not quarrel with this. It is most wholesome for the pedagog. But what some down-town lawyer happens to have said about the law is golden in your ears, sings its far magic like the sweet bell of Yseult. And that devil-doctored shamanistic mark of school and intellectual prestige, the law review, at that you look, and tremble. To cover, to cover quickly, the Bull-Roarer comes! I say you are a queer lot, O my children. Do you not fathom that the only purpose of all disillusion is to make you free?

The road to freedom, in this instance, leads in one way only: to set a problem for yourself, and go after it. If your imagination fails, there are advance sheets. I have heard, even, of instructors who left problems with the class. More, your faculty are affording definite opportunity. The outside paper sets a framework for research, for synthesis, for argument. If you will hold down your words, if you will rewrite, let it grow cold, recast your argument, rewrite again, you may in the process of one paper gain some literacy. As for group-building, literate or not, you still have tongues.

There are three things more which I would call to your attention. One is, that when you practice you will deal chiefly with one state, with one law of but one state. You know this. Stop a while, and realize it. There are statutes in that state. There are decisions. There are judges. There is political organization. There are people. Those statutes, those decisions, those judges, those politics, those people—these concern you deeply. If you have not set about to study all of them, in their interrelations, it is time you did. A little time, each week, making your own notes. Each week, but cumulatively. Think about that. Then do it.

Another is, that you have soaked enough in the undiluted vinegar of law school law. It is time to spice the pickle with some background stuff. What, I care little. Biographies of lawyers or of judges, together with some {138} history of their times. The practices of the Constitution in relation to its words. The records of some cases in relation to the opinion. Visits to the courts, all courts, any courts, not as spectators, but as students, and as critics. The workings of the labor injunction or the juvenile court, as shown in current studies. The Federal Reserve Board and the October market {crash of 1929}. Civil procedure on the Continent. The logic of the logicians in its relation to the argumentation in opinions. The new Encyclopaedia of Social Science. What, I say, I care little—but something you can bring to bear upon your law school law, something you *will* bring to bear upon your law, something you seek yourself, to make your law school law more human, to give it a broader base, a richer soil, a finer flower.

And finally, I would say a word of your instructors. One effect of the first, the plastic year, upon your minds, has almost inevitably been to fit you with a set of ideas as to what types of teaching, what types of instructor, are proper, are fitting, to a law school; yet simultaneously to make you passively receptive, even to these. Thank fortune, you are yet to meet with others who are vastly different. It would be sad if you were not. In meeting the others, however, you can meet them in cooperation or in antagonism. If the latter, it will cost you and the instructor four to eight weeks in merely getting under way. In meeting men with new methods, you can come set to take just what you are accustomed to, and nothing else, by God, no, nothing else! Or else you can come set to find out what *those* men may have to give. And in re-meeting your old—well, may I call them friends?— you can be, you will tend strongly to be, more passive than before. Their bag of tricks you know, and how to rest between whiles. But why content yourselves with the knowing? Why let them palm off on you canned stuff they happen to have stored upon the shelf? Do you prefer it canned? Of course, can opening is easiest for the instructor. You sit back, and he will pour it out. Thick, with a little pepper; and devoid of vitamins. Thick—it runs slowly—slowly enough for you to take it down. He likes it, the instructor. There is a sure esthetic thrill in skillful pouring. There is a pleasure in a skillful job. There is even pleasure in observing your hungry faces as you lap it up.

Of course, you could have it better in the library. Better, and faster. With more case references. A wider body of material at one time. Much quicker work. Much cheaper. More effective. And your class-hours free to get your own perplexing problems solved.

For no instructor is wedded to the can. There is no stimulus to him like that of an eager class. If you react, instead of sitting there like lumps of mud, then so will he. What he wants most, almost the only thing he wants, is to see some results. You give him none, and he must build his own—and hence the can. But in the measure of your expectations, in the measure that you make your expectations felt, in the measure that your minds react to his {139} and *show* reaction, you will unchain the best he has to give. You will unchain stuff better then he knew he had. Bring out your questions, push for answers, follow his arguments through, and test, and challenge. If not in class, because the discussion turns to another theme, then after. You are not reaching what is here for you unless your personal problem comes to its solution. There is a fool false pride abroad, a diffidence at taking up instructor's time. What vagrant idiocy! Let him protect himself! Keep after him. Why do you think he has an office in the building?

I do not mean, with every petty point. I urge group-building, group-jawing, group-rowing, because in the groups so many problems work, all by themselves, to their solution. But if they do not, come group-wise to your man. One man he may turn down; five he will always talk to.

Have I, then, said too much? I said "a fool false pride" at taking up instructor's time. And as to that I still say: stamp it out. But there are those of you who feel some hesitance, and for a finer reason. You recognize that before each of the teaching staff there floats a dream—a reputation as a scholar, to win or to sustain. You feel compunction, then, at breaking in upon his work. And this is good. Yet still I say—let him protect himself. And still I say, there is no stimulus like that of eager students. If you come not to milk him like a cow, but for help in a problem you have struggled with, and hard, then what you bring is worth the time you cost.

There is a further, final reason, why it behooves you to take on for yourselves this job of education, a reason which at the end of the drill year a man should ponder long. It is the stupendous inadequacy, the lack of direction, the inefficiency in legal education. Legal education at large, not education here, peculiarly. Here, as it seems to me, things are better than elsewhere. Certainly they are nowhere better than here. Which is, in one sense, to declare a whole profession bankrupt. What has been said sketches the lines of my thinking on this point. We have but the slightest inkling of whither we should take you. We have but one vehicle worked out to take you anywhere, and that vehicle, unaltered, passes its point of maximum return before the journey is half done. Our teaching technique we have learned one by one in the helterskelter grab bag of experience, and have carried for the most part unaltered into wholly changed conditions, as to size, as to make-up of class, as to material taught. Our machinery for checking our results with you would set an intelligent ass to braying. I say that as a profession we are bankrupt: We are called upon daily to deliver what we have not got. We cannot pay our obligations as they now mature. Bankrupt—if you are to judge our work by the standards of a decent engineer or even of a decent business man—or of the Sales Act.

But from another angle, things are not so bad. We are as well off as the law itself which is our subject of instruction; perhaps, indeed, we are better off. We are as well off, or nearly, as most types of educators. As {140} human institutions go, peculiarly those institutions on the social side, we can stand the current lax test of solvency: we can go on. We can do more; nay, we are doing more. For we have awakened to the need of doing better; we are awake even to the intense difficulty of finding out how to do better.

Meantime, there is no better place for you to go. That is a reason for your staying with the job, as given, here. But surely it is no reason for you to rest content with that job—to turnip in it—to take what happens to be given as all that can be got. If vegetate you must, be an aspiring vegetable. Be a bean, and climb.

X • BEFORE SUNRISE

The time approaches when you will put on fresh raiment, and shake the dust of these halls off your feet, and go down into the market-place. When you have done that, you will have little time for thinking. Having ceased to be a child, you will cease to think as a child, you will, I take it, put away these childish things. Your mind will be on doing; if it should wander there will be no lack of hooks to drag it back. So that it may not be out of place before you go to stop for a moment, to look over, a little, what this profession is to which you go. What is the lawyer and his relation to the life about him? What is the part he plays in this society? Perhaps, too, you will pause with me over some of the things a lawyer does, some of the opportunities which come to him, some of the responsibilities he carries.

And I suppose that the first and the outstanding thing is that the lawyer is not popular. I think he never has been popular. I strongly suspect that there have never been laws or lawyers too heartily approved by the lay population they professed to serve. Certainly radicals have never loved them. "The first thing we will do is to hang all the lawyers"; and lawyers, and records, have been cast for burning since there have been such things as revolutions. Nor does such disapproval rest among the reds. The healthy spirited men of many ages have lifted up their clubs to bring them down upon the lawyer's skull. Cromwell, his law reforms defeated: "The sons of Zeruiah are too much for us." Rabelais, robustious, pungent in his scorn:

> "Who being thus met together, after they had thereupon consulted for the space of six-and-forty weeks, finding that they could not fasten their teeth in it....
>
> "But Pantagruel said unto them, Are the lords between whom this debate and process is yet living? It was answered him. Yes. To what a devil, then, said he, serve so many paltry heaps and bundles of papers and copies which you give me? Is it not better to hear their controversy from their own mouths whilst they are face to face before us, than to read these vile fopperies, which are nothing but trumperies, deceits, diabolical cozenages of Cepola, pernicious slights and subversions of equity....
>
> "Furthermore, seeing that the laws are excerpted out of the middle of moral and natural philosophy, how should these fools have understood it, that have, by God, studied less in philosophy

than my mule."

Or do you prefer the terser account in Ecclesiastes: If thou seest the oppression of the poor, and violent perverting of judgment and justice in a province, *marvel not at the matter*!

And finally, in our own day, we have Sandburg, and what he says deserves attention: {142}

THE LAWYERS KNOW TOO MUCH

The lawyers, Bob, know too much.
They are chums of the books of old John Marshall.
They know it all, what a dead hand wrote,
A stiff dead hand and its knuckles crumbling,
The bones of the fingers a thin white ash.
    The lawyers know
    a dead man's thoughts too well.

In the heels of the higgling lawyers, Bob:
Too many slippery ifs and buts and howevers,
Too much hereinbefore provided whereas,
Too many doors to go in and out of.

    When the lawyers are through
    What is there left, Bob?
    Can a mouse nibble at it
    And find enough to fasten a tooth in?

    Why is there always a secret singing
    When a lawyer cashes in?
    Why does a hearse horse snicker
    Hauling a lawyer away?

The work of a bricklayer goes to the blue.
The knack of a mason outlasts a moon.
The hands of a plasterer hold a room together,
The land of a farmer wishes him back again.
    Singers of songs and dreamers of plays
    Build a house no wind blows over.
    The lawyers—tell me why a hearse horse snickers
    hauling a lawyer's bones.

No, this profession of the law lacks popular appeal; and I suspect it always will. For in the first place, a lawyer is a specialist, a worker in a craft too intricate for easy understanding. Any such specialist, any such master of a mystery, is suspect to the ignorant. Nay, he is suspect to the other specialists. The more highly skilled and delicate and strange his work, the more we may use him in our time of need; the less we love him. Does your heart warm to the surgeon as he draws on his rubber gloves, and asks you whom to notify?

But the lawyer's case is far worse than the doctor's. For the doctor's secret craft consists in fighting nature. The doctor, with increase of knowledge {143} and a touch of luck, can gradually strengthen the percentage of his cures. Not so the lawyer. He is a specialist in the conflict of interests between men. Fifty percent of all the cases that are brought to him are lost —and must be lost, so long as law is what it is.

So long as law is what it is. Not, it may be, forever. For there is nothing sacred, there is nothing immanent, there is not even great utility, in this whole-hog-or-none approach which is so typical of law. In this notion that the purported bona fide purchaser must be left with the whole pie or else lose it all; that he who is contributorily negligent is barred from all recovery; that if the offer for the unilateral contract is revoked before a full performance the contract must either be all good or be all bad. Surely we have in this white-black division an ancient echo, the ghost-voice of pre-medieval centuries, of a procedure too crude to be far trusted. Only one step back of it would be the time when even law and fact were undistinguished, when a man swore merely, or the court decided, on his "right". And in our own later, more refined developments the officials often enough have followed better insight. An "equitable" lien, created by court or by the Betterment Acts, comes in between flat ouster of the owner and flat forfeiture of improvements made in all good faith. The jury, in the teeth of the instructions, will whittle down the verdict of the plaintiff who has also been at fault. Ratable sharing is the aim of bankruptcy; return of a going business to the now insolvent is, at least theoretically, the goal of a receivership. There is some trend, then, toward a more intelligent adjustment, toward the discovery of the more *workable* result, of the result that gives some hope of less bad blood. Much of the urge to settle cases, most of the present drive toward arbitration, all of the creditor's committee handling of insolvencies, run along these lines. But when the case does go to litigation, the point remains. Well nigh up to the hilt, a full half of all such cases must be lost.

It is an invidious business, this shuffling, this gambling, this checker-play with human rights. It is an invidious business to be the mouthpiece of a fighting man who can have victory only as he tramples others down. Small wonder that the trampled do not love the lawyer. But neither do the winners. The lawyer is not only a specialist. He is a specialist in *winning* what even in his client's eyes calls mostly for adjustment. His clients do not understand what he has done, nor how he does it. Even when they flame to the justice of their causes, their lawyer seems to be putting a high cause over by some piddling trick. They cannot follow the merits through the maze of technicality. For the lawyer deals intricately not merely in human conflict, but in the procedure of the legal action. And the procedure of legal action, like any other etiquette, is blind, is hopeless, is repugnant, to its layman. There is much sense in much procedure, along with all the nonsense that goes into it. But you cannot expect a man who has not studied the problem long and deeply to perceive the sense, even if it did not come overlaid with {144} flummery. What turns his stomach, you will note, is not technique. Tricks of his own trade he absorbs with relish. Tricks on the ball field he appreciates and cheers. Tricks that he cannot fathom—these are different. He sees a case in which he has an interest. He sees no reason why technical sleight of hand should stand between him and his victory. And if he is the victor, he respects little the man who won by slipping silken strings before the other fellow's ankles and by pulling silken knots around the other fellow's neck.

Here, then, we have three reasons why the lawyer is not loved. He practices black art. He is a trickster. *Too much hereinbefore provided whereas. Too many doors to go in and out of.* And half of those who go to him are sunk. Three reasons. They are enough. But there are more. Law is the organ of society's woe when order is not working. But law, itself, in its whole drive and purpose, is organized in terms of that same order that, by the same hypothesis, has ceased to work to satisfaction. Law thrusts, law clubs, not merely for the maintenance of order, but for the maintenance of that very order which may be cracking. Law and lawyers must therefore stand to observation at the very point where society has come to press upon the weak, the helpless, the obscure, the wretched. At that very point they stand eternally and struggle for what is old, for what may be outworn, against the claims of anything that may be new and human and appealing. At that point, in aspect, *must* the lawyer stand, stand indeed so conspicuous that sometimes he and his work are all that is perceived. It is not merely an unbounded faith in law which has called forth the flood of under-baked reformatory legislation; it is at least in equal measure that law, and law that cried out for changing, has pressed on the victims like the Iron Maiden. "Woe unto you also, ye lawyers! for ye lade men with burdens grievous to be borne, and ye yourselves touch not the burden with a single finger...." The essential attribute of law is to conserve, to jam new conditions into old boxes, whether they will fit or not; not to change, readjust, or cure. This need not hold of every law, or every lawyer. Lawyers have sometimes been the leaders of reform. Law has been the instrument of change. But do not let events obscure their process. Before each such reform there was a struggle. During the struggle, long-continued, there was suffering. The bulk of the law, the ranks of the profession, stood with locked shields against impending change. When the change came, the bitterness was left. When the change came, it was long overdue. When the change came, it still was, like as not, defeated by the technique of more lawyers. All of which gives a sometimes aloes-flavored grimace to the phrasing: "courts of justice".

For the same reason it is clear that the activity of most skillful lawyers will be upon the side of the Haves and not upon the side of the Have-nots; conscience-sturdy activity, too, impassioned skill; one cannot live with Haves for twenty years without contagion. The best talent of the bar will always {145} muster to keep Ins in and to man the barricade against the Outs. And while in theory legal contests may be equal, the better man, the more skillful man, the man with the longest purse who can hire the better, the more skillful man, has his advantage and will have it in the time to come. Where long-run legal strategy is called for, the marshalling of counsel and of cases through a generation, this advantage will be piled up twentyfold.

By this time you have discovered that I do not think the lawyer popular, and that his unpopularity appears to me as natural as whiskers on a cat.

The curious thing is the extent to which the counts against him prove on examination to be undeserved, or at worst, half-truths; and to disregard in the burst of complaint the merits of the accused.

Look the counts over. What you find is this. For part, the profession is charged with being what any profession should hope to be: expert enough to develop a sort of black art of its own. All that makes law grotesque and dubious is that any man thinks he has adequate knowledge by his common sense to judge of "rights" and "wrongs". What lawyers do must therefore be the diabolical cozenages of Cepola. The common man does not arrogate such knowledge to himself in engineering. The art of engineers is thus white magic more than black.

For part, the charge is one of trickery. Here we tread on delicate ground. So much of that accusation as concerns the mere and more obvious need of some technical order of business, I think we may waive away. Reason enough, as before, to see why the un-understanding are intolerant; no cause for shame. Not so, I fear, some of the other phases. Not so the mazed mass of some procedure, which spells a profession either incompetent in arranging its own business, or wedded to a stubborn ritualism that makes work as three-inch brushes would make work for painters. Not so as to the charge that law procedure, and the combat aspects of the trial, tend to make lawyers forget their clients' interests in their own, and to forget in both the interests—if such there be—of justice.

Apart from procedure, and touching the charges that remain: as to the twisting of rules to win; as to there being no gain at law except at the flat expense of trampling, of putting the boots to a loser; as to the longer purse holding unfair advantages; as to the closed ranks of the law in favor of what is—surely three-fourths of the sting of the charges is drawn, and mud clapped on the wound, when one looks to the obvious truth: that in these matters law and lawyers do not show themselves, distinctively, at all. In these matters the lawyers mirror undistorted the very society that makes the charge. It is clients who wish to win, and to beat down other clients. Nor are lawyers to be held responsible for the clash of interests. Not law or lawyers, but society, gives fighting advantage to the propertied, puts the screws on in favor of the Ins. True, that the law presents a dubious method of adjusting conflict. But true again, that is serves, *somehow*, to settle those {146} conflicts no other machinery has availed to solve at all. Three-fourths of the sting, I say, is drawn. But a part remains. Shall we deny that as we thus meddle trade-wise with the purer pitch of life, some pitch will stick? I have small patience with the man who scorns the man who does his dirty work. I have small patience, either, with the pitch worker who hides behind the skirts of him he serves. "Woe unto you, lawyers! for ye have taken away the key of knowledge: ye entered not in yourselves, and them that were entering in ye hindered."

The worst of the charges, then, seem to me in good part undeserved. The worst of them lie ill in the mouths of most of those who make them. For us in our own hearts they do give cause, they do give heavy cause for searching. Yet not for failing spirit. We have achievements to set off against our flaws.

For who is it who does the heavy work of bringing a limping, halting, clanking legal structure down to date? Who is it manages to unfold enough of that rarest of commodities, human ingenuity, social invention, to make old institutions serve new needs? Which is as much as saying, to make new institutions which are needed. I think if you turn to the work of counsel in the office you will find unlimited, unbelievable, output of that rare ore. The books are full of its traces. Most of our present law can be shown to be its product. Granted that the lawyer may not be the first actor in events, granted that he brings forth few novel needs to serve, he is none the less a precious social engineer. He observes the need that has risen. He finds a way to meet it. It seems to have been the business man and not the lawyer who, in the first instance, brought about bills of exchange and bills of lading. It was, however, the lawyer who devised the mortgage, who made possible the giving of security in goods or land, while leaving the beneficial use of the borrower during the period for which the security was needed; made possible, therefore, the secured production loan whereby a debtor had the chance of financing a new venture out of whose own profits he might hope to meet the debt. *The land of a farmer wishes him back again:*

it was the lawyer who despite the other lawyer built up the concept of the equity of redemption. It was the lawyer who turned the note-of-hand of commerce into the banker's ironclad collateral note, the lawyer who out of the same stock and the ancient covenant produced the bond that forms the base of the investment market. He did not act alone, as I have said. His was perhaps not the first drive, his was not always the full perception of the need. But his the skill, his was the engineering. It was the lawyer who devised the long-term lease for real estate improvement, and the collateral trust for real estate financing, or for financing new equipment for a mort-gaged railroad. And, greatest perhaps of any single line of growth within our law, it was the lawyer who from the outset has shaped the thousand uses {147} of the law of trusts—who made party politics a possibility when to lose an election meant the penalties of treason, who built up the possi-bilities of the permanent charitable gift, who turned the trust to keep family land together in the teeth of rules, who first opened to married women an independent income, who maneuvered by way of trust the first great consolidations, and turned that concept to the new fields of import-ing and motorcar finance. This last step, that of the trust receipt, I find peculiarly illuminating, perhaps because I know its course in more detail. You can see its growth, follow its invention, its steady step-wise spread. First in financing grain from upper New York to the sea. The early litiga-tion that went unnoticed. The crucial case that caught the eye of metropol-itan counsel. The introduction of the device, now modified, elaborated, into the importing business. The major firms that participated in its devel-opment, and the development itself, case by case, in litigation, clause by clause, in the increasing adequacy of the drafting. And in the course of the past ten years we can trace out its spread and readaptation to the financing of automobiles. Again we know the men, the means, the problems. In this one history we can see something of the energy, thought and originality that must go into creation of even such a single, simple tool as this. And this history, we may be certain, is but typical of a course of building as steady, as irresistible, as craftsmanlike, in some ways as beautiful, as that which through the medieval centuries raised cathedrals.

Nor are inventions of the lawyers limited to office counsel. Growth in law, especially growth in case law, has been attributed too lightly in most legal writing to the courts. I would neither deny nor belittle the part that the courts play in the growth. But how many judges do you know of whom it can be said, as it was once of Holmes, "the trouble with that fellow is that he is always deciding cases on points that were not raised in the briefs of either side"? How many judges do you know whose analysis of the case and of the situation is a major fresh creation, a "Let there be light!", rather than that lesser type of building which consists in merely modifying the theory of one advocate or of the other? The job of choosing wisely between the inventions of counsel is a difficult one. The job of consistent wise choice is tremendous. Yet it is not of itself the major work. That has been done, consistently, continuously, by the bar. Webster, not Marshall, made the Dartmouth College case. And when I say invention, I mean invention. To produce out of raw facts a theory of a case is prophecy. To produce it persuasively, and to get it over, is prophecy fulfilled. *Singers of songs and dreamers of plays*—though they be lawyers—*build a house no wind blows over.*

I say, then, that both in the office and in court it is the profession that keeps the law alive. It is the profession that keeps the law from sitting too closely strait-jacketed upon the social body. I have already {148} indicated why the lawyer gets, why he will continue to get, the least of credit for his work. But the fact that he has it to do, puts upon him a responsibility that reaches beyond his clients, beyond his surroundings, that reaches to the future of the people. A responsibility to his kind which there is no escaping. That laymen do not know he carries it, and do not care, makes it no more escapable. His, and his only, is the choice. He can either set himself across the path of progress, he can either check and block, by the exercise of utmost ingenuity, each new forward step. Or he can do the opposite.

Meantime, however, he must survive. It irks me to intrude such thoughts upon a high discussion—but he must pay the rent. Ours is a money economy. The man must have an income. Income and standing up under responsibility; it is a troublous team to ride.

Thus we come to that peculiar engine built up by the profession for the purpose of helping a lawyer ride the team—that system of practices and norms we know as legal ethics. There are two of those norms which look with incisive directness to our problem.

The one is the established view, respectable as few other things are respectable, accepted as such not only by the profession but the public, that a lawyer should believe in his cause. If he believes in his cause he will fight, he will fight more vigorously, he will think more skillfully, his whole self will be unchained by his conviction. That way lies, among other things, success. And as the lawyer becomes the symbol for his cause, and gains weight before the jury when he "stakes his reputation on his case"—so also the finer type of lawyer has through the centuries worked himself up into full belief in his cause before his work took on full value to himself. So much so that the lay-folk speak of an advocate's temperament as of a type, and smile (or jibe) to watch the speed with which most lawyers can achieve conviction.

Believing in one's causes involves, however—comes inevitably and almost imperceptibly to involve—believing in one's client, when one's client brings a considerable succession of cases. The same loyalty which the finer ethic calls toward the cause is bound to develop in the course of time toward the client as well. But in this day of group activity, of corporate practice, the client with the succession of cases is the goal of all delight. He, or it, his or its retainer—if I may be again sordid for a moment—pays the rent. This comes inevitably to mean the substantial identification of a lawyer with a particular client or particular interest. He is a banking lawyer, or a railroad lawyer, or a sugar company lawyer. In such capacity, and with such loyalties, he should of course turn down the cases in which he does not believe. Those, you may notice, will be cases against the banking house, the sugar company, the railroad.

{149} Thus, naturally and easily, one works out a harmonization between one's duty to the public and one's duty to one's pocket. And I wish to make here particularly the point that the ethic of believing in one's case is of peculiar value when one discovers that the case of a poor man is not worthy of such belief.

But there may be a pleasant paunch upon your client. His wallet may look fat. Suppose now that his case does not at first blush seem appealing. Then what to do? Courage, my friend, there is another ethic! There is that admirable ethic of the profession which makes it clear that the lawyer is neither judge nor jury; that the lawyer has neither duty nor right to usurp the constitutional function of the judicial tribunal. It is not for him to condemn a man who has not been found guilty by twelve jurymen. It is not for him to condemn a practice which has not been found unwarranted by the court. It is of the essence of justice that every man be given a fair hearing, be given vigorous representation at the hearing; in a word, that he be assured a fair trial of his case; that he be not condemned until that trial is had, until the court has spoken.

No ethic is more respectable among ourselves.

The public does not always understand it. But reasons of the gravest import and most far reaching effect are and should be urged in its support. To insist upon the identification of lawyer and client is in practice to jeopardize the representation of any unpopular cause, of any unpopular litigant; it is in essence to deny a trial. Shame to those members of the profession who, knowing this, have yet so often shrunk from unpopular causes, have even joined in the pressure against counsel in such causes! If popularity were always rightness, either short range or long, there would be no grave danger in thus lumping counsel and client. But the contrary proves true. And here is also a situation continually met with, in which the lawyer himself finds it impossible to accurately judge the facts. Only either at trial, or long after it, does the true set of facts appear, which contradicts what he himself has believed to hold against his client. Here again a client is entitled to the benefit of the fair trial. He should have it. The bar exists to insure it.

Yet you will tell me these two ethics contradict each other—that one cannot at the same time believe wholly in his cause, and yet secure fair hearing for a cause he does not believe in. Do not be so naive. Already you are almost lawyers. Three years you have been studying the law. Are you still unaware that every doubtful point is regularly answered both ways by authority? Are you still blind to the fact that rules do not *control* decision when the case is troublesome? In every field, on every point, when there is doubt, the law will offer you technique and rules, respectable, respected, to work to *either* goal. There is the Janus-face of Precedent. The same with logic: you can if you will reject the rule because you do not see its end: "We cannot take this step; we do not see {150} where to draw the line." Or, "The rule here contended for would lead to this, and this, which we cannot accept; therefore we must reject it in the present case as well." Or, on the other hand, if you prefer, you can decide the case regardless of such far, imagined difficulties: "It has been urged upon us that the rule proposed would lead to this and this. Such cases are not now before us. It will be time to test them when they come. The present case, in any event, is within the line."

Within the law, I say, therefore, rules *guide*, but they do not *control* decision. There is no precedent the judge may not at his need either file down to razor thinness or expand into a bludgeon. Why should you expect the ethics of the game to be different from the game itself? Of course, from one angle, the two guides are inconsistent. But each, for itself, is true, is sound, is vital—in its place. When to use which? A search for outside answer is an empty quest. Empty, delusive, footless—"Repose", says Holmes, "is not the destiny of man." Choice is your own. Your answer for your choice. There are no rules to shoulder *your* responsibility.

Yet there are rules which can be made to *seem* to shoulder it. For, see, I have set before you two norms of legal ethics, both of which, as I understand it, are completely respectable, accepted, impeccable, and *either* of which is always available. All that is needed, to assure you of success (once you acquire *any* clients) is for you to choose the convenient ethic at the convenient time. You have only to insist upon the need for a fair hearing when a fat client's case looks bad; and to insist upon the need for believing in your case, either when you do by good fortune believe in a fat client's case, or when you find it difficult to believe some starved, pinched fellow. Whatever you do then, you will have done respectably. Men will look up to you. You will sleep at night. Your conscience will be clear. Your income tax will grow.

For your totem, for your ideal, you then can take the squid, the cuttle-fish. Spine he has not, but O, a beak he has. The spine is absent, but the beak is strong. There are ten counted legs, each leg alive with suckers, all waving through the water after prey. The world, the whole world, offers hope for prey. When pressed some time too hard by enemies, most lawyer-like he hides himself behind a cloud of ink. *Why does a hearse horse snicker?*

I may seem to you to have been somewhat lightly ironic, somewhat idly cynical, in what I have just said. I may seem to be mocking at the precious things of life. I should be sorry to have you mistake me. I speak in bitter seriousness. I speak in behalf of all ideals I know. I speak without expectation, but I speak in hope. The unpopularity of our profession, the accusations against it, must not and cannot be permitted to hide its finer service from our eyes. We, and no others, carry the burden of making the law worth having—over the long run, and from day to {151} day. I see so clearly the responsibility. But I see also so very clearly the ease with which it can be shunted, and shunted, even, in all ignorance of the shunting. I see so clearly this two-edged ethic, I see the balm and smugness with which it baits invertebrates among us. The pressure to let the burden slide will fall so soon on you. As things stand, it is a pressure well-nigh irresistible. There will be very few whose eyes it does not close. There will be very few of you who will resist it. But twenty years from now it will give pleasure, it will give foolish pride, it will give honor, to meet those few and take them by the hand. {*page 152 follows*}

THEY THAT COME AFTER

Spring, and the rising sap. New growth, and spring.
Fresh green shoots from the earth, fresh shoots from hardening youngsters.
Spring and the storm: some high old king will fall.
        Room — room — room!
Some overshadowing head will crash to earth...
Surge, sap; rise high! . . And smother the saplings to follow . . .

Spring, and the rising blood. New growth, and spring.
Strong young calves from the herd, fresh growth on hardening horn.
Mating call of the spring: some ancient bull goes down.
        Room — room — room!
Some monarch of the herd is gored to earth ...
Surge, blood; rise high! . . And gore down the rivals to follow. . . .

Spring, and the rising youth! . . New growth, and spring.
Spring—and are men to wait for the old to fall, before youth rises?
Are men trees of the soil, to steal the life from the young till the high
        king crashes?
Beasts of the field, to harem the herd till the monarch falls?
Rise high!

Surge, rise high! Surge from the loins of the elders,
Surge with the counsel and strength of them that have builded before you, —
Builded before you — aye, and misbuilded before you . . .
Surge from the loins of the elders, beside them, beyond them.
        Beside them, beyond them . . . Beside them, beyond them . . .
        ROOM!

• • • • • • •

O, for the bone of our bone that shall rise to replace us!
        ROOM! ROOM! ROOM! It shall rise to replace us!
O, for the brain of our brain that shall bring our doing to naught!

AFTERWORD

After three years or ten or, this time, twenty, one asks oneself: "What would it look like if I were doing it over?" And it is a bit disheartening to realize that what it would come to would be pretty much a shifting of emphasis and arrangement: a fuller development of matters mentioned and passed over; a correction and rounding out of things dealt with too largely in the flat or in a light that hid or twisted some portion of their meaning; a surer sharper drawing of some line that had earlier been ventured vaguely as a guess; while even what might seem "new" would prove on more careful thinking to be stuff already adumbrated in thought and present in flavor. In one way, it is disheartening. One set of ideas seems to be about all any ordinary man can manage in one lifetime, and the time and labor needed to work them into use seems so often to accompany their obsolescence. It has often seemed to me for instance that three-fourths or more of what moves me in all of Brahms' work I know is clearly present in the piano quintet, numbered if I remember rightly Opus 5, and even then a material ripening, deepening reworking of the original job for two pianos. Or again, Kantorowicz showed me in 1928 a notebook from his student days containing the grand plan of what he was to write. Half or more of the items had been checked off; others of the titles—and very little else, indeed—proceeded to appear in following years.

In one way, I say, it is disheartening. But to a man of the law, of that age-old troubled discipline of law-and-government, it should be less disheartening than to most; to us the lesson should in a richer sense be one of lifted courage. So much of our work, so much of our service, so much of men's need for us consists in just these seeming little things: the discovery and insertion of the one apt word or phrase which clarifies an issue or avoids a lawsuit or protects a client or a nation against catastrophe. Or the delicacy and sure power of spokesmanship in a crisis where the outcome turns upon a watch-jewel. Of the sense of balance, timing, tact, which settles a claim to advantage and without ill feeling, or which brings five half-scared, jealous, captious cross-purposers together into a single team, or which finds and holds to the touchstone that saves a Union or a World.

It is these little things, these so very little things, these tiny touches of vision and the deft hand—informed with guts and honor—it is these little things, which take their long life-term to learn, these little things which make us Us, make us worthwhile to our People and to ourselves.

Hence if these lectures were being done over, I am clear that their focus would shift materially off of "the law" as lawyers understand that term and materially onto what the institution of law-and-government is for, and in {154} particular what our own version of that institution is for, and what the part is—the noble and needed part—which the various major crafts of law and the men of law play as their part in that institution. Knowledge of the rules of law (which has occupied so much of the time and attention of our classrooms) would thus move into perspective as being a single one out of a dozen or more necessary parts of equipment for lawyering, and one could begin to persuade properly and cogently against the silly idea that the sound normal road to such knowledge is "a course" or that three years of case-courses can in themselves possibly provide enough of such knowledge for a respectable start on practice. One could really go into the question, then, of intelligent allocation of a student's time as he studies not "law", but to qualify for effective lawyering. Against that background one could—as somebody surely ought to—explain for instance first to the brighter and then to the less bright student the rather different lines of technique which commend themselves to either group for getting moderate or good grades in a case-book course on "the law" of a subject with such minimum time outlay as to open up time for one's true professional education.

It is a queer thing, if one stops to think about it, that our "better" law schools—which remain the better law schools—have allowed themselves to be stampeded out of doing their job. Knowing as they did that full-time centered attention of instructors had real value; knowing as they did that short range rule-of-thumb practical advice could be no substitute for clean thinking, hard work, and sound theory; knowing as they did that mere information on the latest statute or decision in the locality was not enough, they not only moved firmly into theory and into tough study and a faculty focused on the school, but they also permitted the commercial law schools to substantially monopolize the entire realm of the effective crafts of law. Case-study, one of the vital arts, became not one, but *the* vital art, with even the handling of statutes a discipline which has been forced to fight more than thirty years for a reasonable recognition by no means yet achieved. And case-study then developed into a fetish as if it were the only sound way of teaching—or indeed of learning—even the rules and concepts of our law. And the slightest suggestion that a thing learned might prove practical was enough to damn it as heresy against the gospel of "theory" and of "legal thinking."

Whereas the point to be made is that such a craft of law as that of spokesmanship, in any of its phases from appellate advocacy on through to negotiation, is a craft which cries out for the development and teaching of its theory, as it does also for study by *doing* in the light of that theory. What I mean by theory in this connection can perhaps be most quickly suggested by the mere concept "Spokesmanship," taken as a basis for study into activities, their function, their lines of effective method, the reasons for such effectiveness, the problems of decency or legitimacy or both which pose themselves in regard to such effective methods as Hitler's theory of how to lie or in regard to the {155} use of the deliberate red herring or the suppression in appellate argument of cogent authority known to be flatly against you. The specially developed Greek discipline of ancient Greece was not "Spokesmanship" but "Rhetoric"—in essence: the effective techniques of persuasion. Work on the professional legal side was to be developed against that body of tested, communicable techniques worked into orderly arrangement of what, how, where, when, why, which, whither and May I? That is roughly the substance of "theory"—work on the legal side was set for body and meaning against the aspects of persuasion in general, somewhat as today the trial or appellate lawyer has learned to borrow from the arts of advertising, selling, public relations. The specially developed medieval discipline was rather "Dialectic" than Rhetoric; the new feature was a limited and authoritative set of premises within which one had to move, and the crux of the game lay in such a posing of the issue as would ultimately force one's adversary out of bounds. Again the relation to work on the legal side—at least in posing and arguing issues "on the law"—is clear, and study on the legal side could gain body from theory in the wider context. "Advocacy" is another possible line of organization; "Legal Argument" was the one my own study of the field started with, almost twenty years ago. But "Spokesmanship" has come to be for me a more significant focus than any of the above, including and profiting from the essence of each of them while also reaching out to cover such matters as the values of having buffers between contending principals or the differences between the rival goals of victory and reconciliation or the problems and obligations of leadership both in the small and in the large. In a word, Spokesmanship with special attention to work on the legal side seems to me to offer the wherewithal of a full-fledged theoretical-practical discipline with cultural value equal to its professional value, one worth something like four to eight semester units, at least half of its compulsory in any three-year "law" course.

"Counseling" seems to me another line of law-craft under which a dozen sub-crafts gather—at least two of which, "counseling toward litigation" and negotiation, lap over happily, though with completely different background and emphasis, upon spokesmanship. But I should like to stress here again what I have tried to make clear elsewhere: that we misconceive the discipline of counseling and any of its sub-disciplines if we conceive the theory as limited, for example, to such specialties as "estate-planning" or "real estate practice" or "security." I like concrete work held close to earth, just as I like intensive work with cases (much more intensive work than our case-classes commonly permit) around concrete problems. But all such work should be done against a background of solid theory, at least of theory about the sound methods of going at the job; and one of the things needed for right training in counseling is the articulate development of such theory by instructor or student or both, reaching across particular "local" disciplines such as work on estates into the "general" field even as good work on the rules of law reaches {156} out from the local law to include the comparative. I would indeed have the student's work on the counseling side rest solidly on one and another and yet another of the more specialized fields, just as I would add to any "general" case-study a much more intensive treatment of the body of cases in some single jurisdiction; but the two things go together, since concrete counseling work calls for just such high-powered treatment of a single-jurisdiction constellation of authorities and tendencies.

It is thus plain that if I were to do an introduction again this question of some of the major crafts of law and their meaning, and something of their elementary theory, would come in for sustained discussion. Not least, the craft of appellate judging that yields us those reported cases which occupy so much of our attention in school and out, and which are capable of useful study in so many ways other than the mere extraction from them of a superficial picture of "the law" of "a field." For it seems to me vital for students—and indeed for the bar and for the appellate bench itself—to awaken not only to the fact that the rules alone do not decide any case worth puzzling about but to the companion fact, the comrade-and-brother fact, that the courts do not and cannot simply use the leeways of doctrine as they please. Put shortly, the courts are controlled by the tradition of their office with regard to the manner in which they use the leeways which their office opens up to them. There is not only the matter of personal uprightness, nor only the queer but lovely impact upon a man as he dons the robe of a felt pressure to become a something more and better, more responsible, more dispassionate, more restrained, more careful, even wiser, than his mere unrobed self. There is the felt duty to use the law for decency and justice, there is the other felt duty of the craft (with the peculiar tone transmitted by the particular bench) to reach for decency and justice only as *permitted* by the law; which means among other things that the tone and tendency of rules-in-constellation may urge and even force into results entirely without concrete particular authority; and which means that the court must be very slow in consulting its own views of rightness and welfare if they differ perceptibly from those of the community; and which means most especially that *conscious* shift in the content or direction of the law is subject to the law of leeways.

The law of leeways, in our system of precedent, is this: that an appellate court is free, without hesitation and without apology, to make any shift in content and direction of authorities which can be worked by the semi-automatic process by which authorities just take on new light, color, shape—and wording—as they are reviewed against fresh circumstances; but that conscious reshaping must so move as to hold the degree of movement down to the degree to which need truly presses. To ignore the law of leeways is to completely misunderstand the processes of appellate decision and, if you are an appellate lawyer, to double or treble your chance of losing your case. If you are one of those who cherish the illusion that the rules *alone* decide cases, {157} you ignore the law of leeways at the cost of missing the fact of *constant* movement, movement even in the run-of-the-mine case decided by memorandum "on the authority of Wolf v. Lamb." If on the other hand you are aware of the fact of movement, then to ignore the law of leeways is to ignore the fact that judges are not simply people. People they are, and people they remain, but they are people who have been conditioned first as lawyers, who therefore see things and classify things and weigh things like lawyers; and they are also people who have been conditioned second as judges, which makes them very different from what they were when they were merely lawyers; and they are also people who have been conditioned by the tradition of the American bench, and of a particular American bench, which marks them off sharply from French or British or Canadian judges; and they are, finally, people who have been conditioned by the period-style (or styles) of work in law which has had general prevalence during their earlier and later formative years. To think of such heavily and consciously conditioned creatures, so aware of their duty to further condition themselves, as *merely* people, is as curiously blind a procedure as to disregard the fact that each one of them is for all that not only a person but a particular person with an individual equipment in which brains range from brilliance to stupidity, temperament ranges from volatile to phlegmatic, adventurous to routineer, and background of experience ranges from anything to anything.

The individual variations are of course tremendous, as anybody knows, but so is the degree to which those variations can be reduced by conditioning. And one of the queerest phenomena of our own legal system is our failure to do with our trial judges anything remotely reminiscent of the judicial apprenticeship which used to characterize Continental training for the judging office or even to subject our new trial judge to the impact of a bench tradition as we do a new appellate judge, or to joint sittings for a year with various of his more experienced brethren.

But I am concerned here with one special phase of the conditioning machinery which goes not only unplanned but substantially unnoticed: that of the period-style of the law-crafts. It seems to me essential to health of our law and legal work that student, bar and bench should know that the Grand Tradition of the Common Law is our rightful heritage and needs complete and conscious recapture. They should read enough in the reports of the 1830's or 1840's (and a single volume read in sequence is commonly enough) to recognize as a prevailing *style* a handling of material as essentially made up of principle rather than of mere precedent, and of that finer type of principle which has perceptible reason and makes perceptible sense in life. They should come to recognize the court's steady quest for rules which satisfy the needs of the Grand Tradition—each rule with a singing reason apparent on its face, each rule a rule whose reason guides and often even controls application according to the double maxim: *the rule follows where its reason* {158} *leads; where the reason stops, there stops the rule.* They should come to recognize the steady and open checking of results against sense and decency as an of-courseness of our system of precedent when that system is working right; to recognize as of the essence a following because reason dictates following, a distinguishing or developing or shift in direction because reason dictates as the case may be distinction or development or shift.

Only then can student or bar or bench perceive that the conception of precedent as a static something, of movement as queer or improper or "departure," of figuring a court's prospective result without taking full account of the guidance the court rightly seeks *also* from its sense of decency and sense—that such a conception is an aberration which crept upon and into lawyers' thinking in those least happy days of our legal system, the 80's and 90's of the Nineteenth Century. Not every court fell prey to the new formal style of work at the same time. In Maryland, for example, one finds it delayed—in full swing in the 1920's—and the recovery from it delayed as well. But the thinking of the whole bar about the proper way of judicial work had taken shape by 1910 as if the Grand Tradition had never been. It is against a rediscovery of the latter that student, bar and bench can then come, and come at once, to recognize that the picture of our appellate courts over the past thirty years, and increasingly with each of the decades, is one not of departing from the "good" old ways but rather of a groping, almost instinctive struggle to recapture the truly good and older ways which to the discredit of the work of law had slid into the bog.

Of course there is confusion when courts seek to work in the Grand Manner but still seek to write in the Formal Style. For esthetic comfort, work and opinion should match in style. For clarity of mind in judging, a man's verbal tools should fit comfortably into the jobs he is seeking to do with them. For consistency of results, a man needs conscious knowledge of the kind of result he has the job of gunning for—else again and again, and quite unpredictably, he fails to aim or aims in the wrong direction. Finally, for the sure pride of craft and craftsmanship which comforts and strengthens, which gives courage and infuses beauty and vision, for that a man needs not only personal knowledge of his finer craft traditions, but recognition by his fellows that he has such knowledge and that he works with it in the little as in the large.

Here lies the need, here lies the opportunity, here lies the danger. The need is vital because the whole conceptual structure of our "law"-law (concepts, rules, principles) needs reformulation to adjust a preindustrial body of thought to an industrial civilization: consider merely "Contracts," thought of in terms of A and B and C, or "Property," in the image of "my house," when applied to the use, control and revenue structure of the modern investment-seeking corporation. Here there is work for fifty years of top-flight appellate judging.

{159} The opportunity shows in any one of those increasingly frequent opinions in which a vexed area of conflict or confusion is cleared up, a new road charted and stated: "the true rule,"—and the wastage cleaned up to be forgotten. No man who reads such an opinion can doubt as he reads it the thrill that came to the writer as he wrote. Opinions like that are not only as satisfying esthetically as they are doctrinally, but they communicate unmistakably the craft-pleasure found by the author in effective employment of that Grand Manner which is our ancient right.

The danger lies in this: that unless the appellate courts consciously awaken to what their duty is in this regard, unless they see both opportunity and method clean, unless they hook both up with the Grand Tradition in its power and beauty, they are threatened with loss of their own souls, and we are threatened with loss of the greatest asset of the common law. Every opinion must be directed forward, it must make sense and give guidance for tomorrow for the *type of situation* in hand. Only in the light of that are the equities and decencies of the particular case to be attended to, for in the working out of that forward-looking guidance two things occur: first, the authoritative material at hand to work with exercises its due restraint, under the law of leeways, and that gives a court firmness of heart and rock-solidity of work; second, no pressure of the particular case can readily mislead into sentimentality when all is judged against right guidance through the *type* of situation for the future, nor, when guidance through the type of situation for the future is being sought, can a court readily fall into that "first device at hand" line of ground of decision which builds up tricky distinctions and vicious corollaries. But lacking right consciousness of duty and above all of method, an appellate court is tempted into seeing the job primarily as one between the parties. Lacking full realization of the duty and the method, the law of leeways tends to lose its hold because it is not better guidance for the future but only disposition of the present case that is in the forefront of the judge's mind. Lacking full realization of the duty, the method, the tradition, the appellate judge can come and to some extent is coming *to see himself as free*—and that way lies disaster. The bar, in its non-comprehension, has been shouting and cursing at the courts for twenty years now as "departing from precedent" and "without control" and "with no sense of continuity." With time, men can come to take seriously what they are told. For let there be no doubt about this: *the appellate judges* know they move, *they* know the leeways in the accepted doctrinal system which they make use of. More, they know that they must make such use. What they therefore need, as well, is what the bar denies them: a sound consciousness of duty, limits, and high goal in the moving, and a sound consciousness of solid method. All waiting for them in the Grand Tradition of our Common Law.

Of course Utopia is not around the corner. In the highest days of the Grand Tradition, and with what was on the whole a bench of amazing {160} stature and with reasonable time to work, we had our blobs, our blobs aplenty. With modern complexity, personnel and pressure we may expect a percentage greater far. What of that? The method means a lifting of the level of appellate judicial output far above that of today, and means a steady further rise. The simplest piece of that to see rests in the fact that once the whole bar ever gets to realize that a technically letter-perfect case "on the law" is not enough, the number of appeals will go down by half or more, and furnish the appellate bench more time to do an even better job of judging.

* * * * *

There is so much more. Probably, if I had this introduction to do over, I never should have sense enough to stop.

Visit us at *www.quidprobooks.com*.

CPSIA information can be obtained
at www.ICGtesting.com
Printed in the USA
LVOW04s0827030916

503059LV00019BA/1493/P